Keymap
Iron Curtain Trail
From Hof to Szeged
Frames of the detail maps 1:85,000
with city map
D1930388
St. Pölten
Schwechat
Hainburg
Dunajska Luzna
Nove Zamky
Gyöngyös
Hajdúböszörm
Mödling
Dunajska Streda
Baden
Mosonmagyaróvár
Eisenstadt
Komarno
Hajdúszoboszló
Győr
Jászberény
Neunkirchen
Sopron
Kapuvár
Mürzzuschlag
Oberpullendorf
Kőszeg
Pápa
Dabas
Cegléd
Várpalota
Székesfehérvár
Mezőtúr
Nagykőrös
Szombathely
Veszprém
Dunaújváros
Kecskemét
Békés
Békéscsaba
Güssing
Siófok
Kiskunfélegyháza
Csongrád
Szentes
Jennersdorf
Szentgotthárd
Orosháza
Zalaegerszeg
Hódmezővásárhely
Kiskunhalas
Murska Sobota
Lenti
Szeged
Makó
Maribor
Nagykanizsa
Kaposvár
Mórahalom
Ptuj
Cakovec
Baja
Subotica
Kanjiža
Slovenska Bistrica
Varazdin
Komló
Bácsbokod
Mokrin
Nagybaracska
Madaras
Koprivnica
Pécs
Dávód
Bajmok
Senta
Kikinda
Timisoara
Stanišï
Jimbolia
Virje
Ada
Barcs
Bezdan
Backa Topola
Siklós
Sombor
Bjelovar
Beli Manastir
Becej
Krsko
Virovitica
Apatin
Brezice
Donji Miholjac
Kula
Zagreb
Podravska Slatina
Valpovo
Srbobran
49
50
51
52
53
54
55
56
57
58
59
60
61
62
63
64
65
66
67
68
69
70
71
72
73
74
75
76
77
78
79
80
81
82
83
84
85
86
87
88
89
90
91
92
93

Michael Cramer
bikeline®-Guide
European Iron Curtain Trail - From Hof to Szeged

A-3751 Rodingersdorf, Hauptstr. 31
Tel.: +43/2983/28982-0, Fax: -500
E-Mail: bikeline@esterbauer.com
www.esterbauer.com
2nd revised Edition 2017
ISBN: 978-3-85000-727-6

Please quote edition and ISBN number in all correspondence!

Translation: Chris Lines
Cover photo: Michael Cramer
Photo credits: Archiv: 108; G. Paldauf: 108; Markus Belz: 94; Marco Bertram: 20, 22, 26, 36, 104, 114; Martin Kozàk: 12, 10; Michael Cramer: 11, 16, 19, 24, 26, 30, 32, 35, 38, 42, 45, 48, 50, 52, 54, 56, 57, 58, 60, 62, 64, 66, 68, 70, 72, 73, 74, 76, 77, 78, 80, 82, 84, 86, 87, 88, 90, 98, 100, 102, 103, 104, 110, 111, 112, 118, 120, 121, 122, 124, 126, 127, 128, 130, 138, 140, 146, 148, 156, 157, 158, 160, 162, 164, 166, 168, 170; MTI Photo, Matusz Károly: 11

We wish to thank all the people who contributed to the production of this book.
The bikeline-Team: Birgit Albrecht-Walzer, Beatrix Bauer, Michael Bernhard, Michael Binder, Veronika Bock, Petra Bruckmüller, Roland Esterbauer, Dagmar Güldenpfennig, Martina Kreindl, Nora Ludolph, Gregor Münch, Karin Neichsner, Carmen Paradeiser, Sabrina Pusch, Claudia Retzer, Christian Schlechte, Elisabeth Sulz, Martin Trippmacher, Carina Windberger, Carina Winkelhofer, Martin Wischin, Wolfgang Zangerl

Cartography created with axpand
(www.axes-systems.com)

LIVE-UPDATES

LIVE UPDATE

On our web page we offer an online-service, that provides updated information and current changes concerning this cycling guide. This information is brought up-to-date regularly and enables you, in combination with the current edition of this book, to plan your trip in the best possible way. The Live-Update for this book is freely available under:

www.esterbauer.com/db_detail.php?buecher_code=ICTN4_E

Have you noticed some changes or mistakes during your journey concerning the itinerary, the overnight accommodation or the tourist information along the route? Then you have the possibility to bring the bikeline-team up-to-date using the Update-section on our web page. We are looking forward to getting your information and say Thank You in the name of all cyclists.

GPS Tracks

The latest bikeline GPS-Track for this book is freely available under:

tracks.world/?dir=de/trk26ut333

bikeline

What is bikeline?

We are a team of writers, cartographers, geographers and other staff united by our enthusiasm for bicycling and touring. Our project first „got rolling" in 1987, when a group of Vienna cyclists came together to begin producing bicycling maps. Today we are highly successful publisher that offers a wide range of bikeline® and cycline® books in five languages covering many European countries.

We need your help to keep our books up-to-date. Please write to us if you find errors or changes. We would also be grateful for experiences and impressions from your own cycling tour.

We look forward to your letters and emails (redaktion@esterbauer.com),

Your bikeline-team

Preface

To live, breathe and experience history in its purest form – that is the goal of the "European Iron Curtain trail". From the Barents sea to the Black sea, this guide takes you along the Western border of the old Warsaw pact countries across Europe. The route does not just embody European culture, history and sustainable tourism, but also provides the history-enthusiast cyclist with some spectacularly beautiful and varied landscapes and unique habitats in the European Green Belt, which one is sure to find along the border strip.

The maps in the revised edition are more accurately scaled. This volume describes the more than 1,700-kilometre-long southern part of the German-Czech border to the Hungarian border at Szeged. It takes you through the peaks of what was once the Bohemian forests, past Moravia and across the Danube at Bratislava. The southern border of Hungary leads you over Slovenia, Croatia, Serbia towards Szeged.

Maps, route descriptions, extensive historical background information, references to the cultural and tourist offering of each region as well as practical travel and accommodation advice make this cycling guide a truly valuable companion on your journey to discovering the route along the former Iron Curtain.

Map legend

Cycling routes (Radrouten)

Main cycle route, low motor traffic
(Hauptroute, wenig KFZ-Verkehr)
- Paved surface (asphaltiert)
- Unpaved surface (nicht asphaltiert)
- Bad surface (schlecht befahrbar)

Main cycle route, without motor traffic / cycle path
(Hauptroute, autofrei / Radweg)
- Paved surface (asphaltiert)
- Unpaved surface (nicht asphaltiert)
- Bad surface (schlecht befahrbar)

Excursion or alternative cycle route, low motor traffic
(Ausflug od. Variante, wenig KFZ-Verkehr)
- Paved surface (asphaltiert)
- Unpaved surface (nicht asphaltiert)
- Bad surface (schlecht befahrbar)

Excursion or alternative route, without motor traffic / cycle path (Ausflug od. Variante, autofrei / Radweg)
- Paved surface (asphaltiert)
- Unpaved surface (nicht asphaltiert)
- Bad surface (schlecht befahrbar)

Other cycle routes (Sonstiges)
- Other cycle route (sonstige Radroute)

- Cycle route with significant motor traffic (verkehrsreiche Radroute)
- Cobbled street (Kopfsteinpflaster)
- Cne-way connection (Einbahnführung)
- Ferry connection (Fährverbindung)
- Road surface unknown (unbekannter Belag)
- Tunnel (Tunnel)
- Dismounting recommended (Schiebestrecke)
- Train connection (Zugverbindung)
- Planned cycle path (Radweg in Planung)
- Closed cycle path (Radweg gesperrt)
- Cycle lane (Radfahrstreifen)
- Cycle path along road (straßenbegleitender Radweg)
- Road closed to cyclists (Straße für Radfahrer gesperrt)
- Described direction (Beschriebene Fahrtrichtung)
- 5 Waypoint (Wegpunkt)

Gradient / Distance (Steigungen / Entfernungen)

- Steep gradient, uphill (starke Steigung)
- Light gradient, uphill (leichte bis mittlere Steigung)
- 2,4 Distance in km, rounded (Entfernung in Kilometern, gerundet)

Important cycling information (Radinformationen)

- Bike workshop* (Fahrradwerkstatt*)
- Bike rental* (Fahrradvermietung*)
- Covered bike stands* (überdachter Abstellplatz*)
- Lockable bike stands* (abschließbarer Abstellplatz*)
- E-bike charging station (E-Bike Ladestation)
- Information board* (Infotafel*)
- Dangerous section (Gefahrenstelle)
- Read text carefully (Text beachten)
- Stairs (Treppe)
- Bicycle must be carried! (Tragestrecke)
- Constriction, bottleneck* (Engstelle*)
- 17 Waypoint (Wegpunkt)
- Town or city map (Stadt- /Ortsplan)

Symbols only in the city maps (Nur in Ortsplänen)

- Garage* (Parkhaus*)
- Theatre* (theater*)
- Post office* (Post*)
- Pharmacy* (Apotheke*)
- Hospital* (Krankenhaus*)
- Fire brigade* (Feuerwehr*)
- Police* (Polizei*)

* Selection (* Auswahl)

Scale 1 : 85,000

1 cm ≙ 850 m

0 1 2 3 4 5 6 7 8 9 10 11 12 13 14 15 km

Sights of interest / Facilities (Sehenswertes / Einrichtungen)

Church; Chapel (Kirche; Kapelle)
Monastery/Convent (Kloster)
Synagogue; Mosque (Synagoge; Moschee)
Palace, Castle; Ruin (Schloss, Burg; Ruine)
Tower; Lighthouse (Turm; Leuchtturm)
Watermill; Windmill (Wassermühle; Windmühle)
Power station (Kraftwerk)
Mine; Cave (Bergwerk; Höhle)
Monument (Denkmal)
Airport (Flughafen)

Other sight of interest (sonstige Sehenswürdigkeit)
Museum (Museum)
Excavations; Roman site (Ausgrabungen; röm. Objekte)
Zoo; Nature info (Tierpark; Naturpark-Information)
Nature reserve/Monument (Naturpark, -denkmal)
Natural sight of interest (sonstige Natursehenswürdigkeit)
Panoramic view* (Aussichtspunkt*)
Tourist information; Restaurant (Tourist-Info; Gasthaus)
Hotel, Guesthouse; Youth hostel (Hotel, Pension; Jugendherberge)
Campground; Simple tent site* (Camping-; Lagerplatz*)
Shopping facility*; Kiosk* (Einkaufsmöglichkeit*; Kiosk*)
Picnic tables*; Covered stand* (Rastplatz*; Unterstand*)
Outdoor pool; Indoor pool (Freibad; Hallenbad)
Drinking fountain*; Parking lot* (Brunnen*; Parkplatz*)
Schönern Picturesque town (sehenswertes Ortsbild)
Facilities available (Einrichtung im Ort vorhanden)

Topographic information (Topographische Informationen)

Church; Chapel (Kirche; Kapelle)
Monastery/Convent (Kloster)
Synagogue; Mosque (Synagoge; Moschee)
Palace, Castle; Ruin (Schloss, Burg; Ruine)
Tower; Lighthouse (Turm; Leuchtturm)
Watermill; Windmill (Wassermühle; Windmühle)
Power station, Solar power station (Kraftwerk)
Mine; Cave (Bergwerk; Höhle)
Monument; Burial mound (Denkmal; Hügelgrab)
Airport; Airfield (Flughafen; Flugplatz)

Windturbine (Windkraftanlage)
TV/Radio tower (Funk- und Fernsehanlage)
Transformer station (Umspannwerk, Trafostation)
Wayside cross; Boundary stone (Wegkreuz; Grenzstein)
Playing field, Stadium (Sportplatz, Stadion)
Golf course; Tennis courts (Golfplatz; Tennisplatz)
Boat landing; Sluice/lock (Schiffsanleger; Schleuse)
Natural spring (Quelle)
Wastewater treatment plant (Kläranlage)
International border crossing (Staatsgrenze; Übergang)
State border (Landesgrenze)
District border (Kreis-, Bezirksgrenze)
Nature reserve, National park (Naturschutzgebiet, Naturpark, Nationalpark)
Prohibited zone (Truppenübungsplatz, Sperrgebiet)

A13 B12 Motorway/Freeway; Expressway (Autobahn; Schnellstr.)
B236 Highway (Fernverkehrsstraße)
Main road (Hauptstraße)
Secondary main road (untergeordnete Hauptstraße)
Secondary road; Access road (Nebenstraße; Fahrweg)
Track; Ferry (Weg; Fähre)
Road planned/under construction (geplant/in Bau)
Railway/station; S-train station (Eisenbahn/Bahnhof; S-Bahnhof)
Railway disused; planned (Eisenbahn stillgelegt; geplant)
Narrow gauge railway (Schmalspurbahn)
Mountain railway; Cable car (Bergbahn; Seilbahn)
Forest; Park (Wald; Parkanlage)
Marsh/Bog; Heath (Sumpf; Heide)
Vineyards; Allotment gardens* (Weinbau; Gärten*)
Cemetery; Dunes/Beach (Friedhof; Düne, Strand)
Tidal flats; Glacier (Watt; Gletscher)
Rock; Cliff; Scree (Felsen; Geröll)
Quarry; Open cast mine* (Steinbruch, Tagebau*)
Commercial/Industrial area (Gewerbe-, Industriegebiet)
Urban area; Public building (Siedlung; öffentl. Gebäude)
Defensive wall/Wall (Stadtmauer, Mauer)
Embankment, Dike (Damm, Deich)
Canal (Kanal)
River/Dam/Lake (Fluss/Staumauer/See)
Contour line 100m/50m (Höhenlinie 100m/50m)
520 5310 UTM-grid (2 km-grid) (UTM-Gitter)

Inhalt

Atlantic Ocean
Norwegian Sea
Barents Sea
White Sea
North Sea
Baltic Sea
Black Sea
Aegean Sea
Adriatic Sea
Tyrrhenian Sea
Mediterranean Sea
ICELAND
Faroe Is. (Denm.)
UNITED KINGDOM
NORWAY
SWEDEN
FINLAND
RUSSIA
ESTONIA
LATVIA
LITHUANIA
(to Russia)
BELARUS
UKRAINE
MOLDOVA
POLAND
GERMANY
DENMARK
NETHERLANDS
BELGIUM
LUXEMBOURG
FRANCE
SWITZERLAND
LIE.
AUSTRIA
CZECH REPUBLIC
SLOVAKIA
HUNGARY
ROMANIA
SLOVENIA
CROATIA
BOSNIA AND HERZEGOVINA
SERBIA
MONTENEGRO
KOSOVO
MACEDONIA
ALBANIA
BULGARIA
GREECE
TURKEY
ITALY
SAN MARINO
VATICAN CITY
MONACO
ANDORRA
ALGERIA
TUNISIA
Åland Is. (Finl.)
Corsica
Sardinia
Sicily
Mallorca
Moscow
St. Petersburg
Helsinki
Tallinn
Riga
Vilnius
Minsk
Kiev
Chişinău
Warsaw
Berlin
Prague
Vienna
Bratislava
Budapest
Bucharest
Sofia
Belgrade
Ljubljana
Zagreb
Sarajevo
Podgorica
Priština
Skopje
Tirana
Rome
Bern
Paris
Brussels
Amsterdam
London
Copenhagen
Oslo
Stockholm
Istanbul
Odesa

The author

Michael Cramer was born on June 16, 1949 in Gevelsberg, Westphalia and attended the Reichenbach grammar school in Ennepetal. He studied music, sports and education in Mainz from 1969-74. From 1975-95 he taught at a school in Berlin-Neukölln.

From 1989-2004 he served as transport spokesman for The Greens in the Berlin House of Representatives. Alongside his work as an MP he took several teaching positions relating to transport and urban policy at the Otto Suhr Institute of the Free University of Berlin. Michael Cramer has been a member of the European Parliament since 2004 and he has been serving as the chairman of the Committee on Transport and Tourism since 2014. He also continues to pursued several journalistic activities through publications in journals and books.

According to the author, three key events from his youth acted as the catalyst for his intensive study of the German-German history. The first was in 1961 when the Wall was built and he went on his first holiday without his parents to the North Sea resort of St. Peter Ording. There, he did not just marvel at the beach sailers but was also able to listen to the legendary 80-year-old Count Luckner (1881 – 1966), who was said to be able to tear telephone books apart as well as bend and flatten 5-Mark coins with his bare hands. Whilst on holiday he read a newspaper with the headline: "Berlin Wall – is this the start of World War III?" At once he remembered the stories his parents and teachers had told him about the war period and grew increasingly anxious that he too, might live to experience such terrible times. Two years later he journeyed with his football club TuS Ennepetal to West Berlin and played against BFC Südring. Whilst there he ate his first curried sausage - which did not yet exist in West Germany - played for the first time Mini-Golf in the Hasenheide – which back then was not possible in Ennepetal - and drank his first Fassbrause lemonade – something that cannot be found today in West Germany. His aunt gave him a camera for the trip and the first pictures he took were of the Wall at Bernauer Straße.

Every time he returned to Berlin thereafter, he went to Bernauer Straße and recorded how the Wall changed. Initially, only the windows were bricked up on the ground and the first floor. A short while later, however, the windows on the other floors were also bricked up. Eventually, the houses that stretched to the first floor were replaced by the "modern" Wall.

A year later he read his first book on politics: "Child of the revolution" by Wolfgang Leonhard (*1921 - 2014), who in 1935, as a child of Communist parents, fled from Nazi Germany with his mother, Susanne Leonhard, to seek refuge in the Soviet Union. After a short time, however, his mother was arrested and exiled to a labour camp in Siberia. Her son Wolfgang was brought up as a "socialist" in children's homes and boarding schools. As a committed communist, he was part of the "Ulbricht Group", which after the war was sent from the Soviet Union to live in occupied Germany.

From July 1945 to September 1947 Wolfgang Leonhard worked for the Central Committee of the Communist Party (from 1946 known as the SED) and was active in the department of "agitation and propaganda" and also taught from 1947-49 history at the "Karl Marx SED school" in Kleinmachnow. In 1948, Wilhelm Pieck, the man who would later become GDR president, helped him retrieve his mother from Siberia and bring her to Germany. Susanne Leonhard (1895-1984) first lived in East Berlin and then in the spring of 1949, moved to West Germany. She was arrested by US intelligence CIC (Counter Intelligence Corps) and detained until April 1950. As a committed anti-Stalinist socialist, she declined to work for the US as a spy. In 1956 she published the book "Stolen Life. The fate of a political emigrant in the Soviet Union". In 1949, her son Wolfgang broke with Stalinism, fled via Prague in the "non-aligned" Yugoslavia and has been living in the Federal Republic of Germany since the 1950s.

After studying in Mainz, Michael Cramer moved to Berlin (West) in 1974 and confirmed the oft-quoted observation: "Either you pack your bags and leave Berlin after six months or you stay and live forever in Berlin." He stayed.

In the summer of 1989 he cycled along the 160 km long "Patrol route" around West Berlin, which had been created by the Western Allies after the Wall. It was impossible to get lost because you just stayed on the West Berlin side and followed the Wall. Then the Wall fell and he was able to repeat this tour around the Wall in the spring of 1990 on the patrol road between the front wall and the hinterland wall. It was during one of these such cycling rides that the idea for cycling tours involving the Berlin Wall was born.

However, it took another ten years until it could take shape. After the fall of the Wall, the slogan in Berlin was: "The Wall must go". The responsibility for this task fell upon the shoulders of the GDR border guards who were in charge until 2 October 1990 and who carried this out with typical Prussian-Socialist thoroughness. On the 40th anniversary of the Wall, Michael Cramer returned to his original idea and in the summer of 2001, organised public "Wall-forays". The Senate and House of Representatives of Berlin decided to protect the remaining Wall by making it a listed monument, added signposting to the Berlin Wall and making it cyclist-friendly. These measures were completed in 2007.

The book "Berlin Wall Trail" was first published in 2001 by the Esterbauer publishing house, and detailed a route of 160 kilometres along the former border to West Berlin. It was presented by Volker Hassemer, who had served for many years as the Berlin Senator for Urban Development and Environmental Protection. This book has since been revised several times and was also printed in English in 2003.

The book "German-German Border Trail" first appeared in the summer of 2007 - in English 2008 - and was presented at the European House in Berlin by Wolfgang Thierse, the then President of the German Bundestag (1998-2005). He quoted the former President of the European Commission, Jacques Delors (1985-1995), with his statement: "The European Union is like a bicycle. If you stop riding it, it will fall over." The three volumes of the "Europa-Radweg Eiserner Vorhang" were published in 2009 and as "Iron Curtain Trail" in English in 2010. They were also presented in the European House in Berlin by Hans-Gert Pöttering, the then President of the European Parliament (2007-2009). The revised version of the southern part from Hof to Szeged with a unified scale of 1:85,000 was published in 2014 and presented by the EU Commissioner for Regional Development, Johannes Hahn, in the European House in Vienna.

Berlin Wall Trail

212 p., 1 : 20,000, **ISBN:** 978-3-85000-458-9, **€ 13,90**

Iron Curtain Trail

The Iron Curtain divided the continent into East and West and extended from the Barents Sea through Europe to the Black Sea - a distance of 10,000 kilometres. Until the peaceful revolutions in Eastern Europe, it was the physical and ideological border between two mutually hostile blocs. It did not just divide many neighbouring states, but also divided Germany into East and West. Few things remain of the former death strip today. The few relics that are still there remind us of our past but no longer separate us.

Therefore, it is imperative to make the memories visible! We know that there is little in the way of shared memories between the West and the East, that the experiences of Europeans east and west of the border differ, not least because their perspectives were often shaped completely differently depending on the official policy in both parts of Europe. The Warsaw Pact countries were set up with the goal in mind of "protection against the class enemy". For the West, the East represented a lack of freedom in real socialism. Visible memories already exist with the "Berlin Wall Trail", which has been signposted since 2001 by the Berlin Senate and made with cyclists in mind.

To compliment the various stops along the former Wall, the "Berlin Wall History Mile" was launched, a permanent exhibition with artistic designs of the crossings in four languages (German, English, French, Russian), with about 30 panels detailing the history of the division of Berlin, the Wall construction and when it came down. Photographs and short texts describe events that took place at each location. The "Berlin Wall Trail" became part of Berlin's tourism program and is the first project that combines soft tourism and city tourism. In Berlin you can experience history, politics, nature and culture.

It was not just Berlin that was divided for decades, it was the rest of Germany, too. The memory of the present 1,400-kilometre inner German border strip must be preserved. With this in mind, on the 30th June 2004, the coalition parties of the SPD and Bündnis 90/Die Grünen brought forward the motion in the German Bundestag (DS 15/3454) to convert the former death strip into a habitat. The "Iron Curtain", they argued, should be developed for sustainable tourism and a European Green Belt (Green Belt Europe) should run along it. The German Bundestag voted unanimously in favour of these plans in December of 2004.

The "German-German cycle track" on the "Green Belt" runs through 150 nature reserves and encompasses numerous flora-fauna habitat areas (FFH), including the three biosphere reserves of Schaalsee, Elbaue and Rhön as well as the Harz National Park. The route leads from the Baltic Sea to the Czech border with numerous rivers and lakes along the way and covers not just the height of the Harz mountains but also the Thuringian Forest. There are many monuments and border museums to discover, as well as some remaining watchtowers.

But also Europe was divided for decades. The Iron Curtain ran from the Barents Sea on the Norwegian-Russian border to the Black Sea on the Bulgarian-Turkish border. Today, it no longer separates us but is rather a symbol of a common European experience in the reunified Europe. This is another reason why the European Parliament approved in 2005 my resolution by a large majority in the European Parliament from all countries and all political groups to include the "Iron Curtain Trail", in its report on "New perspectives and challenges for sustainable tourism in Europe". It is part of a collective memory, with which the much-valued and often praised European identity can be promoted.

Europe's division does not begin at the end of World War II, but rather with Hitler's seizure of power on 30 January 1933 and the beginning of World War II on 1 September 1939, as German soldiers marched into Poland. Had it not been for Nazi Germany and WWII, Europe would never have been divided.

Despite their ideological differences, the anti-Hitler coalition was united in a common struggle against Nazi Germany. The respective own interests soon came to the fore, however, after the unconditional surrender of the German army. Already on March 5, 1946, British Prime Minister Winston Churchill who had been voted out of office after the war, stated in his famous speech in Fulton/Missouri that a division of Europe had occurred and that part of Europe now found itself behind an "Iron Curtain". The Cold War had begun.

The leaders of the Warsaw Pact countries were not willing to grant political freedom and proved unable to solve the economic problems resulting in repeated uprisings. The first in the

Signposting at the Iron Curtain Trail

Soviet sphere of influence happened on 17 June 1953 in the GDR. This was followed in June of 1956 by the Poznan demonstrations in Poland and in October the Hungarian Revolution, the Prague Spring in Czechoslovakia in 1968, the workers' uprising in 1970 in Poland, Charter 77 in Czechoslovakia in 1977 and in 1980 the emergence of the Solidarity movement in Poland, that with 10 million, had more than three times as many members as the Communist state party. The activities of Solidarity movement, the successful orientation of Hungary to the west, the "Singing Revolution" of independence movements in the Baltic states, the "Velvet Revolution" in Czechoslovakia, together with the increasingly strong opposition movement in the GDR and the dismantling of the barbed wire on the Hungarian-Austrian border by the two Foreign Ministers Gyula Horn and Alois Mock on 27 June 1989 paved the way for the fall of the Berlin Wall on 9 November 1989 and the Iron Curtain in Europe.

Following the successful example of the Berlin Wall Trail and the German-German Border Trail, a hiking and biking trail was envisaged along the former Iron Curtain on the former death strip, to help us retrace the footsteps of this shared European history. The 10,000 kilometres "Green Belt" from the Barents Sea to the Black Sea have been under the patronage of Mikhail Gorbachev since 2002, who in March 1985, with a majority of just a single vote, was elected General Secretary of the KPdSU. The former president of the Soviet Union has been the President of Green Cross International (GCI) since 1993. The importance of the Green Belt for conservation and its value as a symbol of the union between East and West is internationally recognised today. Once Member States in cooperation with the European Parliament and the European Commission fully develop the project, you will be able to learn even more about European history, politics, nature and culture.

Twenty countries are participating in this project, including 15 EU Member States. Starting at the Barents Sea the hiking and biking trail extends along the western border of the former Warsaw Pact countries to the Black Sea. You begin by cycling along the Norwegian-Russian and Finnish-Russian border until you reach the Baltic Sea and continue along the shoreline of Russia, Estonia, Latvia, Lithuania, Kaliningrad, Poland and the former GDR. The route from the peninsula Priwall at Travemünde to the Saxon-Bavarian-Czech border triangle follows the former inner-German border strip. Then it leads over the heights of the Bohemian Forest, past Moravia and the Slovak capital Bratislava, and here one must cross the Danube. The route takes you along the southern border of Hungary across Slovenia and Croatia. Between Romania and Serbia it largely follows the course of the Danube through Bulgaria, Macedonia and Greece and ends on the northernmost tip of Turkey on the Bulgarian Black Sea coast.

The route passes through several national parks, each with a variety of interesting flora and fauna and combines a beautiful assortment of unique landscapes that have remained largely untouched due to its remote border location and the former exclusion zones. It also connects countless memorials, museums and open-air facilities, which remind us of Europe's division and how it was overcome by the Peaceful Revolutions in Eastern Europe.

As with the "Berlin Wall Trail" and the "German-German Border Trail" the European "Iron Curtain Trail" partially makes use of paved patrol roads on the border. Many countries and regions in Europe are still working on the project and numerous sections have already been signposted and expanded.

Of course there are many ways in which you can move around in the Green Belt by bike. You can be on the western or the

Alois Mock and Gyula Horn cutting through the Iron Curtain

eastern side, closer to the border or further away, on paths with perforated plates or on asphalt. The proposed route was selected based on the following five criteria:

- as close as possible to the former border
- as comfortable as possible
- avoid busy roads
- frequent cross the former border
- integrate as many historical testimonials as possible

The suggested route is to be taken as a "work in progress". It should go without saying that the local people know more about their area, and there is always the possibility of construction works. And of course, a detour is sometimes suggested to take in a nearby tourist attraction. This has been done sparingly, however, because otherwise the whole route would become very long. With this in mind, the author and the publisher hope the readership of this book will take this into account, but are nonetheless pleased to accept suggestions and improvements based on the criteria mentioned above.

This edition of the European "Iron Curtain Trail" would not have been possible without the support of other individuals and institutions. I would like to thank Roland Esterbauer and his team, who has supported the project from the beginning and professionally implemented everything.

In this edition of the "Iron Curtain Trail" I was accompanied along the Czech and Slovak border by Radka Žáková, Siegrid Weiß and Peter Šebo, along the Austrian-Hungarian border by Barbara Neuroth and on the Hungarian-Croatian section by Lidija Mišćin and Robert Rigo.

For the coordination of the project as well as the editing of the books I was greatly supported by Philipp Cerny, Alexander Kaas Elias, Jens Müller, Sara Ott and Erdmute Safranski, whom I would also like to thank very much.

I would like to pay special thanks to the European initiative europeangreenbelt (www.greenbelt.eu), which together with conservationists from the Central and Eastern European countries brought the project "Green Belt" to life - now one of the most successful and at the same time emblematic European projects.

On 23 September 2014 a "Memorandum of Understanding" was signed in Slavonice by Gabriele Schwaderer for the European Green Belt Initiative, Daniel Mourek for the European Cyclists Federation and Michael Cramer for the European Parliament with the aim to protect the Green Belt and enable cycling in it.

As part of both projects, the signing institutions undertook to support sustainable tourism, the protection and preservation of the special flora and fauna as well as the awareness of the history and culture. They are unified in their conviction that these goals can only be reached together with the population. Sustainable tourism in particular strengthens the local economy which is also supported by improving the existing infrastructure.

I would also like to thank Mikhail Gorbachev, who as President of Green Cross International, gave his full support as patron of the "Green Belt" project.

And last but not least I would like to thank Marianne Birthler, Vaclav Havel (1936-2011) and Lech Wałęsa who are serving as patrons of the European project "Iron Curtain Trail".

More than 25 years have passed since the fall of the Iron Curtain in Europe. In Wilhelm von Humboldt's words: We know that "Only those who know their past have a future", which is why we have to first deal with the past. Therefore, we maintain with gratitude the memory of the Peaceful Revolutions in Eastern and Central Europe in order not to forget the decades of division on our continent.

With all this in mind, I wish you great pleasure along your journey of exploring European history, politics, nature and culture.

Michael Cramer

About this book

This bike tour guide contains all the information you need for cycling along the European Iron Curtain cycle path: Accurate maps, a detailed route description, a few accommodation options and the most important information concerning tourist attractions.

The maps

The detailed maps are on a 1: 85,000 scaled. In addition to the route, the maps also give you information on the sort of ground you can expect (paved or unpaved), gradients (light or heavy), distances and cultural, tourist and gastronomic facilities en route.

However, even the most accurate maps cannot replace a quick glance at the directions. The recommended main route is always in red and violet, variations and excursions, are shown in orange. The exact meaning of each symbol is explained in the key on pages 4 and 5. .

The text

The text part essentially consists of the route description, which contains the recommended main route, and many historical stories.

This text is interrupted by orange paragraphs dealing with variants and excursions.

Furthermore, all the important places for better orientation of the text are highlighted.

The description of individual places and historical, political, cultural or natural interesting facts and happenings along the route contribute to a rounded travel experience. These text blocks are printed in italics so as to distinguish themselves differently from the route description.

TIP

Text portions in violet highlight points that indicate daytrips, interesting sights or activities a bit off the route.

Iron Curtain Trail 1

Part 1: Along the "Green Belt" from the Barents Sea to the German-Polish Border

220 p., 1 : 75,000, 100,000, 400,000
ISBN: 978-3-85000-277-6,
€ 15,90

Iron Curtain Trail 2

Part 2: Along the "Green Belt" from Usedom via the German-German Border Trail to the Czech Border

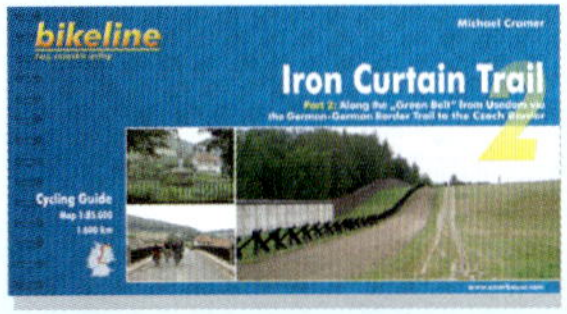

272 p., 1 : 85,000
ISBN: 978-3-85000-278-3,
€ 13,90

Iron Curtain Trail 3

Part 3: Along the Green Belt from the German-Czech Border to the Black Sea

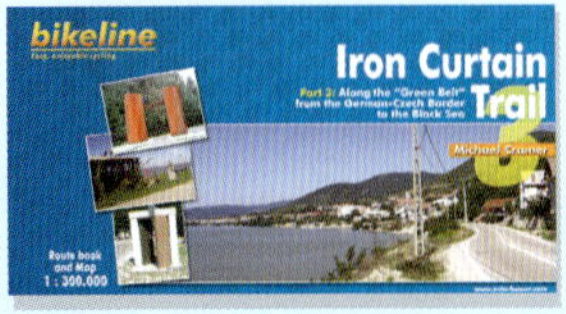

180 p., 1 : 300,000
ISBN: 978-3-85000-279-0,
€ 15,90

From Hof to border triangle 14 km

There are many train connections in Hof, which is why it is best to start the tour at the main station. Not only that, the city also has a lot to offer.

Hof

Postcode: 95028; Area code: 09281

Tourist Office, Ludwigsstr. 24, ✆ 815-7777 www.hof.de

Museum Bayerisches Vogtland, Lower Gate 5a / 5b, ✆ 815-2700, OT: Di Su 10 16 o'clock. The main focus of the collection is on the feudal and industrial history of the city. Two natural history departments include examples of almost the entire livestock population in Europe. In the new building there is a large special exhibition entitled "flight and expulsion".

The author at Dreiländereck

St. Lorenz Church (12C.), Lawrence Road. The St. Lorenz Church is the oldest church in the city of Hof. Inside is the famous Hertnid of stone altar, which probably dates back to the Bamberger workshops in the 1480's.

St. Michaelis Church, Church Square. The church is from 1230. After the great fire of 1823 it was rebuilt, successfully combining Gothic, neoclassical and Biedermeier elements to create an impressive religious building.

Town Hall, Ludwig Street, and the corner of Kloster street. The palatial style of the original building which was originally built in 1563-66 and subsequently rebuilt after numerous fires is a beautiful example of German urbanism.

Fernwehpark on the Michaelis bridge. Located right on the Saale Cycle Route, there is Europe's unique collection of place-name signs from around the world. Additional attractions are the "Signs of Fame" – greeting signs of celebrities from the worlds of show business, sports and politics.

Bürgerpark Theresienstein is the oldest public park in Germany and is in the north of the city. The landscape park is in the style of a classical English garden and represents 200 years of garden architecture. It includes zoological, botanical and geological gardens and was voted one of Germany's most beautiful parks in 2003.

The **recreation area Untreusee** with over 60 hectares of water is 3 km from the Saale Cycle Route in the south of Hof.

HofBad, Oberer Anger 4, OT: Mon-Thu 9-21, Fri, Sat 9-22 pm, Sun / holidays 9-21 pm

Outdoor pool, Ascher Str 32, OT:. In mid-May-mid-Sep, Mon-Sun 7:30 20:00

Wheelhouse Hensel & Koller, Wunsiedler Str. 16, ✆ 5402730

Bike Station, Ernst-Reuter-Str. 64, ✆ 141,444

The old town in Hof that we see today originated from the Rekkenze settlement which surrounded the Lorenz Church (built in 1080). Otto I, Count of Andechs and Meran, founded the Neustadt (New town). in 1230, which still bears the name Hof today. In 1373 the viscount of Nuremburg acquired the Regnitzland as well as Hof. The city then belonged to the first burgrave of Nuremberg, later to the margrave of Brandenburg-Bayreuth and finally fell to the Kingdom of Prussia in 1792, and in 1806 to the French. It was only in 1810 that Emperor Napoleon I of France gave the Regnitzland and Hof to the Kingdom of Bavaria, thus ending the 400-year-old Hohenzollern rule.

In 1823, a large city fire destroyed almost all the buildings of the Neustadt. During its reconstruction, contemporary architectural elements were used which gives the city a youthful appearance, as it corresponds to their actual age.

A great economic and industrial boom started for Hof and its textile industry with the opening of the railway in 1848.

Hof has about 45,000 inhabitants and is a popular destination for day trips. The city is characterized by its high density of bakeries and butchers. It offers a wide variety of food including bratwurst, ham and sausage to typical Franconian dishes and snacks in restaurants. In addition to these culinary delights, several outstanding cultural events attract plenty of visitors to the city.

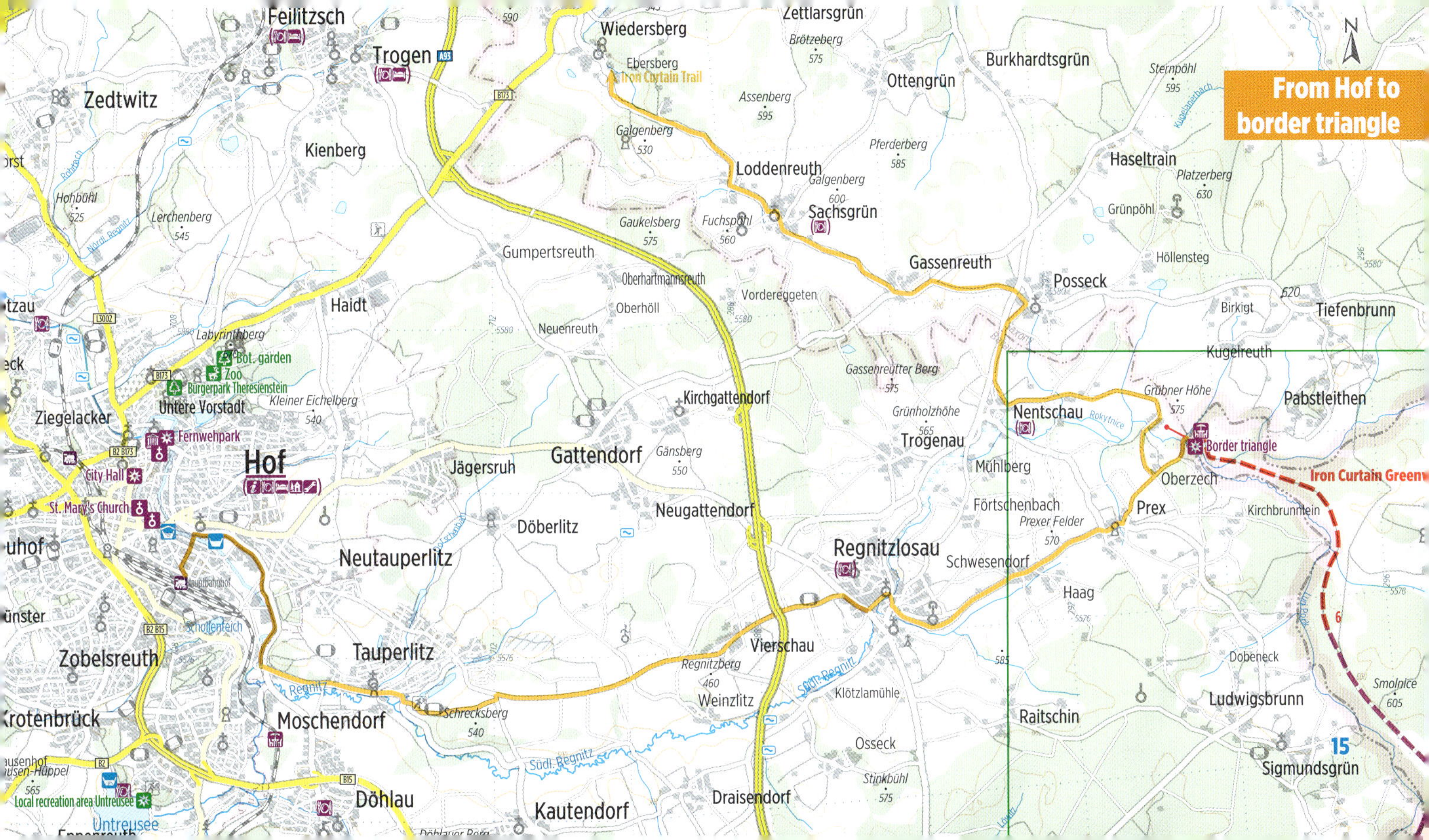
From Hof to border triangle
Iron Curtain Trail
Iron Curtain Green
Border triangle
Hof
Feilitzsch
Trogen
Zedtwitz
Kienberg
Wiedersberg
Ebersberg
Zettlarsgrün
Brötzeberg
Burkhardtsgrün
Ottengrün
Assenberg
Galgenberg
Loddenreuth
Sachsgrün
Pferderberg
Haseltrain
Platzerberg
Grünpöhl
Sternpöhl
Hohbühl
Lerchenberg
Gaukelsberg
Fuchspöhl
Gumpertsreuth
Oberhartmannsreuth
Vordereggeten
Gassenreuth
Posseck
Höllensteg
Birkigt
Tiefenbrunn
Haidt
Oberhöll
Neuenreuth
Labyrinthberg
Bot. garden
Zoo
Bürgerpark Theresienstein
Untere Vorstadt
Kleiner Eichelberg
Ziegelacker
Fernwehpark
City Hall
St. Mary's Church
Kirchgattendorf
Gassenreutter Berg
Kugelreuth
Grübner Höhe
Pabstleithen
Nentschau
Grünholzhöhe
Trogenau
Gattendorf
Jägersruh
Gänsberg
Mühlberg
Oberzech
Neugattendorf
Förtschenbach
Prexer Felder
Prex
Kirchbrunnlein
Döberlitz
Neutauperlitz
Regnitzlosau
Schwesendorf
Haag
Zobelsreuth
Tauperlitz
Vierschau
Regnitzberg
Weinzlitz
Klötzlamühle
Dobeneck
Ludwigsbrunn
Smolnice
Raitschin
Moschendorf
Schrecksberg
Südl. Regnitz
Osseck
Sigmundsgrün
Stinkbühl
Local recreation area Untreusee
Untreusee
Döhlau
Kautendorf
Draisendorf
15

From the central station cycle along the so-called "filthy rich Bavaria corner" on the stand-alone asphalt bike lanes, then the bicycle routes in the road, partly through streets with more traffic and then onto the Saale Cycle Route and the Vogtland bike trail over Tauperlitz along the southern Regnitz to Regnitzlosau. From there towards Schwesendorfer Graben through Prex towards Oberzech. Behind the village, turn left onto a paved forest road that after a total of 14 kilometres leads to a little meadow at the border triangle.

Border triangle

On the right side there is a memorial cross for the Unknown Soldier of World War II. Straight ahead of you, you can see the border signs on both the German and Czech sides.

From Border triangle to Cheb 41 km

Push your bike across the meadow and a small creek bridge on the Czech side to find a picnic area and some signs.

TIP Around Hranice and Aš you can find here a further protuberance of the country in miniaturised form: The Czech Republic is only 200 to 500 m wide here for over a distance of 1,500 m.

Turn right on the 20km long **Iron Curtain Greenway**, a permanent forest road towards the town of Aš. After a few kilometres, starting from the turn-off to Hranice - there keep to the right - the route is paved and is called **bike path 2058**.

Signal wall, 1950

TIP Unfortunately, there are also numerous potholes – you find yourself on the former border patrol area.

The history of the Czech Republic

The Czech Republic was created on 1 January 1993 as the successor state of Czechoslovakia. The territory mainly comprises of the former so-called "Bohemian crown lands" of Bohemia, Moravia and Moravian-Silesian.

In the 9th century Bohemia was divided up between several "Slavic tribes". Charlemagne tried repeatedly to militarily conquer the area, but with little success. After the fall of Great Moravia, Bohemia voluntarily submitted to the king of the kingdom of Ostfranken, Arnulf of Carinthia. However, it retained a special position in the Holy Roman Empire, evident by the position of the King of Bohemia staying with the ruling Přemyslid family.

After about 400 years of Přemysliden dynasty, in 1355 Charles IV was crowned King of Bohemia, by the emperor of the Holy Roman Empire. Prague was his town of residence. Between 1471 and 1526 the Bohemian crown was in the hands of the Polish dynasty Jagiellonian. On account of the Bohemian Estates in 1526 choosing the Habsburg Ferdinand I as King of Bohemia, the land belonged to the Habsburg territory. Autonomy and confessional disputes then provided a catalyst for the Thirty Years War (1618-1648). "Peace of Westphalia" was agreed and with that it was also decided that the creed of the ruler should also determine that of his subjects ("cuius regio eius religio"). The Protestant faith was therefore suppressed in the Catholic Habsburg Empire. From the late 18th century the Czech national consciousness flared up once again. However, until 1918 the area remained in the dominion of the Habsburgs.

After the First World War finished in 1918, the so-called First Czechoslovak Republic was created. In the Munich Agreement in 1938, the regions with German population majority (Sudetenland) were awarded to the German Reich. The southern part of Slovakia and the Carpathian Ukraine fell to Hungary, the Těšín area was occupied by Poland. Despite the attempts to appease Nazi Germany, German troops occupied in March 1939 the so-called "rump Czechoslovakia" and established it as the Protectorate of Bohemia and Moravia under German administration. The massacre of the imperial army in the villages of Lidice and Ležáky and the concentration camp in the Czech lands paid witness to the cruel handling of the persecuted Jews, political opponents and minorities. American, Soviet and Czechoslovak troops liberated the country in May 1945.

After the war ended in 1945, the Czechoslovak Republic (SR) restored the 1918 borders aside from the Carpathian Ukraine, which were taken by the Soviet Union. Due to the various decrees by the Czechoslovak President Edvard Beneš (1884-1948) millions of Sudeten Germans were expropriated and expelled. 400 villages just on the borders with Austria and Bavaria alone, were levelled.

The Czechoslovak Republic (CSR) - since 1960 Czechoslovak Socialist Republic (CSSR) - was a member of the Warsaw Pact and the Council for Mutual Economic Assistance in the influence of the Soviet Union behind the Iron Curtain. The "Prague Spring" in 1968 under Alexander Dubček represented an attempt of creating "socialism with a human face". He was crushed by the military intervention of the Warsaw Pact states, for Herbert Marcuse, the "greatest tragedy since the Second World War" and for Jean-Paul Sartre, a "war crime". The reformist government was then replaced by one more willing to tow the party line.

But the resistance had been only temporarily broken: A civil rights movement called "Charter 77" under the leadership of the writer Vaclav Havel (1936-2011) turned even more against the regime. When Mikhail Gorbachev relieved the pressure through his policies of glasnost (transparency) and perestroika (reconstruction), the resistance increased their protests. On 24 November 1989, the "Velvet Revolution" forced the Communist government to resign. On December 28 Alexander Dubček was elected President of Parliament and a day later, Václav Havel was elected the fourth president of Czechoslovakia, which was renamed the Czechoslovak Federative Republic and Slovakian (SFR) on April 23. The first free elections were held on 5 July 1990, confirmed by the Havel in office.

The negotiations between the Czech Prime Minister Vaclav Klaus, who won the elections in the Czech part of the country, and his colleague from the Slovak part, Vladimir Meciar, led to the division of Czechoslovakia into two

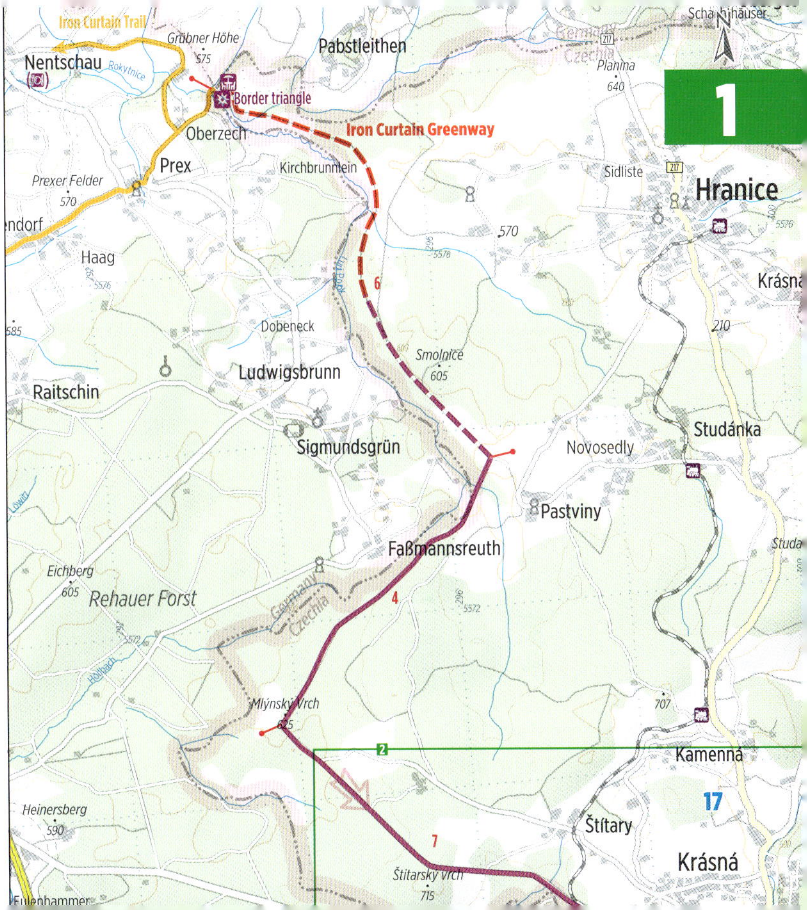

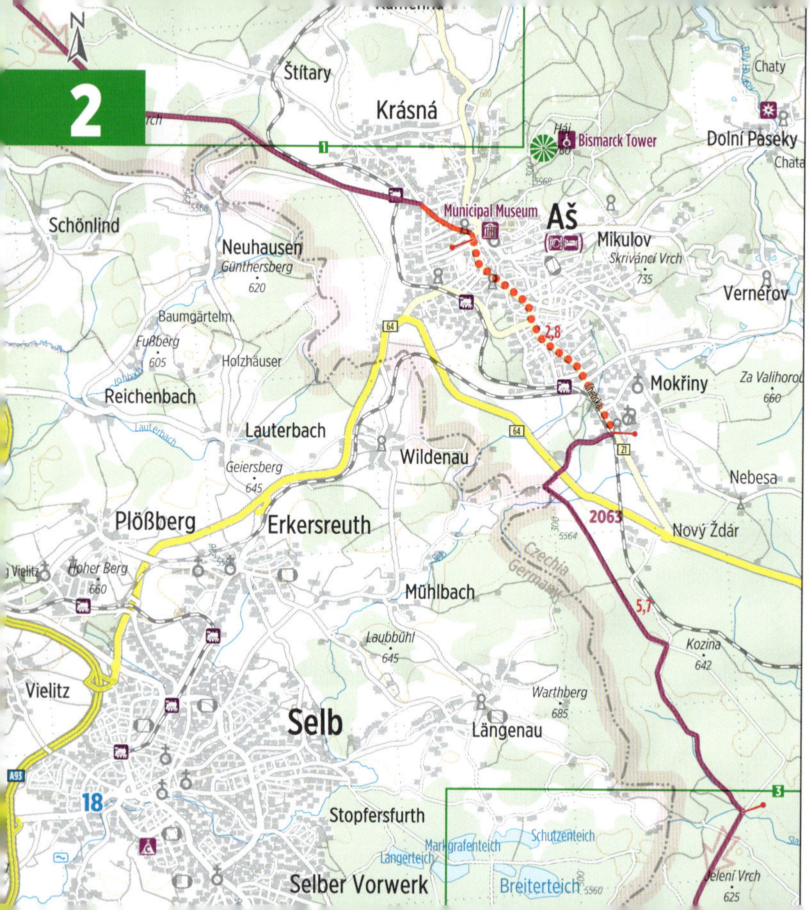

independent states - the Czech Republic and the Slovak Republic - on 1 January 1993.

The Czech Republic became a member of NATO in 1990 and on 1 May 2004 a member of the European Union.

The Iron Curtain in the CSSR

According to the information we have today, 145 people were shot between 1948-1989 on the border between Czechoslovakia and Germany and Austria while trying to escape and 96 were electrocuted by the electric fence. More than 41 people lost their lives either by drowning whilst trying to swim across the Danube, crashed their vehicles into turnpikes, were shot down in flying objects they had constructed, or driven out of fear of the border guards to commit suicide. More than 50 other dead people were pulled from the border rivers, but there are no files on these people.

The border zone which could only be entered with express permission was initially ten to fifteen kilometres wide. Around 2,500 "politically unreliable people" were resettled from the area. The totally depopulated exclusion zone was two kilometres wide. Every sign was dismantled up to eight kilometres inland. In 1964 the ban on the restricted area was removed and the border zone reduced to a one to three kilometre wide strip.

It was hoped that the expansion of the border regime after the takeover by the Communists in 1948, would help in guarding against agents of hostile intelligence services and hold back the ever-increasing tide of people trying to cross. The border was secured by about 20,000 soldiers, the soldiers had machine guns, jeeps and dogs to help them prevent any escape.

In 1950 a "bulwark against imperialism" was built along the border of Czechoslovak soldiers. A fifty-metre strip was cleared, watchtowers built and a barbed wire fence erected. A part of the border strip was sprinkled with fine sand, so that each footprint could be seen.

Initially, the wires were placed under 5,000 volts high voltage so that even the lightest of touches was deadly. But because animals and debris from trees often triggered a false alarm – and because some soldiers guarding the area were also killed by mistake - the voltage was lowered from 1965. However, *even then, a mere touch was enough to alert the next border post.*

Very little can be seen today of the former settlement **Újezd (Mähring)**, which was on the 3 km southwest clearing in the middle. In 1994 a war memorial was rebuilt in this former settlement of this most westerly point of the Czech Republic. The **Štítary** train station, which is reached when going in a south-easterly direction, was formerly just one of four districts (**Ängerlein**) whose village signs were destroyed.

Remain on the 2058 until you reach Aš (Asch).

Monument to the victims of the Iron Curtain

Aš

The narrow and high Neo-Renaissance town hall seems a bit out of proportion compared to its surroundings. Originally, it was closely surrounded by old town houses, but these have been lost as a result of war or because of the extensive depopulation through the expulsion and construction of the border zone. Today, it forms the focal point in a park-like environment. The small-town market square in front of it is hard to make out anymore, and the once prominent Protestant church of the Holy Trinity behind it is equally hard to find. Asch was able to keep its Protestant faith after the Thirty Years War, but despite this, the church constructed in 1622 was later rebuilt in the Baroque style, the style of the Catholic Church. After a fire in 1960, only the outer walls survived, which were in turn later removed. The remaining wall height is just good enough to mark the outline.

150 metres to the southeast, close to the Nikolai Church, one can find the city museum in a former Zedtwitz family palace. On the north-eastern Háj (Hainsberg) is one of three surviving Czech Republic Bismarck-towers, from which one can enjoy a wonderful view

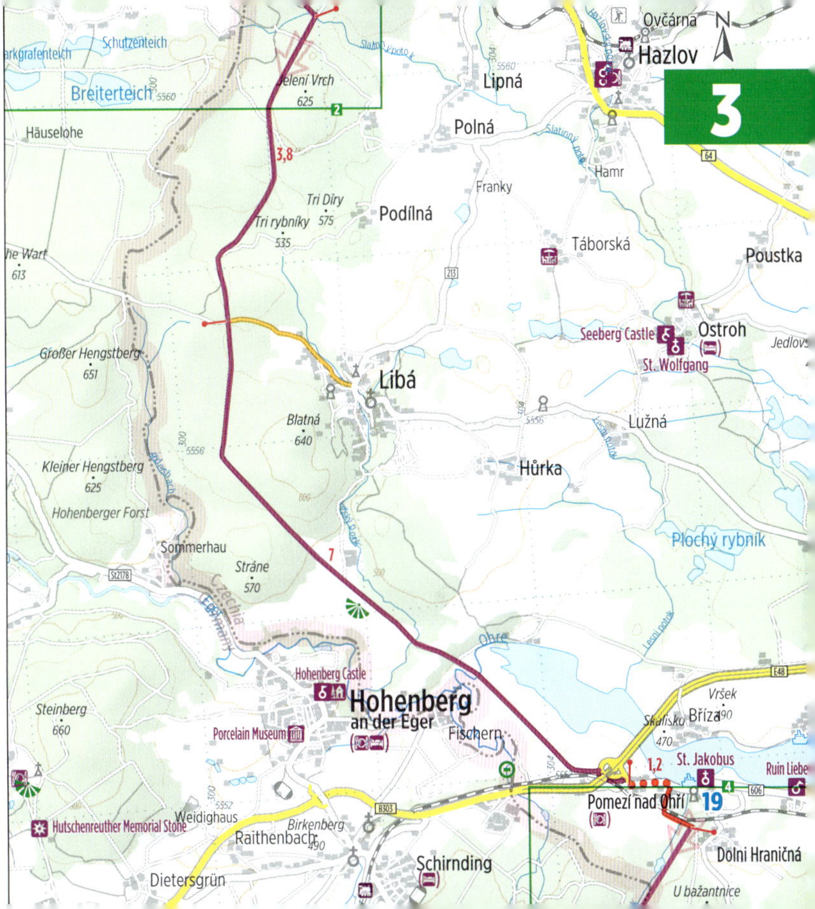

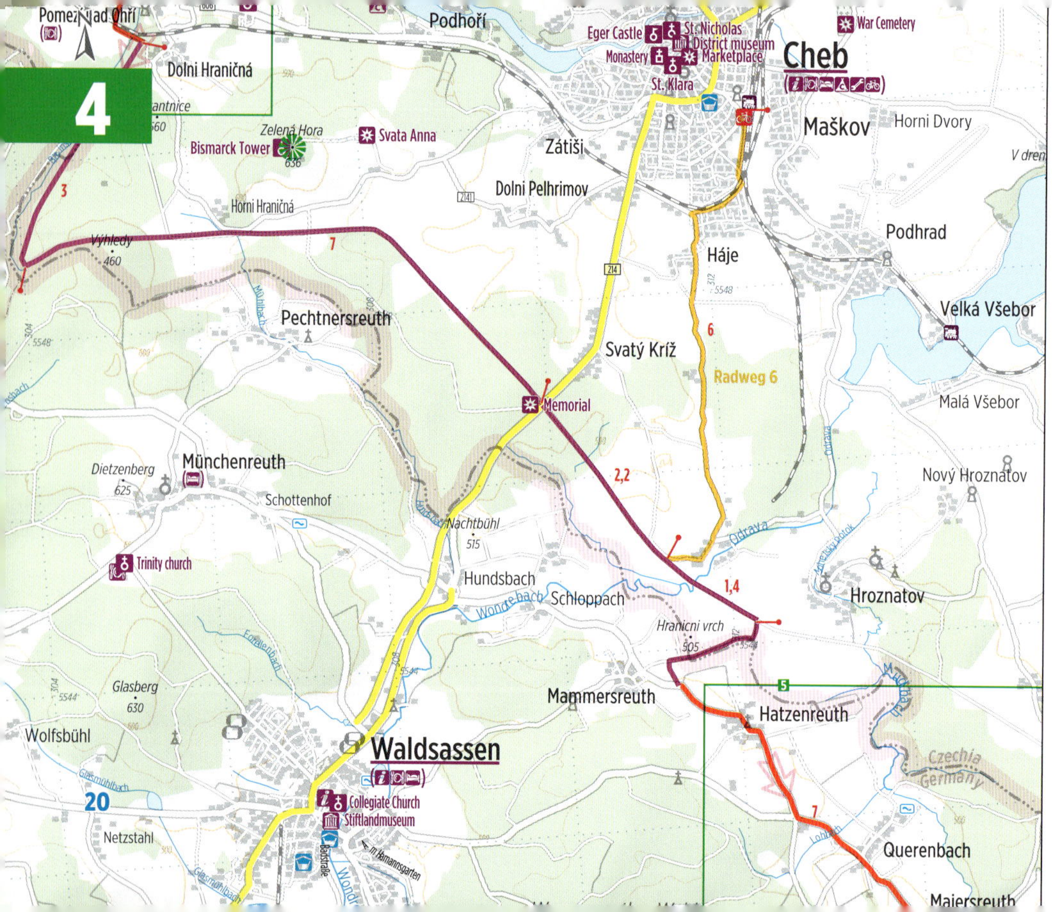

of Fichtel, Elster and Erzgebirge. In Asch, there are a few accommodation options to choose from, e.g. Hotel Radnice (✆ +420/354/526954).

Leave the town and make for a southerly direction on the main road (**Chebská**) until you reach the train station, from which you can take a direct train to Cheb. Pass under the tracks, keep to the right and join **cycle path 2063** into which you turn right. At the border you encounter the previous patrol route of the border guards, which is signposted as 2063 and **Iron Curtain Greenway**. In parts it is quite steep uphill and downhill.

EXCURSION After about 5 km the path 2066 branches towards the left towards Libá (Liebenstein).

Libá

The rococo palace that was built by the Zedtwitzer in place of a destroyed castle is completely run-down through Army use.

The "European Iron Curtain Trail" continues straight ahead.

VIEW Here you have a beautiful view of the Bavarian town of Hohenberg with their well-preserved castle, which lies on the other side of the valley opposite.

The patrol, which is marked as the Iron Curtain Greenway with two yellow and one red arrows is lined with concrete slabs and leads steeply down to the rather adventurous-looking old steel bridge over the Ohre. It continues through the meadows and fields crossing **Pomezí nad Ohrí / Schirnding**. Pass under the **E48 highway** and turn immediately right into the paved patrol road.

EXCURSION If you want to visit Cheb (Eger), you can take the 606 road which leads you along the south bank of the Skalka Reservoir. A better connection to the city but one we recommend a little later, is cycle path 6, which runs along a former railway line.

At the border cycle to **Highway 214**, where a memorial reminds us of the opening of the Iron Curtain.

Monument to the victims of the iron curtain

This **memorial** of Antonín Kašpar was inaugurated on 27 June 2006 with the participation of the first Czech foreign minister after the fall of the Wall, Jiří Dienstbier. It is dedicated to the people who died whilst trying to escape across the border. The main message of the broken/blown-up chains should be clear. The names of 82 people from 1948 to 1981 killed on the western border are listed. At the inauguration of the 56th anniversary of the execution of dissident politician Milada Horakova, 20 people demonstrated, mainly comprising of former staff of the border regime..

Milada Horáková

The lawyer and politician was active in the anti-Nazi resistance during the Second World war and for years was imprisoned by the Nazis. After the war, she pursued a political pluralism and sat as a Member of the "Popular Socialist Party" in the Czechoslovak Parliament. After the Communists came to

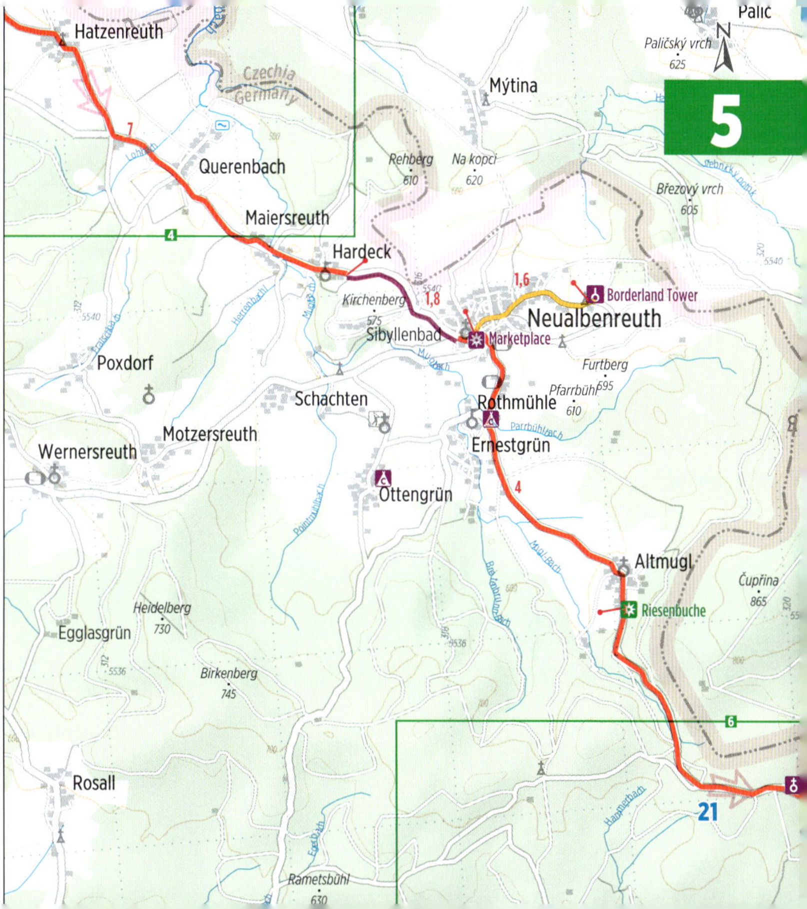

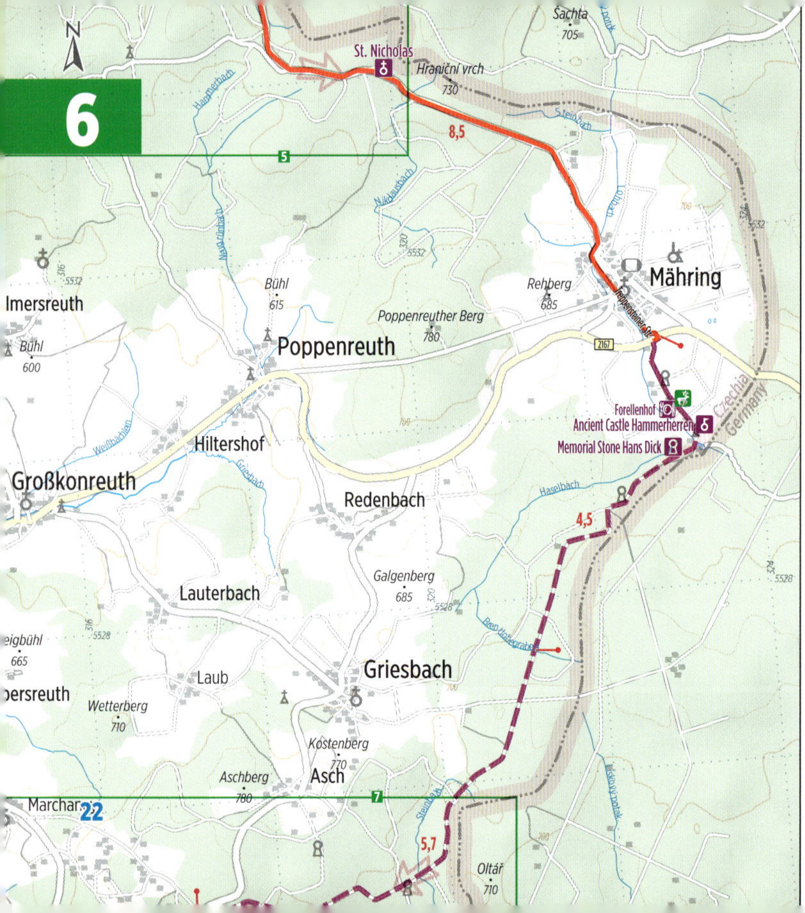

power in February 1948, she resigned her mandate out of protest.

In a nine-day show trial Milada Horakova was sentenced to death and executed on the 27th June 1950 - the only woman who was executed in communist Czechoslovakia for political reasons. The conviction was overturned in 1968, but she was not pardoned until 1990. There is a memorial stone of her in the Vyšehrad National Cemetery in Prague.

Cross highway 214 and cycle straight along the patrol road.

EXCURSION At the next opportunity cross bike path 6, which leads to a former railway track from Cheb to Waldsassen. If you want to visit Cheb - and this is highly recommended - turn left and continue cycling to the station, where there are also direct trains to Nuremberg and Prague. The same path will bring you back to the main route.

Cheb

Pedestrian zone. For the 950th anniversary of the first mention of the city a new pedestrian area was inaugurated, in which the history of the city's timeline is etched out. Special events are displayed alongside their respective years: E.g. 1061 the city was first mentioned or: "In 1938, after signing the Munich Agreement, Freikorps occupied Eger on the 1st October". The end of the pedestrian zone is marked by the "Gate of Time". Marian Karel's installation is a wall of steel that rotates a few degrees every hour so that at night the pedestrian zone is symbolically blocked off.

War Cemetery. This is the biggest collection of war graves in the Czech Republic. Since 2010, in the rear part of the cemetery, in the shade of old oak trees and birches, you will find 5,600

Borderland tower near Neualbenreuth

German and Czech war dead buried, only 2,700 of which have been buried. Among the people buried there are also 473 German and Czech civilians. In contrast to other former eastern bloc countries, the Czech Republic has no agreement with Germany regarding the creation and maintenance of war graves abroad. The remains of the dead were previously scattered throughout the country. It is thanks to the Lord Mayor Jan Svoboda, that this war cemetery was realised. The city was occupied by German troops in 1938 and remained a part of the German Reich until 1945..

The 35,000 inhabitant-strong city has a German name derived from the river (the Czech name originally means "bend"). It was created at the foot of a castle which was built in 1120 to manage the Bavarian Nordmark which itself was built on the foundations of a 200-year-old Slavic settlement. The starting point for a tour is the elongated-triangular square with its two fountains, in the midst of which a Roland and a Hercules keep watch. Opposite this you will find the "Information centre" for tourists. The sumptuous Baroque town hall excites just as many visitors as the Egerer Stöckl (Špalíček) does, a group of eleven Jewish merchant houses which miraculously survived a great fire in the 13th century.

Behind this is the Pachelbel house, where Prince Waldstein, called Wallenstein by Schiller – was murdered in 1634 because he had become too much of a threat. It now houses the county museum, which in addition to some memorabilia regarding the commander, also shows a documentary about 20 border villages of Cheb which were abandoned and destroyed after 1945.

Friedrich Schiller stayed in the Metternich House whilst he finished his Wallenstein Opus as he wanted to stay in authentic surroundings.

In mid-2008 the Gothic Nicholas Church restored the spires destroyed in the war so that they now tower again above the market square. 300 metres to the west on the river bank, is a castle which Friedrich Barbarossa had converted into an imperial palace, before it fell to the king of Bohemia. The Black Tower, built of lava rock, is particularly striking with its almost three-metre thick walls. For architecture enthusiasts, a special highlight is the Romanesque double storied twin chapel. It was accessible from both the lower levels and the higher levels of the Pallas. The ground floor was reserved for common people

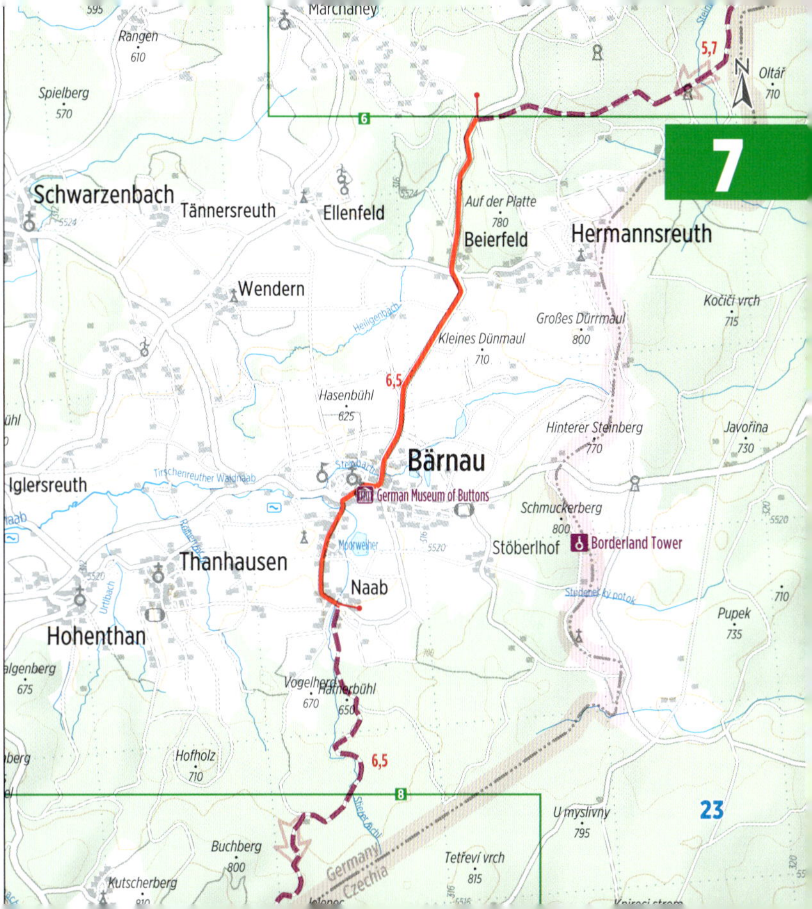

and the area above for the nobility, who could participate in the service via an octagonal ceiling opening.

From Cheb (CZ) to Bärnau (DE) 44 km

From the train station, take bike path 6 towards Waldsassen.

Turn left shortly before the border on the former border patrol road, which is signposted as **cycle path 2056**. At the next intersection, turn right and continue cycling to the border, where you once again turn right and cycle along the border towards Mammersreuth. In Germany, turn immediately left and you'll get to the road to Hatzenreuth into which you turn left.

Hatzenreuth

Once you reach Hatzenreuth, turn left in the road towards Neualbenreuth. Behind the village, turn left onto the asphalt path in the field, and at the next opportunity, keep right until you reach **Querenbach** where you once again turn right. On this street with little in the way of traffic, the route takes you left and you go through **Maiersreuth** to Hardeck.

Hardeck

Cross a stream and continue cycling on a bike path running safely parallel to the road until you reach the charming location of Neualbenreuth.

Neualbenreuth

Market square with timbered-houses in Egerland style.

Borderland tower. The place is located in the hilly countryside around the 939-metre-high mountain Tille, which was once calculated as the centre of Europe.

EXCURSION The tower road leads to the tower which is about 2 km away.

The route follows the road south through open land to Altmugl.

Altmugl

Giant beech. The trunk has about 7.70m circumference but nobody can guess the actual size of the tree. The top had to be cut 1999.

The trail goes through the forest for about 4 km. After 2km the Czech border begin to get closer to the road.

TIP Here we find on the left hand side the little Niklas Church belonging to the former Högelstein village which ceased to exist since the Hussite wars. The current construction is only just over a 100 years old and adds to the charm of the area.

Mähring

The market town of Mähring is located directly on the German-Czech border (the border crossing is located in the district of Treppenstein) and benefits from their proximity to the Bohemian spas in a place where tourism is becoming increasingly important. Due to St. Anne's Church location during the division of Europe by the Iron Curtain, it provided alongside the usual services, a connection to their old country for people who had been expelled. Ever since it was first mentioned in 1162, Mähring has been seen as a "Gateway to the East".

Memorial stone for Hans Dick

In Mähring, turn left off the main road and into **Treppensteiner Straße**. Continue for 500 metres until you hit the east-west link **road 2167** into which you turn right and 80 metres later you leave it again by turning left.

A narrow strip of asphalt stretches to **Treppenstein**, a former castle and today a large game reserve. Right next door, the delightful Forellenhof offers some good traditional meals. Continue on a well-maintained gravel forest road staying close to the Czech border. At the next intersection you will find a large upright stone commemorating "Hans Dick, died 18.09.1986 - shot by Czechoslovak Socialist Republic border guards."

Hans Dick

The last victim of the Iron Curtain between Bavaria and Bohemia was shot by Czechoslovak border guards on 18 September 1986. From what we know, Hans Dick was on his usual walk through the forest along the border, when suddenly he heard a series of screams and shots ringing out. A group of Czechoslovakia border guards were pursuing two fugitives from Poland. A border guard, several hundred metres deep in German territory strafed Hans Dick with his automatic assault weapon from behind. After the soldiers had noticed that they were already on the territory of the FRG, they laid the seriously injured Dick on a stretcher and carried him across the border. In distant Pilsen Hans Dick died of stomach wounds. Although mounting evidence suggested that the offender could be found amongst their ranks, the Czechoslovak side remained silent. Under pressure from the federal government, which intervened at the UN, the body was handed over.

The President of Czechoslovakia, Gustav Husák apologised and Hans Dick's widow received compensation of 100,000 D-Mark. The border guards were given disciplinary sanctions. After the fall of the Iron Curtain court proceedings were opened against three border guards, but all resulted in acquittals.

Behind the memorial turn left, pedal slightly uphill and follow the path straight along a right hand bend until you come across a country road, in which you turn left and follow the slope down to Bärnau.

Bärnau

Bärnau, which belonged to the Waldsassen monastery, was expanded in the middle of the 14th century into a city. Since 1628 it has been a part of Bavaria and could be described as structurally weak during the 19th century. Nonetheless, factories and light industry emerged, specifically for Bärnau, the production of buttons. No fewer than 70 companies produced pearl buttons. After a while a technical button school and an international trade fair even emerged. The competition from cheap plastic and die-cast buttons could not be withstood however, and today there are but a mere handful of button factories. For more information on the more glorious times it is worth a visit to the German Button Museum, which exhibits various materials and manufacturing methods.

This cozy town is worth a stopover. If you can do without electricity and running water, why not stay in the borderland tower (built 1913) over the summer. It can be found south of the small border crossing at 800 metres

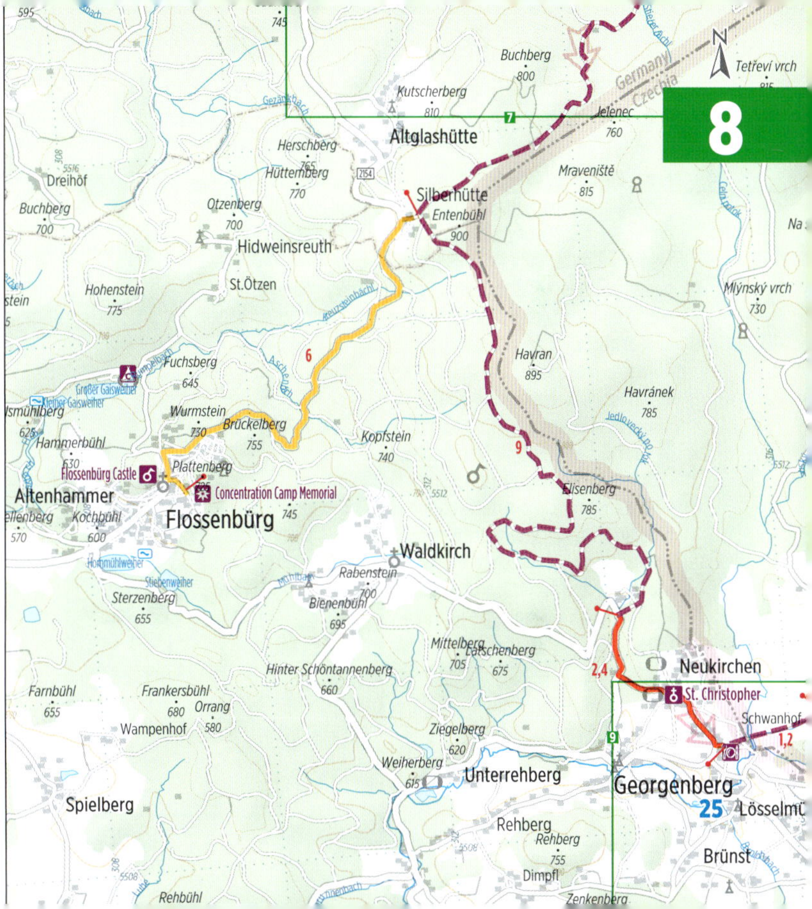

above sea level. On the road leading to it, you can pay a visit to the old Steinberg church on the left.

From Bärnau to Waidhaus 37 km

A small road leads through the fields to **Naab** in the south, where you can orient yourself using the orange-red-orange markings on your right towards Silberhütte. The route, which leads through forests and past secluded wooden cabins, is a little bit bumpy and winding but very scenic.

Silberhütte

In the centre of this well-known cross-country skiing area, you come to the **2154** main road to Flossenbürg.

EXCURSION Even though the route turns off before the town, a trip to the memorial in the former concentration camp of Flossenbürg is an important reminder of the dangers of human cruelty and is recommended for historical reasons.

Flossenbürg concentration camp

Flossenbürg Concentration Camp Memorial, Gedächtnisallee 5-7, OT: 9-17.

Without even seeking to hide what they were doing, the Nazis established a camp mostly for people deported from the occupied territories in Eastern Europe. In the nearby quarry they had to extract granite for Hitler. From 1943, military production, particularly for the aircraft company Messerschmitt was added. Between 1938 and 1945, about 100,000 people were imprisoned in Flossenbürg and in more than 80 sub-camps. Up to 1,000 slept in a shack in which there was only room for 300 inmates. A plaque here informs us of the fate of the resistance fighter Dietrich Bonhoeffer who was executed here shortly before the war's end. In total 30,000 prisoners were murdered. The Nazis worked them to death, starved them or froze them to death. The death march to Dachau in 1945 as the Allies were closing in, left a trail of more than 5,000 corpses.

Three Linden near Hranice

After the camp's liberation authorities built prisoner accommodation and a residential estate on the site, which reveals the arrangement of the barracks today. Even commercial use of different parts of the camp was not taboo. Only in June 2006, this "prototype of the forgotten camp", the remaining Nazi buildings and the quarry was declared a monument. A year later - after two generations - a permanent exhibition was set up for the first time, which was awarded the European Museum Prize in 2014.

Flossenbürg Concentration Camp Memorial

John Demjanjuk (1920-2012)

The Nazi war criminal John Demjanjuk was present in several concentration camps and from October 1943 was a guard at the Flossenbürg camp. His service number 1393 was the same number that he used in the Sobibor extermination camp. After the Second World War he emigrated from Germany to the USA. From there he was transferred in 1986 to Israel, where he was sentenced to death for crimes in Treblinka extermination camp. In 1993 the conviction was overturned and he returned to the United States.

In May 2009, Demjanjuk was extradited from the US to Germany where he stayed until his death. After the Munich prosecutor had collected enough evidence he went on trial on 13 July 2009 for aiding and abetting murder in at least 27,900 cases. He was found guilty and sentenced on 12

May 2011 by the regional court in Munich as an accessory to murder. John Demjanjuk was the last living war criminal who had to stand trial.

The European Iron Curtain Trail bends off in Silberhütte before 2154. The Green Roof bike path continues south. It continues along the border through a wooded area toward Neukirchen.

Neukirchen

Church of St. Christopher with a 45-degree twisting tower

Remain on the signposted Green Roof bike path, turn left in front of Neukirchen and cycle to the **Waldheim border crossing**.

Waldheim – the divided village

The Bavarian-Bohemian border has led through Vorder-Waldheim since time immemorial. At number 11, an inn, was said to have served Bavarian beer on the one side and Czech beer on the other.

After the communist government of Czechoslovakia had declared the area along the heavily-guarded border between Bayern out of bounds, the village was evacuated and demolished in the 1950s. Today a footpath exists between Vorder-Waldheim and Přední Zahájí on the border of Bohemia.

Before crossing the border there is a restaurant on the Czech side and then there is a short distance on an unpaved forest road to the **border patrol path 2238**, in which you turn right. Continue through hilly terrain in order to reach a picnic area with information about the razed village of **Hranice**.

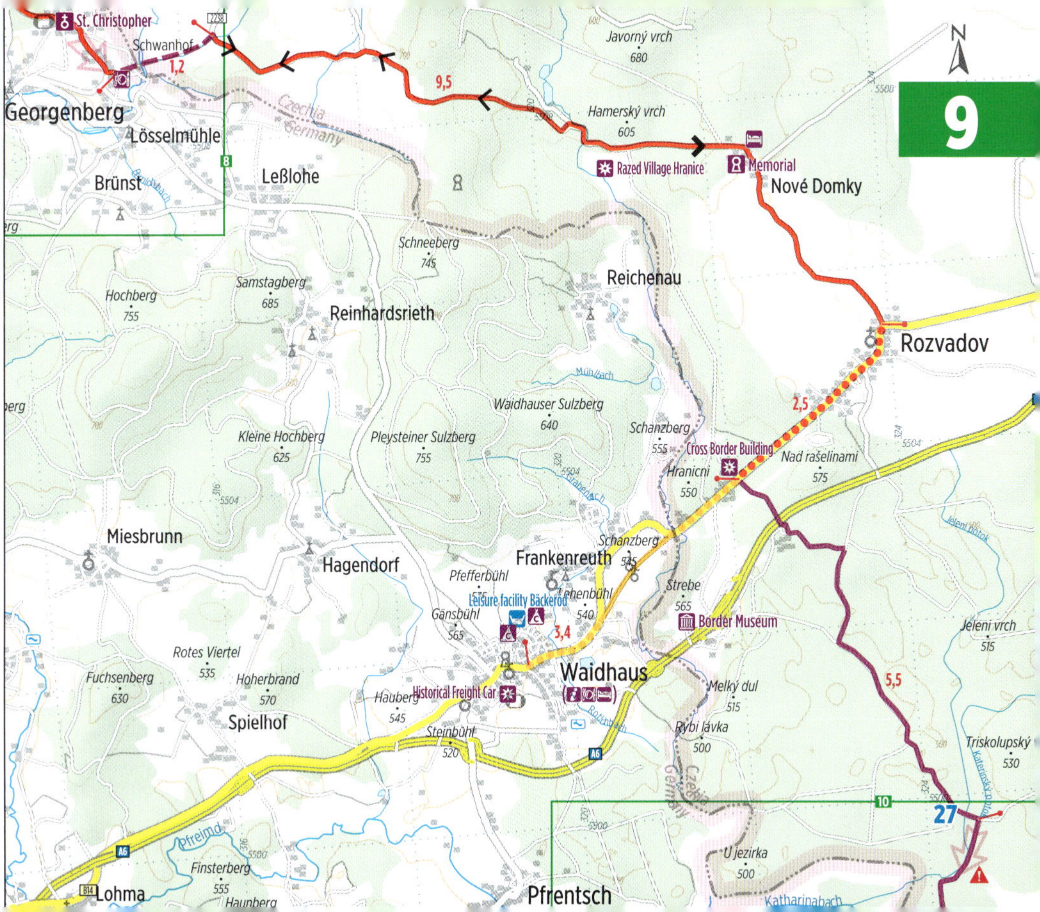

Razed village Hranice

In order to get free line of sight and fire, the whole village was razed. Today grass grows over where it once stood, but three monuments with commemorative plaques remind us of the past.

Ignore the many right turns and remain on the 2238 to Nové Domky. After a steep uphill part one can see on the right side a memorial commemorating the opening of the Iron Curtain.

Iron Curtain memorial

At this point on the trail, the foreign minister of Czechoslovakia and the Federal Republic of Germany symbolically cut through the border fence. Former member of the opposition Jiří Dienstbier (1937-2011), who was sent to prison for three years for the signing of Charter 77, was the first non-communist foreign minister since 1948. He had only taken office on 10th December and on 17th December together with Austrian Foreign Minister Alois Mock made the cut between Hatě and Kleinhaugsdorf and then with German Hans-Dietrich Genscher on 23 December 1989.

Nové Domky

Stay on the 2238 and in **Rozvadov** you will hit the road to Waidhaus, in which you turn right. Shortly before the former border control building on the Czech side, turn left onto the asphalted former patrol road which is signposted as Iron Curtain Greenway.

EXCURSION If you wish to cycle to Waidhaus, which is 4 km away, where there are also a few restaurants and options for accommodation, continue straight ahead. In order to get back to the main route see below.

From Waidhaus to Waldmünchen *53 km*

From Waidhaus cycle across the border to the Czech Republic and turn right behind the former border building right into the Iron Curtain Greenway.

After crossing a bridge over the motorway, immediately leave the road and turn into a damaged asphalt road on the left, which is signposted as the Iron Curtain Greenway. Turn right onto the better-paved road.

TIP The blue and white triangles on the nature trails contain interesting information about animals and plants.

On the level path, keep straight and continue along the old patrol road, a paved path in good condition, which can be navigated well. After crossing a stream, turn right, following the signposts towards Železná.

ATTENTION ⚠ Before the next left bend, the path is in a bad condition.

Then we come to the well-paved **bike path 36**, in which one turns right and reaches the next stop.

Železná

Today you will find a colourful market spread out across where was once Eisendorf (Železná), a place where 90 percent of the buildings were torn down. The historic St. Barbara's Church from 1770 has alas disappeared as has the cemetery, which had to give way to a barracks. A small snack shop and a small park compliment a pretty pond.

In Železná turn right – you will also find the restaurant Praha here - and cycle across the border to Tillyschanz. After the border, you can find a cycle path on the left side.

TIP This is shown as a **Pan-European Cycle Route** from Paris to Nancy, Strasbourg, Heidelberg, Nuremberg and Pilsen to Prague. There is also a mention of the Way of St. James.

Once it is possible, turn left onto the unpaved but relatively comfortable **R 13**. At the next intersection Triangle keep left and cycle along the **Leuchtenberg Tour**.

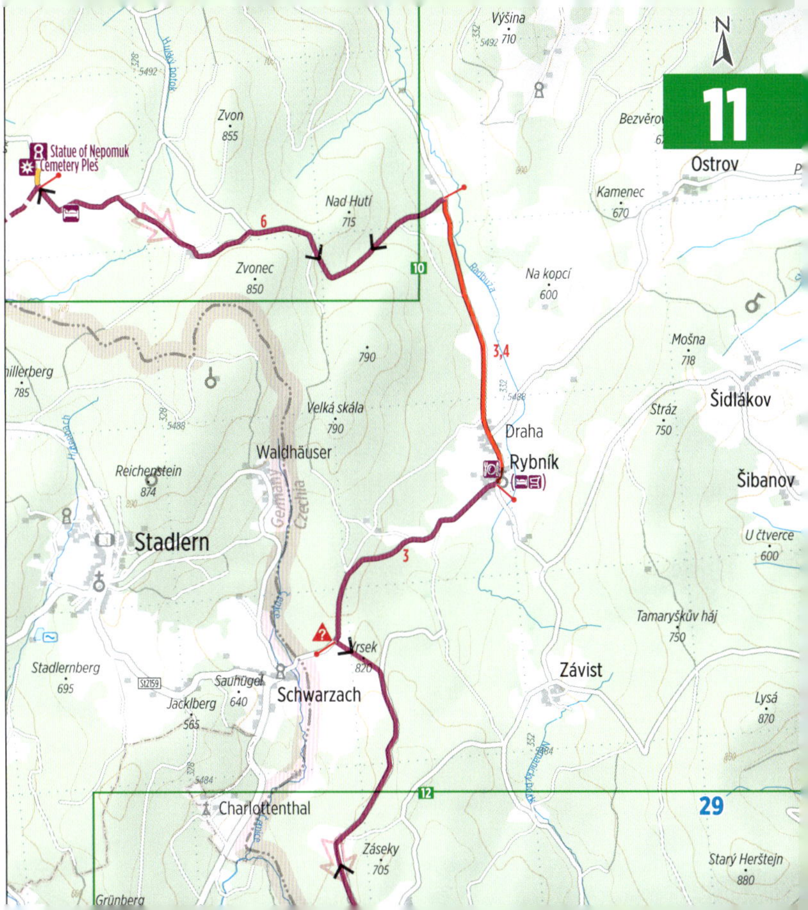

At the major junction the R 13 continues to the right, but you should continue straight ahead on the Green Roof bike path until you come across a paved road, into which you turn left.

Behind **Polster** turn right at a house in the street, and then - after the last house - left into the unpaved but again, reasonably comfortable path. After about 1 km the route takes a steep uphill turn and then you come across a paved road with no traffic, in which you must turn left towards **Friedrichshäng**. On the **R 36**, that's also called the **Johann-von-Nepomuk-Weg**, the path continues across the border, where the road is not paved, but is easy to navigate. It then branches off to the right, downhill onto the asphalted R 36.

EXCURSION If you want to check out the Nepomuk statue - John of Nepomuk is the patron saint of bridges - travel straight a little further. Just before you reach it you can also see the Pleš / Plöss cemetery. There you can still see the gravestones and the foundations of the church - the only evidence of the ruined village that still exists today.

Memorial stone for the victims of the world wars in Plöss

Pleš

The settlement was first mentioned in 1606 and in 1839 had 54 houses and 483 inhabitants. Despite the almost barren soil and the high altitude in Plöss, there used to be 10 large farms with good animal rearing, while the rest of the inhabitants were involved in trades such as forest workers, after the former glass pearl hut went downhill.

After 1945 the village was inhabited at a much slower rate. In the 50s immigration to the border zones was stopped altogether. All houses up to the forester's house and the former mountain hotel were destroyed, the latter converted into a barracks. The smuggler Zika was an inhabitant of the lodge for a time, who was shot whilst trying to cross the border in the early 1950s. In the 1970s, the demarcation was moved inland and the barracks were demolished. What remains now is only the former forester's house, which was converted into a bed and breakfast in 1990.

Continue following the path downhill, which is signposted as the Iron Curtain Greenway and is in very good condition. You will be rewarded for the climb with a beautiful and fun descent. At the bottom of the road, turn right to Rybník.

EXCURSION If you continue just a little further down the dirt road, you will arrive at a small bridge.

This small bridge, destroyed during the floods in 2002, and subsequently rebuilt, was very important for the people from the district Bischofteinitz that were displaced 1945. Some went back several times, picked up their cattle and belongings and then went back over to Pleš Schönsee.

Turn right and cycle along the Iron Curtain Greenway towards **Draha**. There turn right onto **cycle path 2141** until you reach Rybník.

Rybník

Waier is only sparsely populated, the parish church of St. Anna was demolished after its fall into ruin in 1964 and the town is dominated by a large agricultural development operated by the University of Pilsen since 1982. It is nonetheless possible to have a drink or bite to eat and stay the night.

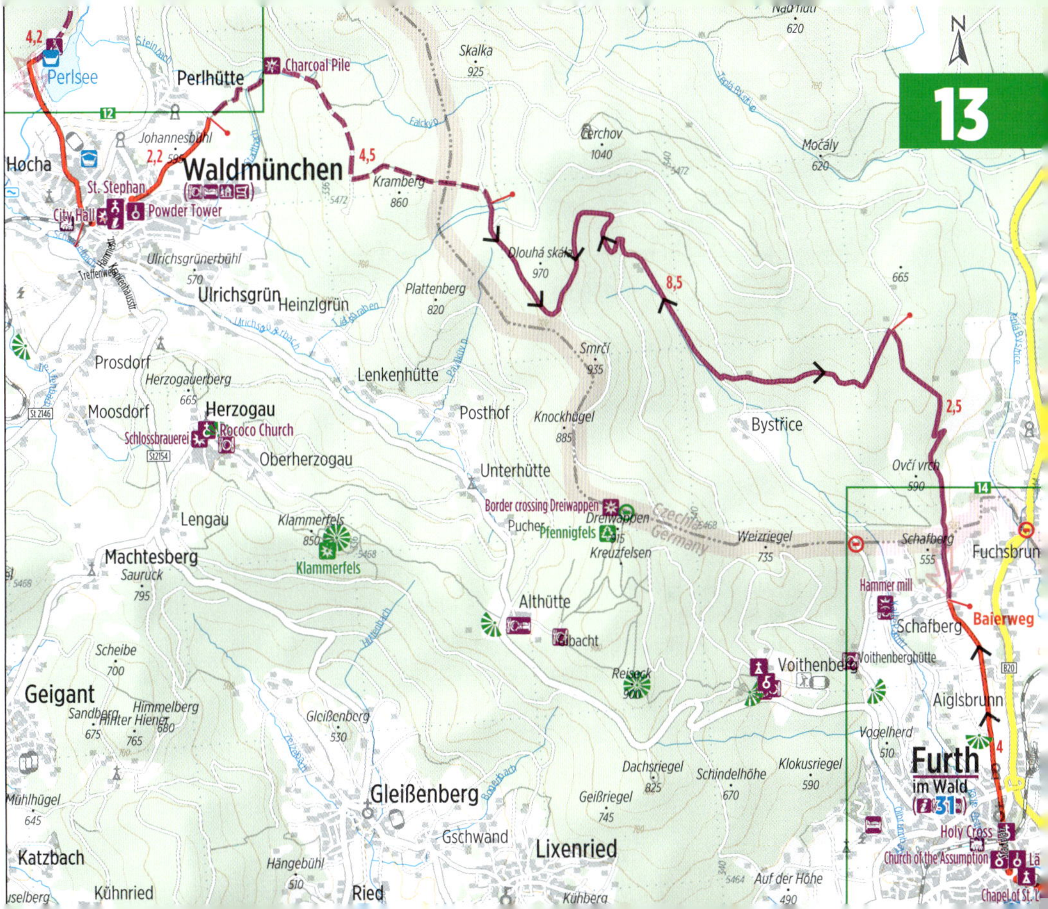

Border crossing in Finkenhof-Lucina

Just before leaving the village, turn right at the intersection and stay on cycle path 2141. At the next intersection go straight towards Schwarzach in the direction of the Czech-German border. Remain on bike path 2141 and turn left.

TIP This turning is not signposted as Route 36 ⚠.

At the triangular crossroads after the slope, where a sign points towards the villages Padorf and Hranica, turn right. The 36 Road then branches off to the left, but continue straight ahead on the partially damaged asphalt but well-signposted 2141 and you'll see big pavement slabs which lead you to Finkenhof on the Czech-German border.

Finkenhof

After the border cycle along the road and turn right after the sharp left bend into the unpaved forest road towards **Hammerfest**. There, keep to the right and continue cycling on the C 33, C 34 and C 8 through Buchwalli towards **Perlsee**. At the end, turn left into Waldmünchen.

Waldmünchen

The town with 7,000 inhabitants obtained its city rights in 1250 and has had many different rulers throughout the years. Her fate in a nutshell: stormed by the Hussites in 1434, several devastating fires in the town, looting and plague during the Thirty Years War. 1742 brought a bit of luck: The Pandur Colonel Trenck took the city during the Austrian Succession War, but thanks to the intervention of a priest and some school children decided not to sack the city. This event has been celebrated in the form of a festival with 300 amateur performers since 1950 'Trenck the Pandur before Waldmünchen", which takes place in July and August with wild riding scenes and blazing bonfires.

The health resort offers numerous accommodation possibilities and refreshment stops and shopping. The Türmerstube (watchman's room) in City St. Stephan's Tower is particuarly interesting, which was inhabited until the 1923. A border museum has existed here since 2001.

Direct trains to Cham and Prague are possible from the local train station

From Waldmünchen to Furth im Wald — *21 km*

From the square take **Böhmer Straße** before turning right into **Garten Straße**. Then keep right and turn into **Arnsteiner Straße**, from where you turn right into **Vossstraße**. At the car park, follow the signs towards Devil's Bridge (Teufelsbrücke). After 100m the trail goes steeply uphill and you cross the Kohlmeier forest path.

At the next branch in the road keep left, passing the water wheel and following the orange sign. After the waterfall the trail is again steeply uphill - you may have to get off and push - and at the next corner, turn right and continue going straight uphill. Once at the top cross a road and cycle straight into the trail, which is signposted **Brombeerweg** or **Kirchhofsteig**. Finally, you will also find the orange symbol with the number 34.

The Cerchov border crossing is also signposted. (At 1,041 metres, the mountain is the highest in the Upper Palatinate Forest). The level path has a few bad areas but the border crossing can be reached after 7 km. Then it goes uphill a little bit and you come across the Iron Curtain Greenway No. 36, into which you turn right. There follows a long ascent, which is not avoidable even with a different route.

But you will be rewarded with a wonderful downhill ride on an asphalt road. Once at the bottom, keep to the left. Following the number 36 sign, the route is gentle but again, steadily uphill. Take the right turn in cycle path 2014 towards Furth im Wald. Continue downhill on the asphalt surface, across the border and into **Schafberg** and then onto **Baierweg**.

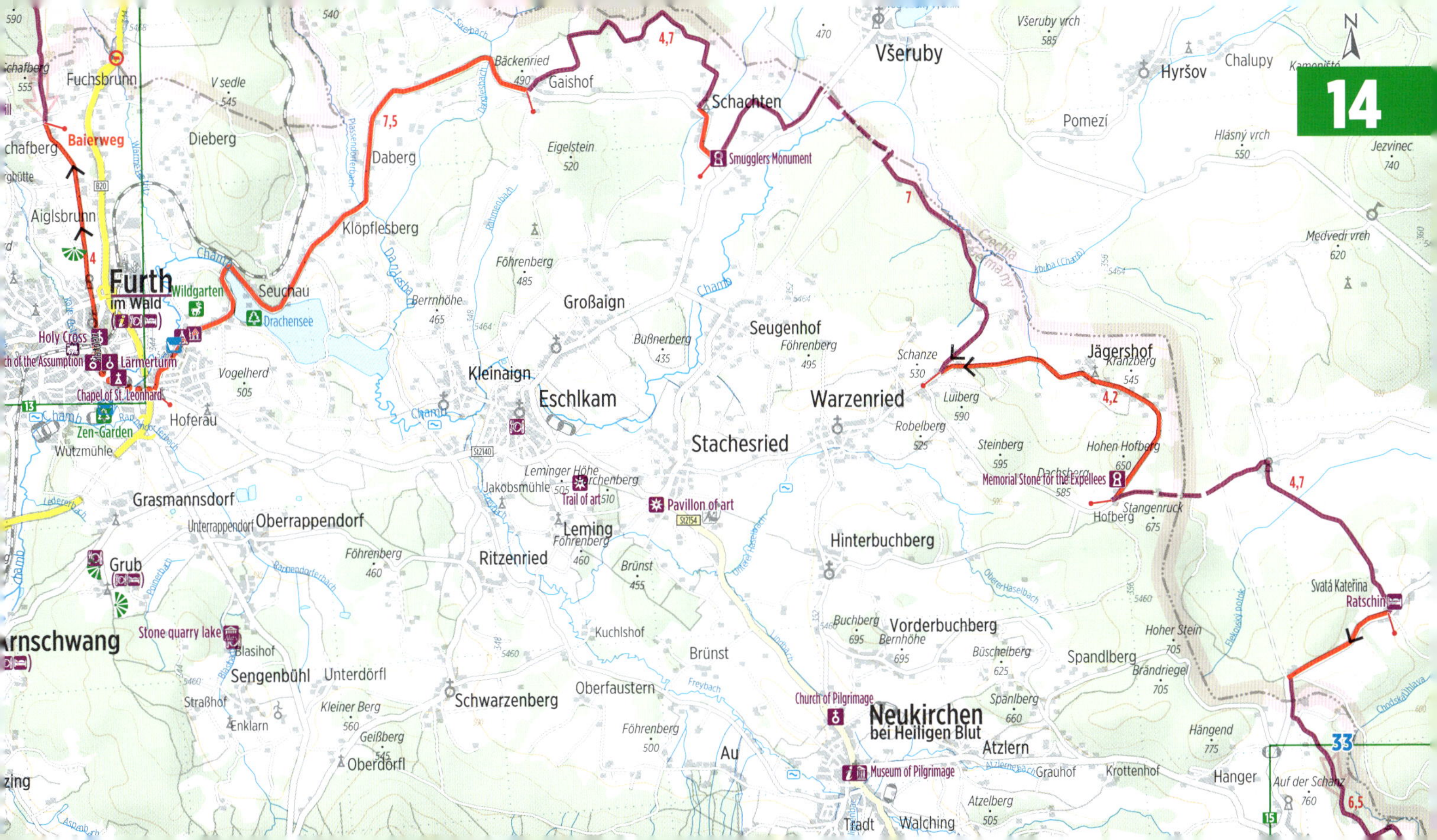
14
Furth im Wald
Fuchsbrunn
Baierweg
Aiglsbrunn
Wildgarten
Drachensee
Seuchau
Holy Cross
Lärmerturm
Chapel of St. Leonhard
Zen-Garden
Wutzmühle
Hoferau
Vogelherd
505
Dieberg
V sedle
545
Daberg
Klöpflesberg
Bäckenried
490
Gaishof
Eigelstein
520
Schachten
Smugglers Monument
Všeruby
Všeruby vrch
585
Hyršov
Chalupy
Pomezí
Hlásný vrch
550
Jezvinec
740
Medvedí vrch
620
Czechia
Germany
Föhrenberg
485
Berrnhöhe
465
Großaign
Bußnerberg
435
Seugenhof
Föhrenberg
495
Schanze
530
Jägershof
Kranzberg
545
Kleinaign
Eschlkam
Warzenried
Luiberg
590
Robelberg
525
Stachesried
Steinberg
595
Hohen Hofberg
650
Memorial Stone for the Expellees
Dachsberg
585
Stangenruck
675
Hofberg
Leminger Höhe
505
Jakobsmühle
Trail of art
510
Pavillon of art
Leming
Föhrenberg
460
Grasmannsdorf
Unterrappendorf
Oberrappendorf
Föhrenberg
460
Ritzenried
Brünst
455
Hinterbuchberg
Svatá Kateřina
Ratschin
Grub
Stone quarry lake
Blasihof
Arnschwang
Kuchlshof
Sengenbühl
Unterdörfl
Brünst
Buchberg
695
Vorderbuchberg
Bernhöhe
695
Büschelberg
625
Hoher Stein
705
Spandlberg
Brändriegel
705
Straßhof
Enklarn
Kleiner Berg
560
Schwarzenberg
Oberfaustern
Church of Pilgrimage
Neukirchen bei Heiligen Blut
Spanlberg
660
Geißberg
545
Oberdörfl
Föhrenberg
500
Au
Atzlern
Hängend
775
Museum of Pilgrimage
Grauhof
Krottenhof
Hanger
Auf der Schanz
760
Atzelberg
505
Tradt
Walching
7,5
4,7
7
4,2
4,7
6,5
4
33
13
15

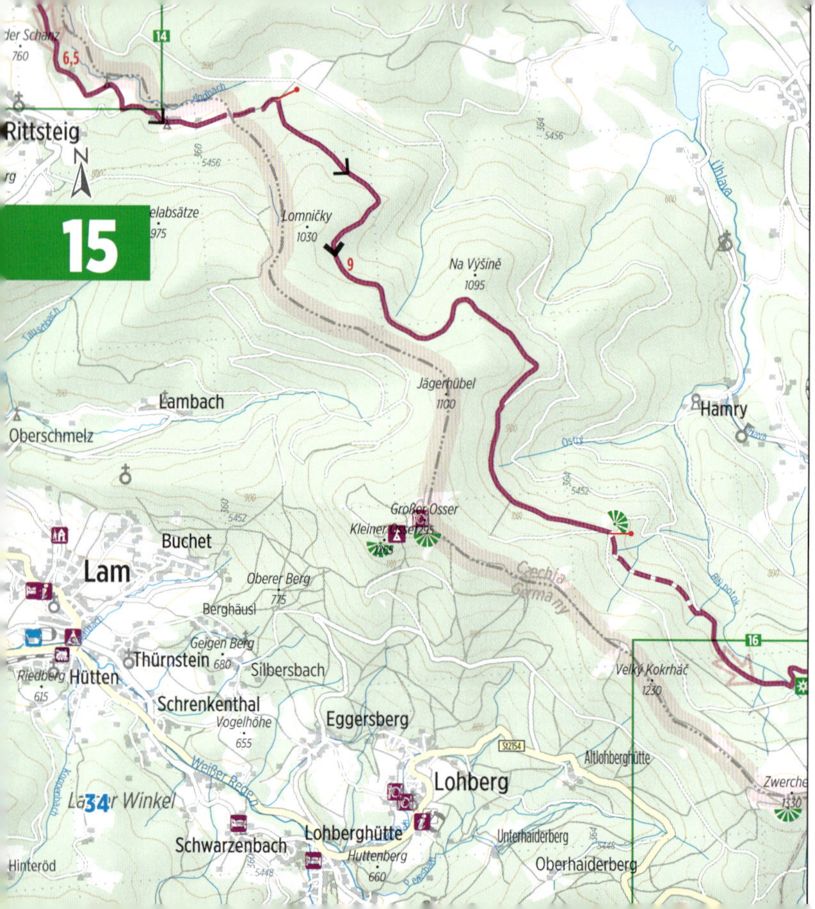

Baierweg

Baierweg belongs to one of the many old exploration and trade routes. One that runs from the Danube to the crest of Bavaria and through the Bohemian Forest establishing a link between Bavaria and Bohemia (Czech Republic). Its development is closely linked to the Counts of Bogen who used this path in order to transport their goods as safely as possible. The Blue diamonds, a symbol of the Baier path, comes from the Bogener family (11-12. Century), and from this the familiar blue and white Bavarian diamond pattern emerged.

From Schafberg the path goes down to Furth im Wald, where on the left you can see a memorial to the dead of the two world wars just before the entrance sign. Continue straight to the town square.

Furth im Wald

- The **Lärmerturm** houses several museums, including the **First German Dragon Museum**.
- Baroque **parish church of the Assumption**
- **Historic stone tunnels under the city**, OT: May-Sept, 13-16 pm, tour of Kramer Straße.
- **"Further Drachenstich"**, 2nd-3rd Sunday in August, the popular drama is considered to be the oldest in Germany. It consists of a parade with over 1,000 participants and 250 horses, and a play in which a dragon who symbolises evil, dies.

Furth has been designated a city since 1332. Direct trains to Schwandorf and Pragu are available from the local train station.

From Furth im Wald to Bayerisch Eisenstein 61 km

Road 2014 is already signposted on the square. Cycle past the Town Hall by **Torf road**, turn left into the **Eschlkammer road**, cross the Chamb and turn left into **Daberger road**. On the signposted Chambtal bike trail, which is also referred to as **2014**, take the **C 3** around **Drachensee**.

Gaishof

The signposted **Rittsteigweg** bends to the left and leads you to the border. Shortly before the forest the route takes you right along the former Iron Curtain. In the West you can see meadows and cornfields and in the East, a forest. Continue along the former patrol road and if you look closely you will see a stone marking the border, on the front

Smugglers monument near Schachten

of which the Bavarian coat of arms is painted and on the back, the Czech lion.

Schachten

At this point you will find yourself back on the road you left in which you now turn left. At the **Smugglers monument** turn left, then turn right at the next opportunity until you come to a road, in which you turn onto the bike path on your left. Shortly before the border, you will find a milestone with "Santiago de Compostela 2825 km" written on it. Turn right into the signposted Rittsteigweg. On the eastern side of the road you will see the border posts. Stay on the paved Rittsteigweg and keeping going straight whilst keeping right.

After the ascent, just before Warzenried, turn left downhill towards Jägershof. Just before you turn left again, you will see a memorial stone dedicated to the mostly young people who died in World War II which does nt mention the invasion of Czechoslovakia by Nazi troops in 1938. You will reach Hofberg, where the path takes you left to the pedestrian border crossing.

Shortly before the border the road is not paved anymore. The pedestrian border is marked by a big stone, where you will also see the Czech-German border stone. After the border, keep straight on the non-paved road, ignore the first branch to the right and continue straight until the road is paved. Continue to the right, on the paved part which is signposted **2055** to Svatá Kateřina.

Svatá Kateřina

Ratschin, ✆ +420/376/571863, overnight accommodation

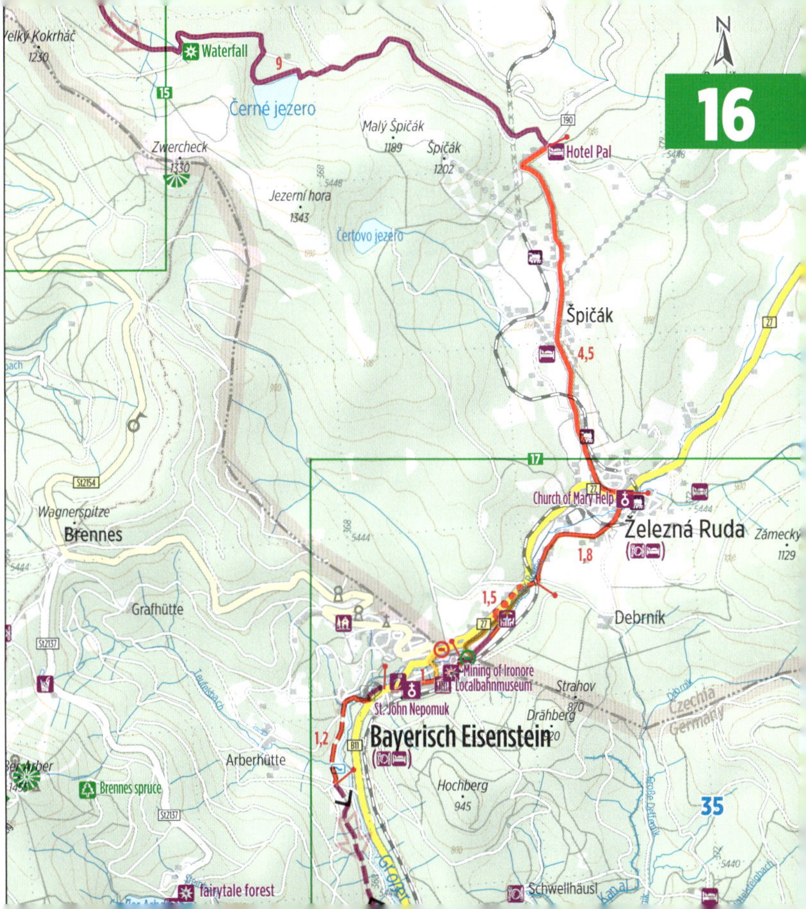

Here, turn right and continue cycling uphill to the border. After the climb, there's a fun ride down. Shortly after the crossing for bikers and hikers and before the first house, turn left into the paved road that leads you up and down hill and hits another road in which you turn right into Rittsteig. Ride left uphill to Helmenhöfen and cross the border, where a sign reads: "Prohibited for all types of vehicles except for customs, police and BGS". This is rather odd because the way is also signposted as bike path R. If pushing your bike across is also prohibited, is anyone's guess!

After the border the trail continues once again for a short time on an unpaved road uphill and then flattens out. The path then hits the tarmacked **2055 cycle path** (co-financed by the EU) in which you turn right. This part of the route is incredibly beautiful, even if it does go steeply uphill until you reach 1,050 m - the highest point of **Šumava (Bohemian Forest)**. Continue cycling straight on the 2055.

You can enjoy a wonderful view on a large square with three large trees, to which four streets lead. Turn right into the third street where you can follow the signs to the Black Lake (Černé jezero) and the round trip hammer no. 1 and no. 2. Watch out for wildlife along this stretch as it would not be surprising to see a deer dart out in front you. The paved road also has a few not very comfortable parts.

Keep to the straight passes waterfalls and comes at a lodge to a large waterfall, via the poet Klostermann wrote a book.

Karel Klostermann (1848-1923)

To the Czechs, he was considered the poet of Šumava, but for the Germans, he had no chance against Adalbert Stifter. He also wrote most of his works in the Czech language. After the expulsion of the Germans, streets, alleys and squares were named after him.

Ride straight downhill on a paved road.

Černé jezero

Between these two glacial lakes, the Černé jezero (Black lake) and the Čertovo (Devil's lake), one needs to overcome an altitude of 1,159 metres, the watershed between the Black Sea with the Danube and the North Sea with the Vltava.

Cycle along the lake, keeping to the left and staying on the paved road until you come to the Hotel Pal on a road, in which one turns right downhill in the direction of Železná Ruda.

Train station and border in Železná Ruda/Bayerisch Eisenstein

Cycle on the road without cycle lanes through **Špičák** - here you can find some bicycle-friendly accommodation (Pension Aura Špičák 2, Tel: +420 376 383 471, Mobile: +420 608 241 655) - and reach Železná Ruda. At the entrance, take the first street on the left and continue to the centre.

Železná Ruda

- **Informační turistické centrum,** Klostermanovo nám. 295, ✆ +420/376/397033, www.sumava.net/itcruda
- Baroque **parish church of Mary Help** of the star with its hexagram floorplan and central onion dome (1729-33). The late Baroque altar cross is made of polished and engraved ruby glass.

Železná Ruda is situated in the Sumava National Park, and benefits from its proximity to the 1,200-metre-high Špičák (Spitzberg) and the local ski resorts. The site has a number of stately mansions.

At the church, turn right, cross the railway tracks and turn off the main road to the left. Then on a paved bike path continue to the Bayerisch Eisenstein border station.

VIEW: Wonderful views of the Great Arber, which at 1,455 m is the highest mountain in the Bavarian Forest.

Border station Železná Ruda/Bayerisch Eisenstein

The border station was built in 1877, half on German and half on Czech territory, for the shortest ever railway connection between Munich and Prague. The border between Germany and the Czech Republic runs straight through the station area with the reception building. After the end of World War II cross-border rail traffic came to a

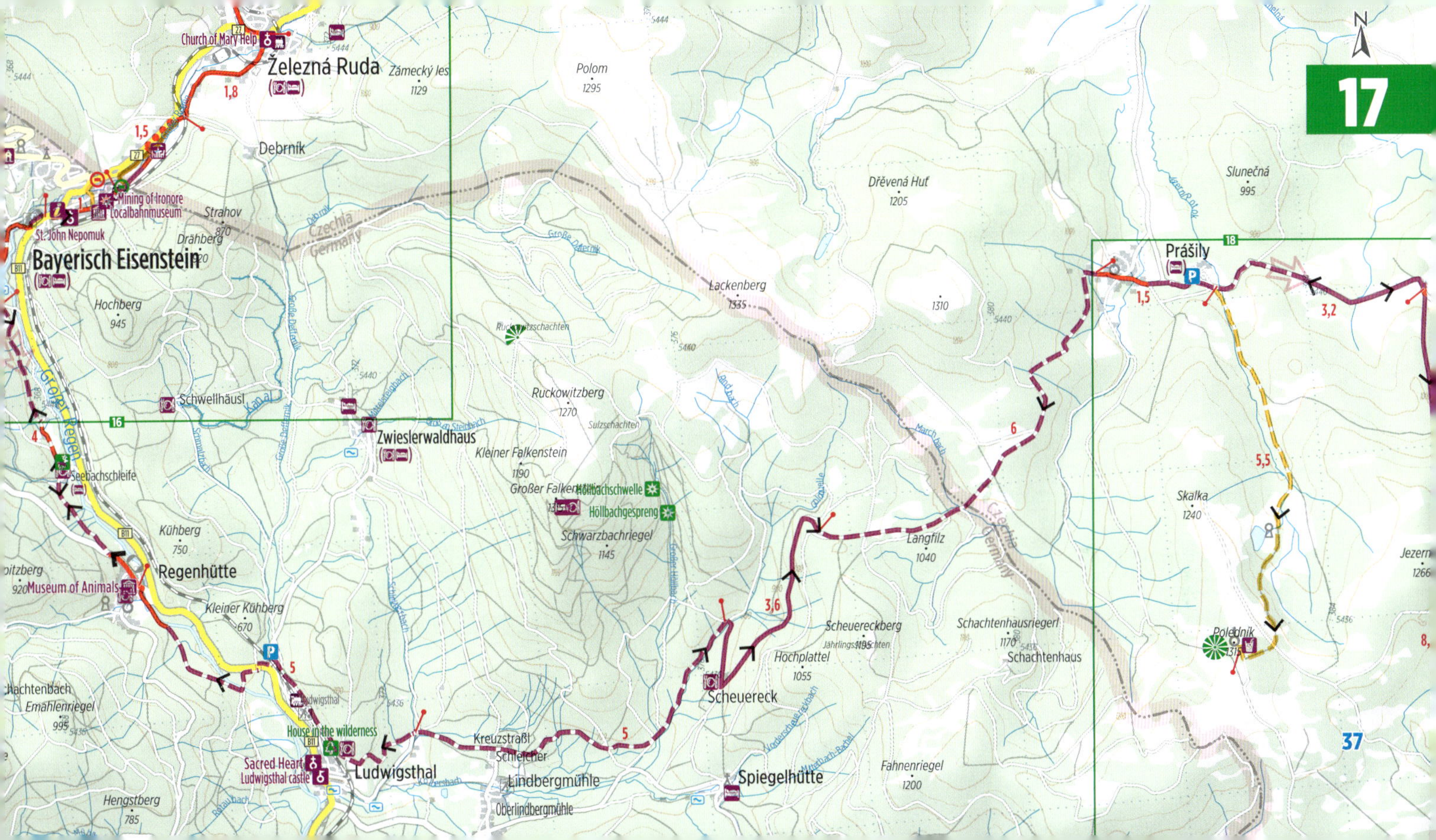
17
Church of Mary Help
Železná Ruda
Zámecký les
1129
Polom
1295
Debrník
Mining of Ironore
Localbahnmuseum
St. John Nepomuk
Strahov
870
Dráhberg
Bayerisch Eisenstein
Czechia
Germany
Hochberg
945
Lackenberg
1335
Dřevená Huť
1205
Slunečná
995
Prášily
1310
Schwellhäusl
Zwieslerwaldhaus
Ruckowitzschachten
Ruckowitzberg
1270
Sulzschachten
Kleiner Falkenstein
1190
Großer Falkenstein
Höllbachschwelle
Höllbachgespreng
Schwarzbachriegel
1145
Seebachschleife
Großer Regen
Kühberg
750
Regenhütte
Museum of Animals
Kleiner Kühberg
670
Langfilz
1040
Skalka
1240
Scheuereckberg
Schachtenhausriegel
1170
Schachtenhaus
Hochplattel
1055
Scheuereck
Poledník
1315
Jezerní
1266
Emahlenriegel
995
House in the wilderness
Sacred Heart
Ludwigsthal castle
Ludwigsthal
Kreuzstraßl
Schleicher
Lindbergmühle
Oberlindbergmühle
Spiegelhütte
Fahnenriegel
1200
Hengstberg
785
1,8
1,5
4
5
6
3,6
5,5
3,2
16
18
37

complete standstill. In 1953 Czechoslovakia erected a wire fence across the railways and the tracks were broken up. The reception was divided by a wall. On June 2nd, 1991, in the presence of Chancellor Helmut Kohl, the station was opened for rail traffic once again. Since that time, it has been possible to jump onto a regional train and continue your trip to another state. Direct trains to Plattling and Prague are also available here.

Bayerisch Eisenstein

Neo-Baroque **Church of St. John Nepomuk** with wooden rococo sculptures

The area owes its name to the former mining of iron ore. In the 18th century, however, the glass industry was the main driving force of the economic boom. Today, due to the heavy snowfall it has proven itself a popular destination for winter tourism. The church is also worth a visit, but the greatest attraction in Bayerisch Eisenstein is the border station.

From Bayerisch Eisenstein (DE) to Modrava (CZ) — 43 km

From the station, cycle on the **Bahnhofstraße** to the main road (**Hauptstraße**), turn left and right behind the petrol station turn right into the signposted and initially paved **Regental-Radweg**. After a short while the paving stops but the road is still navigable. Eventually you will hit **Arber Straße**, into which one turns left.

Regenhütte

After the passage way turn right at the exit onto the signposted cycle path.

Cycle over a beautiful moss-covered bridge, cross the next road and over the wonderful old railway bridge and turn right at the car park into an unpaved, but nonetheless decent National Park bike path. After a slightly uphill cycle ride you will reach **Haus zur Wildnis** (house in the wilderness).

House in the wilderness

Since 2006, the visitor centre has provided information on the Bavarian Forest National Park and the Šumava and the neighbouring regions on both sides of the border. The development of the National Park forests in relation to the wilderness is sharply in focus. Visitors can expect a variety of exhibitions, a great 3D cinema, games room, the National Park gift shop and certified organic food.

Bavarian forest National park and Národní park Šumava

There is a national park located to the south Bayerisch Eisenstein. The "Bavarian Forest National Park" in the west was founded in 1970, and the "Národní park Šumava" in the east was founded in 1991. The 190 km long low mountains between the Czech Republic, Germany and Austria - also known as the "green roof of Europe" - was known in the

Iron Curtain Trail near Regenhütte

early 20th century as the "Bohemian Forest" and was one of Europe's largest forests.

In the romantic opera "Der Freischütz" (The marksman) by Carl Maria von Weber the forest is equally celebrated as it is in the entertainment program "Musikantenstadl". The two world wars, however, have divided this area. During the Cold War, the German and Czechoslovak forest area were separated by reinforced barbed wire fences. On the Czechoslovakian side, large parts were designated "forbidden border zones" and equally inaccessible. Since 1989, the entire area, which the locals say is always "three quarters winter and the remaining quarter is cold", has been freely accessible again – thanks to the Schengen agreement you can even enter the Czech Republic now without any border controls.

Recognised by UNESCO as a Biosphere Reserve National Park with primeval remnants of mountain forests, glacial lakes, bogs and floodplains the national park makes up one third of the largest contiguous forest area in Central Europe.

Thanks to conservation and a favourable climate of the last 35 years, a number of unusual, diverse natural forests are starting to thrive again after

large parts of the forest on the southwestern slopes had been destroyed by air pollution and bark beetles towards the middle of the 20th century.

And a special phenomenon can be seen here, namely that after 20 years the border does not appear to not just be in people's minds but also the animals have not forgotten. Scientists like Rothirsche equipped a series of animals with a satellite transmitter and began tracking their movements. They observed that both the deer on the German as well as on the Czech side, travel up to the former border and then reverse. Although there are no barriers anymore prohibiting the deer from straying any further it seems that the memory of the border fortifications continued to be passed down from generation to generation. When this will change, no one knows.

Bavarian Forest National Park

The Bavarian Forest National Park is the oldest national park in Germany. It was founded in 1970 in Bavaria and covered just 130 square kilometres. In 1997 this was extended to 240 square kilometres. The park contains some areas of dense

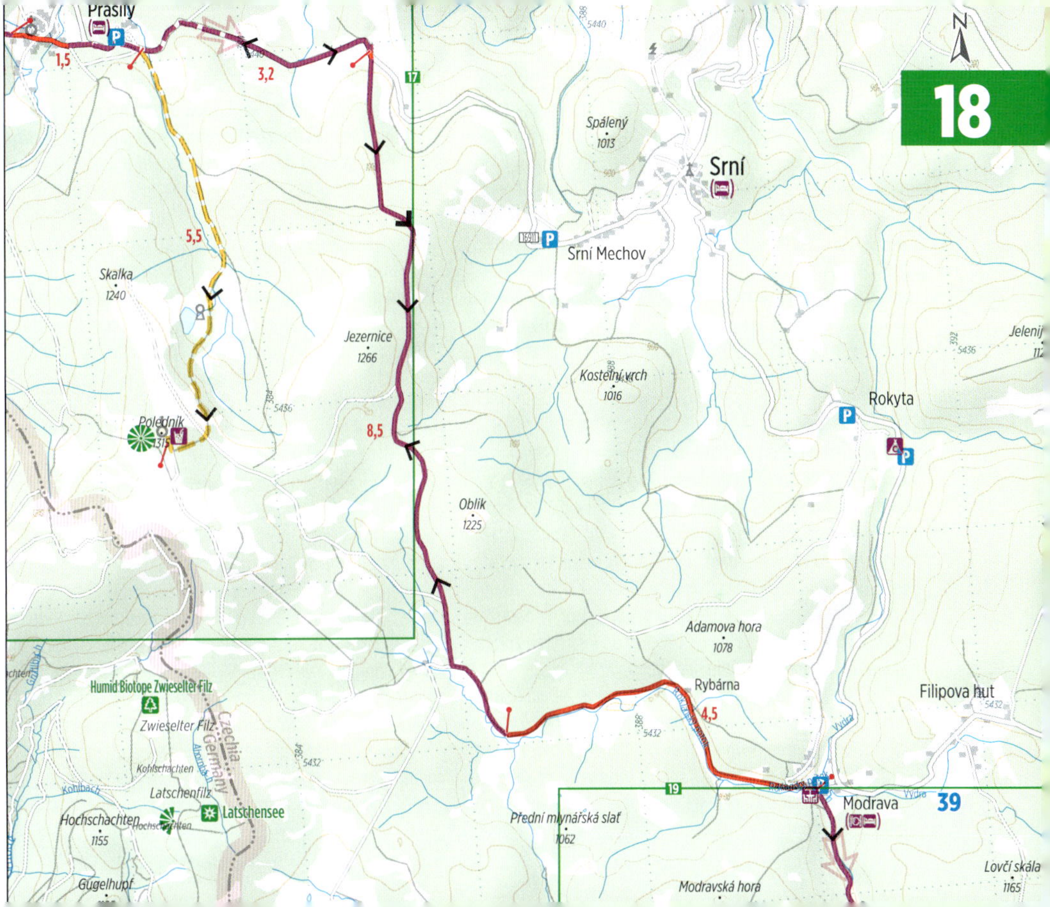

foliage, lakes and fells and extends to an altitude of 700-1450 metres. The park experiences 160 days of frost every year. The highest mountains of the Bavarian Forest in the area called "Woid" by the locals are the "King" of the Great Arber (1,455 metres), which is, however, only three feet higher than its "subject", the Great Rachel (1,453 metres). Overturned and overgrown trees remind us of the cycle of life. Meanwhile, the Lower Bavarian forest pulls in hundreds of thousands of visitors each year. The lynx, considered extinct in this area 150 years ago, has since the 1980s, returned. Even wolves have been sighted again. And long-lost beetle and fungal species feel at home in their habitat.

Národní park Šumava

The Šumava National Park was founded in 1991 and at almost 70,000 hectares, is almost three times as large as the on the Bavarian side. The highest mountain at 1,378 metres is the Plechý, the favourite old haunt of Adalbert Stifter. From here he looked down at the Plöckenstein lake which seemed to him to be like a "fossilised tear". A 14-metre high obelisk was erected on the tenth anniversary of his death in 1877. The forest area, which is divided up into three zones, makes up 81 percent of the national park.

The "Pure nature" zone includes the most valuable and most stable parts of the landscape - jungle-like forests, moors, glacial lakes. Nature has developed here undisturbed and without human intervention for thousands of years. It covers roughly 9,000 hectares which is 13 percent of the National Park area. The "Guided nature" zone makes up the majority of wooded and open areas, from the natural areas and the modified to the greatly damaged areas. The goal of this zone is to maintain the natural balance of the area and encourage a gradual approach to natural forest ecosystems. It covers 57,000 hectares, 83 percent of the national park area.

The border zone includes the areas substantially altered by humans, including settlements. The use of these areas should be permanently preserved and promoted for housing, services, agriculture, tourism and recreation, so long as it does not contradict the National Park objectives. This area is approximately 2,800 hectares comprising 4 percent of the national park area. The zoning in the Šumava National Park is regarded as a dynamic process. The area ratio of the pure nature area has been gradually increased by connecting areas of the guided zone.

From Haus zur Wildnis, continue on to **Ludwigsthal** and after passing a willow tree continue downhill towards Scheuereck. In **Schleicher** you will come across a paved road, into which you turn left. Continue on an upward slope on a paved road. The National Park cycle path runs gradually uphill along Kleiner Deffernik. At a sharp bend, continue over the bridge. You can see from the stone crossing points that this river was expanded in the past to transport wood. After 27 km on level ground you will reach Scheuereck..

Scheuereck

Here you can find food, drinks and homemade cakes.

Turn left onto an asphalt road and for around 4 km cycle up a steep hill towards Prasily. Just before the top, you will see a sign for the border crossing. The asphalt road makes way for a non-paved road. Keep going straight ahead. After the peak, the trail leads you down to the border and from there it is only 4 km downhill to Prášily.

You can see on the left side the remains of the deserted houses of Schwarzenbach. The forest road leads into a paved road and at the junction go straight ahead. To the left there is a monument for the student O. Kareis who drowned there in 1927.

Prášily

The sparsely populated area was declared a closed military zone after 1948, and Prášily was at the centre of a military training area. Traces of tank tracks and firing range paraphernalia can still be seen as can deserted villages which were shot to pieces by artillery. After the withdrawal of the military in 1991, the church was re-established and with their remaining 25 houses has been striving ever since to create good enough infrastructure to restore its once sterling reputation as a winter sports centre.

On the outskirts, behind a large triangular intersection, turn right into the forest onto an asphalt road, which is signposted as **cycle path 33** and runs at a safe distance parallel to the road.

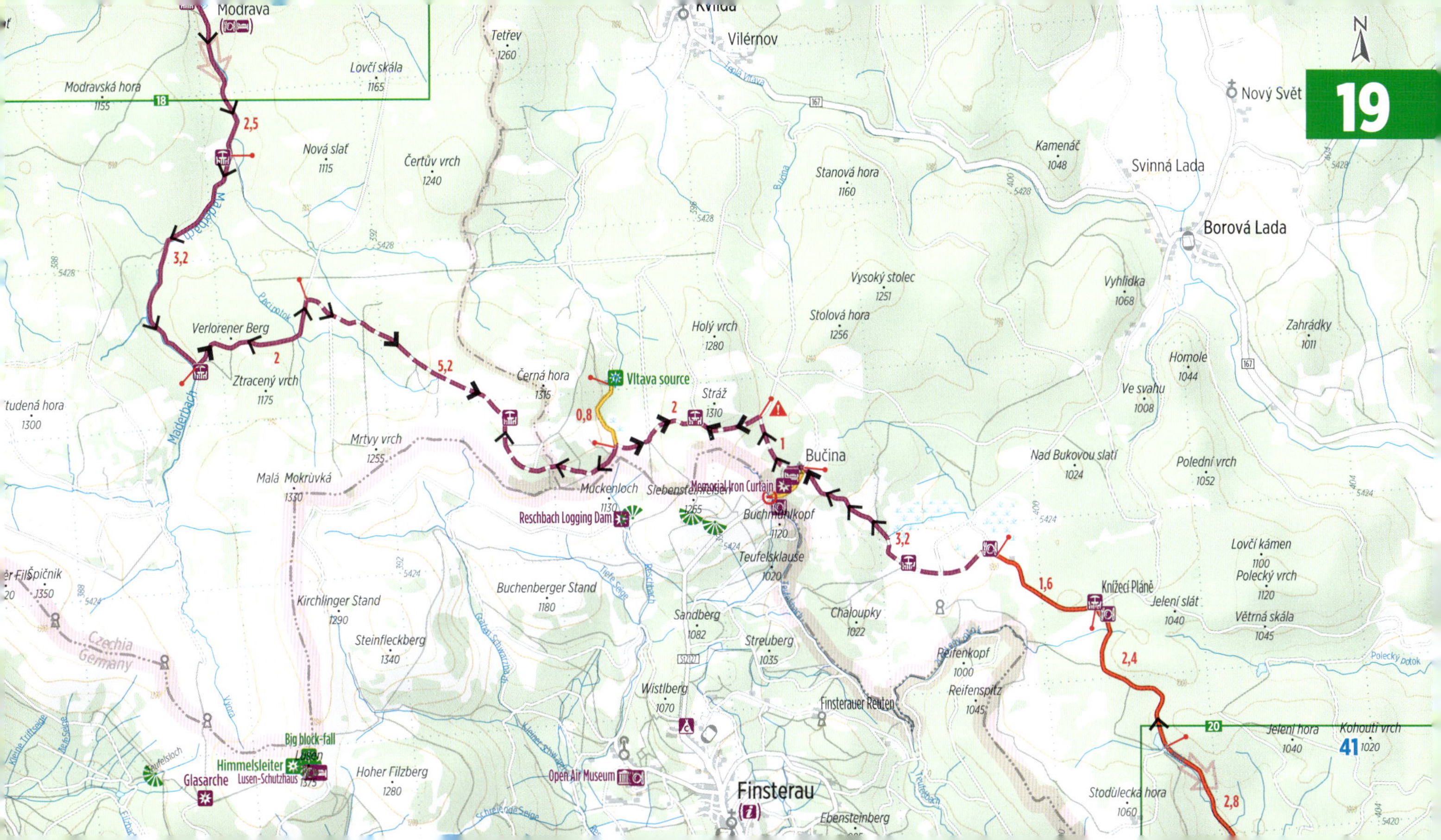
19
Modrava
Tetřev
1260
Lovčí skála
1165
Modravská hora
1155
18
2,5
Nová slať
1115
Čertův vrch
1240
Kvilda
Vilémov
Teplá Vltava
Nový Svět
Kamenáč
1048
Svinná Lada
Stanová hora
1160
Borová Lada
3,2
Verlorener Berg
2
5,2
Ztracený vrch
1175
Černá hora
1315
Vltava source
0,8
Stráž
1310
1
Bučina
Vysoký stolec
1251
Stolová hora
1256
Holý vrch
1280
Vyhlídka
1068
Zahrádky
1011
Homole
1044
Ve svahu
1008
Studená hora
1300
Mrtvý vrch
1255
Malá Mokrůvka
1330
Mückenloch
1130
Siebensteinfelsen
1265
Memorial Iron Curtain
Buchwaldkopf
1120
Reschbach Logging Dam
Nad Bukovou slatí
1024
Polední vrch
1052
Teufelsklause
1020
Lovčí kámen
1100
Polecký vrch
1120
Knížecí Pláně
1,6
Jelení slát
1040
Větrná skála
1045
Chaloupky
1022
Sandberg
1082
Streuberg
1035
Buchenberger Stand
1180
Kirchlinger Stand
1290
Steinfleckberg
1340
Špičník
1350
Czechia
Germany
Reifenkopf
1000
Reifenspitz
1045
2,4
Wistlberg
1070
Finsterauer Reuten
Big block-fall
Himmelsleiter
Lusen
Lusen-Schutzhaus
1373
Glasarche
Hoher Filzberg
1280
Open Air Museum
Finsterau
Ebensteinberg
20
Jelení hora
1040
Kohoutí vrch
41 1020
Stodůlecká hora
1060
2,8
Polecký potok

EXCURSION

If you want to cycle to Poledník, cycle across the parking lot to board and turn right into unpaved bike path 2113. At the end of this turn right and follow the trail up a fairly steep hill to Poledník.

Poledník

The 1,315-metre-high Poledník was located in a restricted military zone. At the end of the 1960s, a concrete tower for radar purposes was built there. After the dissolution of the exclusion zone in 1989, the military equipment was dismantled and the tower, at a height of 37 metres, was transformed into a viewing platform. This was opened in July 1998, and with over 227 steps provides an extensive view over Šumava and the Bavarian Forest and even as far as the Alps. Next to the tower you will find a cabin where you can obtain a quick snack.

On bike path 33, cycle straight on until you reach **2118**, into which one turns right. The path small gentle slopes upwards before flattening out. At the next right turn is a sign for cyclists, yellow-green-yellow in horizontal stripes - the sign for the bicycle path - although the central strip can also be red or blue. However, the number and the local reference point to this path is unfortunately missing. Once you reach 1,105m height, it goes downhill. Once at the bottom, turn left and follow the sign "Modrava 6 km". At the first intersection, turn right and continue cycling straight to the centre.

Modrava

The city on the old Gold Trade Trǻil was founded in 1757. In the 18th century, the glass industry dominated here, as it did throughout the region. From the beginning of the 19th century, with the start of intensive logging, lumberjacks began to settle here, and the Chinitz-Tettauer Schwemm canal (Vychnicko-Tetov kanál) was used from 1801 to 1958 to transport wood.

Since 1826 and after the establishment of the Bienertsäge sawmill, pines were processed into resonating wood for the use in musical instruments. One wing of the building was preserved, the half-timbered building with turrets today serves as a rehabilitation centre.

After the Second World War the church lost nearly all of its 2,000 mostly German inhabitants. Due to its vicinity to the border, most had already fled before the forced expulsions reached the village. Today, only 52 people live in the village.

West of Modrava are the Maderer felts (Modravská slať), the largest raised moors of the two national parks which have been under protection since 1933. The nature reservation containing 3615 hectares of forests which have a significant black grouse population forms the heart of the Šumava but cannot be accessed by visitors. The felts are a major water reservoir that feed into the stream Rachelbach. Over plank walkway is the Tříjezerní moor (Dreiseenfilz), 19-hectare moor located north-west of the village.

The Bergfichten forests south of Modrava were destroyed in 1995 by bark beetles and have been left to nature for natural reforestation.

Hotel Klostermann stands on a hillside on the other side of the river.

Bark beetle

The bark beetle is not a pest – it belongs as much to the trees as the Bavarian Forest. Both have a limited lifespan. If the spruce trees become too big and too old, they emit a scent that attracts the bark beetles. The bark beetles drill holes in the bark of the old trees and lay their eggs in there. The larvae feed on the tree until it becomes unstable and falls. The bark beetle therefore helps the next generation of trees to emerge. However, through the change from mixed forests into monocultures – spruce wood trees were better for business than other trees – acid rain, climate change with warmer winters and an increase in natural disasters the population of bark beetles has increased like never before. Since the dying trees were no longer sufficient to sustain

Old wood infested by bark beetle and new wood in the south of Modrava

them, they began looking for even healthy spruce for their offspring. In effect, the bark beetle is nature's revenge for the timber industry's greed. The Bavarian Forest National Park was established in 1970 and was the first national park in Germany. Forestry was initially approved for years but in a limited capacity. It was not until 1983 when violent storms felled about 70,000 cubic metres of wood that the Bavarian government decided under Minister Hans Eisenmann to leave 30,000 cubic metres untouched.

In the mid-1980s and early 1990s violent storms and high winds created even more favourable living conditions for the bark beetle. In subsequent years, the population increased so much that to find a non-affected, healthy and still standing spruce was the exception. Some parts of the population did not understand the order not to do anything; the adjacent wood farmers feared for their economic livelihood. The dispute revolved around whether the infested trees should be cut down and specific measures taken against the bark beetle, or whether one should trust nature to solve the problem independently without human assistance. It was argued that the bark beetle is actually a helper who corrects the wayward conversion of vigorous and healthy mixed forests into vulnerable monocultures. After all, the beetles infest only the spruce – they do not touch the other trees.

Now that many of the old spruce forest monocultures in the National Park are largely dead, as expected, the number of beetle numbers has been declining significantly for some years now. With the regrowth of young rowan, spruce, fir and beech a young forest has emerged in many places again which in some areas now resembles a pristine primeval landscape.

The result is not to the liking of some locals, because a different type of forest to the one they were used to has now been created. Not only this, the forest farmers who live in part from the forest industry, of course, fear that the beetle is accessing their forests from the National Park. To prevent this, measures have been taken in the form of a 500-metre-wide protective strip around the National Park - the maximum flying distance of a bark beetle is said to be much lower. Apart from that, there is also now a law which dictates that every bark beetle infested tree in Bavaria be cut down and

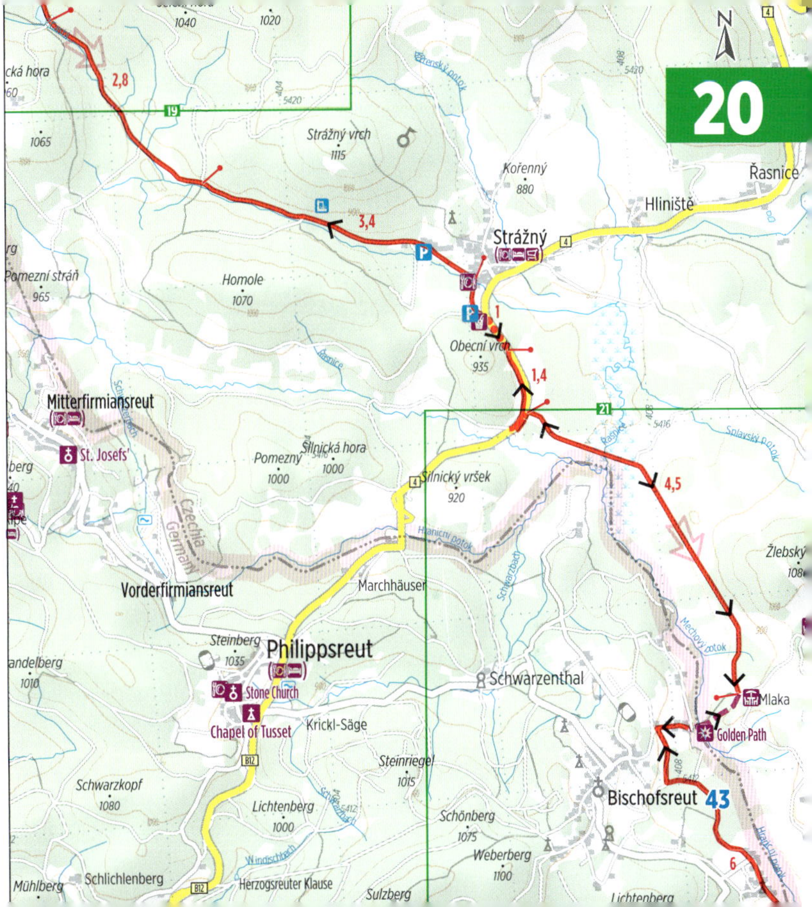

removed from the forest apart from in the national park! This heavy-handy measure has understandably caused a lot of resentment. In large parts of the national park the native forest farmers still which to fight the bark beetle, which continues to go against the "let nature be" mantra from supporters of the national park. However, the nature zones will again be set up gradually until 2027, which is an absolutely necessary measure in maintaining the national park. This is because in a national park, 75 percent of the area must be called a natural zone.

The hope remains that in the Bavarian Forest National Park, nature itself deals with the changed environmental conditions and solves the human-caused problems.

From Modrava (CZ) to Haidmühle (DE) 41 km

From Modrava the bike path continues at the entrance in a southerly direction, and is signposted **1023** to Bučina and leads gently along the river **Modravský potok** (Mader Bach). At the next crossroads, turn left and uphill on the **1042** towards Horska Kvilda. At the next crossroads, turn right. Road **1023**, a cross between asphalt and gravel is signposted to Nove Udoli - unfortunately there is no signposting to the German Haidmühle. From here it takes you uphill to the highest point, where the road also becomes paved. After the exit turn right at the next intersection to Bučina.

EXCURSION The Vltava spring is well worth a visit. For this, stay on the paved path for a further 700 m.

The Vltava (Moldau)

The Vltava (historically from the Germanic Wilth-Ahwa, which translates as "wild, raging water") is also called the "Bohemian Sea", and is the longest river in the Czech Republic and flows into the Elbe. The Moldova is 430 km long and drains an area of 28,000 km². It originates from two source rivers, the warm Vltava near Aussergefild (Kvilda) in Šumava and 50 km further on the Cold Vltava near Haidmühle in the Bavarian Forest, in which it also receives small streams from Bavaria. The Grassy Moldova (Rasnice) is a tributary of the Warm Vltava.

At Mělník, the 430 km-long river Vltava and the river Elbe, which is 258 km shorter up to that point, converge. Usually, the name of the longer source river is adopted. However, the rivers Aare, Rhine, Warta and Oder as well as Havel and Spree are the exceptions that prove the rule. Otherwise, Dresden and Hamburg would be located on the river Vlatava.

Except for cuts in the upper Vltava at Oberplan (Horni Plana) and to Budweis and Prague it flows through a mostly narrow valley. In the past there used to be a lot of rafting and other water-related tourism there. Starting in 1936, but mainly between 1954 and 1962, several reservoirs were built such as the Lake Lipno and Orlík Dam, which at a total length of 190 km give the river a completely different character. These are known as the Vltava reservoirs cascade. Hydroelectric power plants were installed producing a total capacity of 700 MW which is mainly used to cover the shortfall during peak times. From the penultimate reservoir around 20 kilometres north of Prague, the Vltava can be navigated by boat again.

Uwe Rada's book „Die Elbe" impressively describes the flow of Europe's history.

The Moldau by Bedřich Smetana

The river Vltava provided the inspiration for the most famous romantic symphonic poem from the work "My Country" by Bedrich Smetana (1824-1884). In "The Moldau", he provides, among others, two flutes, representing the river's two sources and its course through the Bohemian countryside, the thundering water in the now sunken St. Johann rapids, the wide bottom of Moldova, their run at Vyšehrad, through Prague and its confluence with the Elbe. Smetana also refers to the surrounding river culture which, for example, included hunting and country weddings.

Having returned from the Vltava source, follow the road to Bučina. It is uphill and you will see the dead spruce caused by the bark beetle, and even some newly grown trees.

ATTENTION ⚠ The way to Bučina is a big ask - you must cycle very carefully.

Finally the trail takes you downhill again and at the next branch in the road, turn right into the **Vltava cycle path**.

Arrive in Bučina, cross the paved bike path 331, which is also signposted as a National Park bike path.

Bučina

Memorial Iron Curtain: At the border crossing, parts of the Iron Curtain with watchtowers have been reconstructed. Refreshments.

Buchwald was declared a military zone after the people were expelled and for a long time nobody was allowed to live there. The 26 buildings present were demolished in 1956 - all with the exception of a hotel. The destroyed cemetery and the chapel were re-built after the opening of the border again and inaugurated latter in 1992. Hikers can now spend the night in the hotel again which in 2010 was substantially refurbished.

Border crossing near Bischofsreut

EXCURSION A small detour to the Iron Curtain Memorial is worthwhile.

CONNECTION In Bučina there is the possibility to go with the "Igel bus" to the station in Spiegelau. The bus does not just take cyclists with it, but is part of the public transport system that is free of charge for all our guests who have stayed on the German side in a national park community.

Back at the crossroads, turn right and continue cycling on the paved **bike path 1023** to the next intersection in **Knížecí Pláně**. Turn right, passing a restaurant and cycling on the signposted 1023 Vltava Cycle Path. Unfortunately, a reference to the city Strážný is missing.

Strážný

Strážný (formerly Kunžvart, German Kuschwarda) lies at the foot of the 1,115-metre-high Strážný (Schlösselberg), and has 472 inhabitants to its name. It has had market rights since 1844. The community on the Gold Trail was established 1672/1689. Built in 1781, Trinity Church was demolished due to disrepair in 1965 and the cemetery was levelled. Today, there are a seafood restaurants and shops. The historically important

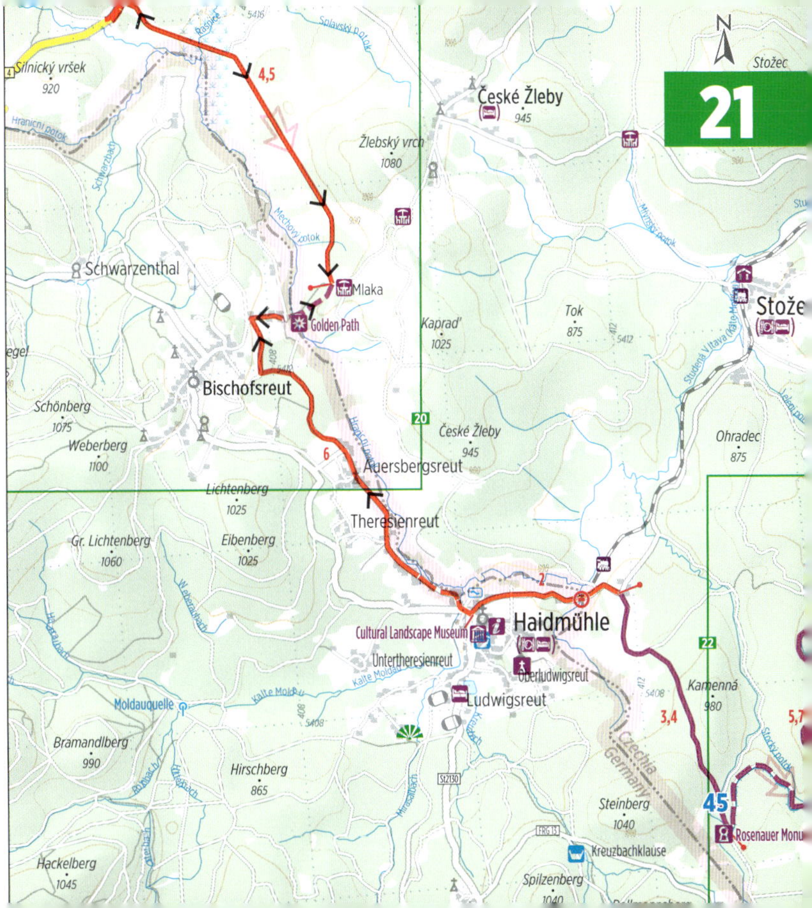

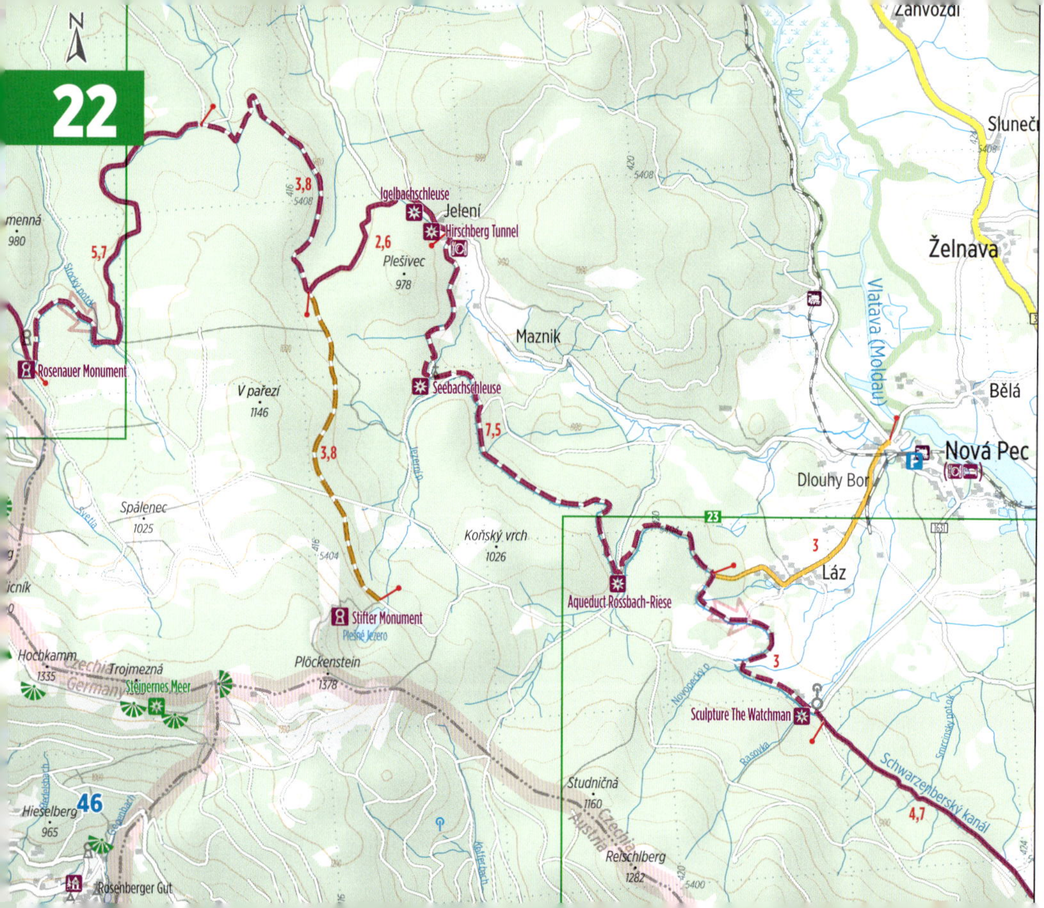

street from Passau to Prague (B 12 in D, National Road 4 in CZ) has existed since 1833.

The path from Strážný to bike path 1023 is only possible over the very dangerous highway where there are no bike lanes. Since underpath is neither marked nor fully built, it is advisable to cross after the bridge on the old road, which crosses the motorway and then to turn back a bit and then turn right.

The road is paved and signposted Nové Údolí. An indication of the border crossing would not hurt but sadly there is not one at the time of writing. The trail is slightly undulating. In **Mlaka** there is a big board. Once you see it, turn right towards Bischofsreut onto the fortified forest paths and cycle down the 1000-year-old **"Golden Path"** across the border into Germany. A landmark stone, funded by the European Union, can be seen there and there is some interesting historical information on the panels.

TIP The road on the "Golden Path" is worth it - even if the surface could be improved.

Cross the stream Harlandbach on the historic stone bridge. The trail goes uphill on a paved road. Turn left into the signposted path in the Danube National Park to Haidmühle. From here it goes downhill. At the next corner, turn left onto the unpaved but comfortable path and at the next corner turn right into the signposted route to Haidmühle. Just before the road near the houses, the road is paved. Then turn left, and from the road you can the stream and the border signs below and will reach Haidmühle after a little while.

Haidmühle

Cultural Landscape Museum (KUlturLAndschaftsMUseum KULAMU). The museum, founded in 2003, is the first of its kind and is in various ways an interesting insight into the cultural landscape that existed as a result of the separation in the Cold War. The relics resulting from the border situation have been restored and brought back to life.

The municipality has a relatively short history as it has only existed since 1770. It lies on the Cold Moldova and is a nationally recognised health resort standing 830 metres high. There is a wide range of accommodation to choose from.

From Haidmühle (DE) to St. Oswald b. Haslach (AT) 53 km

At the entrance, turn first left into **Max-Pangert Straße** and left again into **Neuthaler Straße** that leads you to the border crossing for hikers and cyclists. Here you see a railway bridge with the shortest route in the world.

The shortest railway route in the world

In 1990, the railway line was taken all the way to the border from the Czech side, however, the continuation to Passau is difficult on the German side due to decommissioning. This led to the shortest international railway in the world with a length of just 105 metres. On the remaining piece of the old railway embankment you can travel with a little train from the Czech Republic into Germany from a few metres. The journey takes a full 24 seconds! A small railway museum is housed in three old freight cars.

After the border you can find the Czech Railway Station, with trains to Čičenice and Volary. The connection to Waldkirch has not yet been restored - more than two decades after the fall of the Iron Curtain.

Ilztalbahn

It was the association "Support the Ilztalbahn" (founded in 2006) that managed to push through, despite enormous resistance, regular transport links between Passau and Freyung on the environmentally-friendly

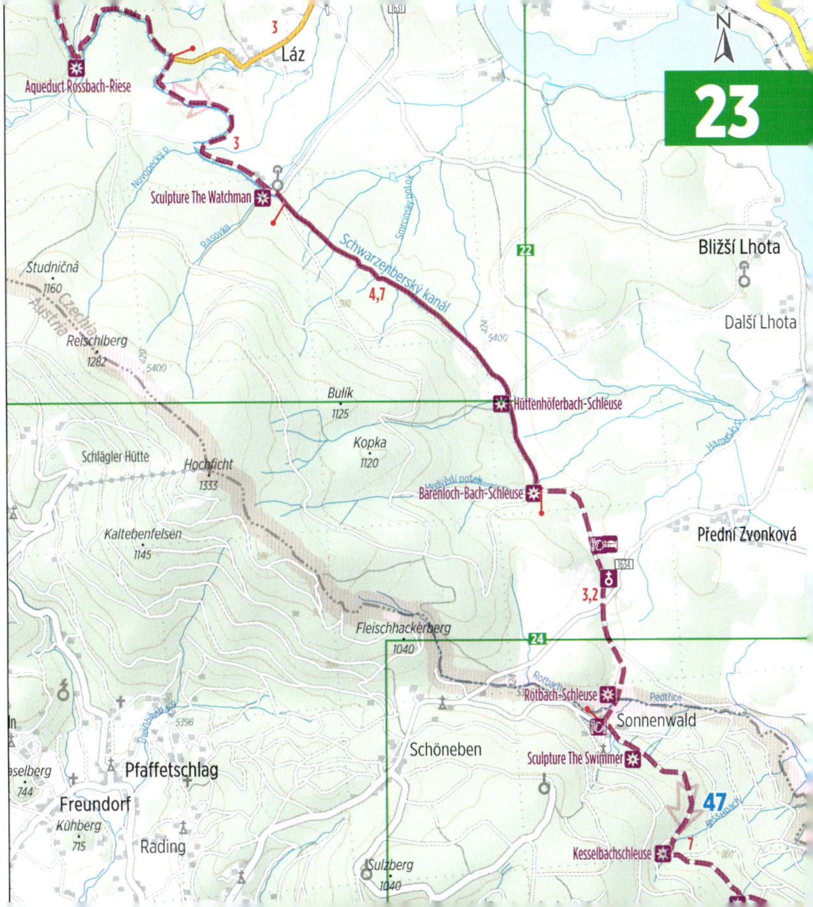

rail tracks in 2011. Before the war, this section was part of the direct connection from Munich via Passau to Prague. Although from the Czech border station Nové Údolí the trains now go again via České Budějovice (Budweis) to Prague, the 20-kilometre-long gap closing on the German side is missing as is supposedly also the money for the 9 km route between Holzhau and Moldava and the 7 km between Altenberg and Dubí. The 660-metre(!)-long gap between Sebnitz and Dolní Poustevna was only bridged in 2014 and the 10 km gap between Selb and Aš only in 2015. Even here, things that belong together, need to grow together once more.

Cycle uphill, passing the station until you hit the road that leads to Stožec and there turn right. Pass a memorial stone for the village Nové Údoli Laikal, 1795-1956, on your left, which was razed after the war and of which only the name has remained as a border crossing today. Because the road is blocked, even for cyclists, the route takes you left. But after 20 m you should turn right towards the Rosenauer monument - dedicated to one of the Schwarzenberg canal engineers. After a while the road becomes wider, more comfortable, and the cycle track better signposted. The path through the forest, which is also paved by the time you reach the first big bend, is 850 metres above sea level. It is on the left side of the canal.

Schwarzenberg canal tunnel

Schwarzenberg canal / Schwarzenberský plavební kanál

This engineering feat was once – like many other buildings of the 18th and 19th century - celebrated as the "eighth wonder of the world". They manage to tame the main European waterways. On the one hand the Main, Eger and Saale, whose water flows into the North Sea via the Rhine, Vltava and Elbe on the other hand the Naab, which flows into the Danube to the Black Sea.

Construction began in 1789. The canal was fed in the beginning by several streams (Hirschbergen) in the northwest Jelení Vrchy on the northern slope of the Bohemian Forest, which then became the main suppliers of firewood for Vienna. North of the Haslach big trunks were taken from the Great Muehl and carried to the Danube. The business flourished so much that already in around 1820 a northwestern extension of 52 kilometres was undertaken and the canal in Jelení Vrchy was channelled at an altitude of 790 metres through a 419-metre long tunnel.

It was the first canal tunnel in Central Europe and 1,200 people were involved in its construction. Loggers had to be recruited and many new villages emerged in the border area. 300 drift workers were charged with the task of making sure that the logs found their way.

The construction was made possible by the princes of Schwarzenberg and the idea came from the forest engineer Joseph Rosenauer (1735-1804), who is on several memorial stones. Until 1892 it was used for the transport of timber to Vienna.

After 100 years of work which sent 8 million cubic metres of firewood on its way, demand dropped in favour of Silesian coal. Therefore, on the Czech side a system was developed in 1900 for the transportation of logs and was still in operation until 1961. Today large parts have been restored as a historic structure and are used for tourists to shop and for festivals. The steep steps in Morau, east of Sankt Oswald are among the most impressive parts, because the water gushing here is particularly noisy and frantic. The historic road accompanying the canal is marked as a bike path, and has numerous information boards about the history of this masterpiece, which goes through the most beautiful areas of the two national parks.

EXCURSION Over the Plöckensteinsee, about 1 km north-east of the border triangle Germany-Austria-Czech Republic, a monument commemorates Adalbert Stifter. It consists of a 14.5-metre high obelisk made of granite and was inaugurated in 1877 for its ten-year anniversary.

Adalbert Stifter

The painter, writer and educator Adalbert Stifter (1805-1868) ("painter-poet") was born in Horni Plana (Oberplan), which is located 13 kilometres east of the monument on the Vltava River dam. In long, complex sentences, he brought his native love for his home onto paper and "the breath of air, the trickle of water, the growth of the grain, the green Earth, the shining of heaven" were described.

After the Second World War and the beginning of the Cold War, the border of the former Czechoslovakia was closed to Austria and Germany and fortified. The border fence ran in some parts several hundred metres away from the border. The monument was just a few metres in front of the fence between the border and border fortifications. This made it inaccessible to the public for decades. It was only from 1989/90 that it could be accessed again. Today, the monument can be reached by hiking trails from all three countries.

Pass **Igelbachschleuse** until you reach a place where the canal is guided through the **Hirschberg tunnel**. At this point turn right uphill. On the other side of the tunnel, where the canal is quite frothy, there is a guest house. The road continues a little bit downhill, then turn immediately right and continue cycling parallel to the canal. There you will see an exhibition on the Schwarzenberg Canal, which was restored here in its original condition. The road along the canal is no longer paved, but nonetheless in decent condition. Pass **Seebachschleuse** and later the **Rossbach-Riese** aqueduct giant. Via a bridge the canal crosses the stream which runs at a right angle to the canal.

EXCURSION If you want to visit Nová Pc, where there are plenty of restaurants and accommodation, take the next left when the road branches.

Nová Pec

According to historical word-of-mouth, the first house was said to have been built here in 1577. The first written mention of any buildings were of

two courtyards in 1653. The railroad ran for the first time in 1892 from Budweis to Salnau and from 1910 to Haidmühle. There were about 66 homes and 476 inhabitants in Nová Pec / Nová Pec around the year 1900.

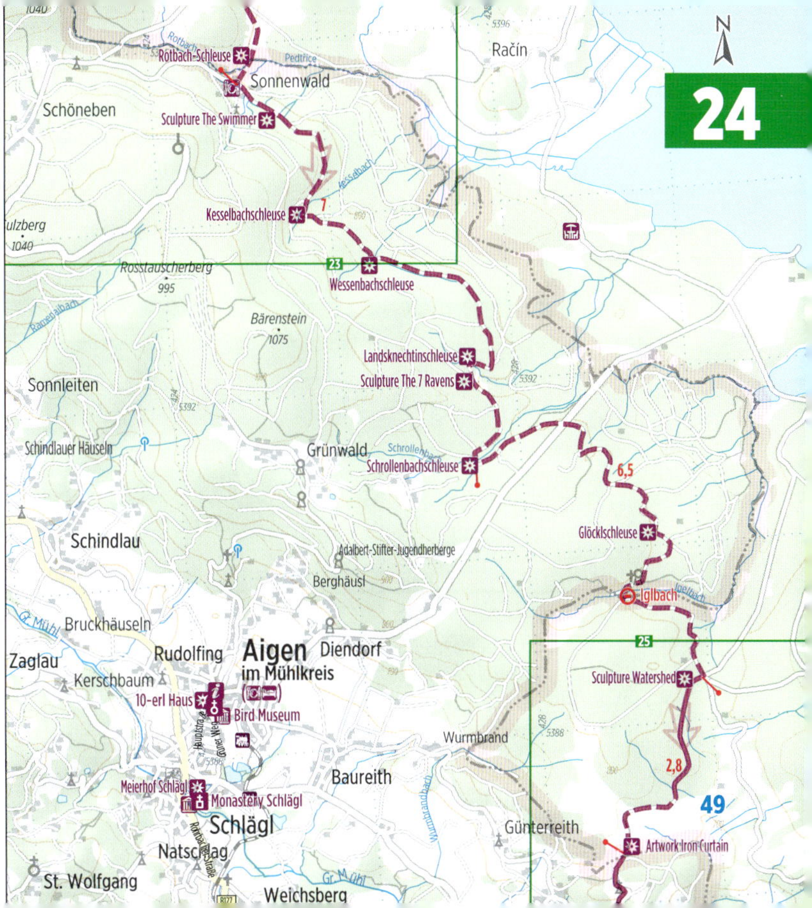

Lipno-reservoir

In the area of the upper Vltava River there was a natural lake, that until the completion of a reservoir, was a wild, raging, white water due to its massive stone blocks. Between the Devil's Wall (Certova stena) and the Luc mountain the lake broke through and created the Vltava riverbed.

The reservoir is 48 km long, at Cerna 10 km wide and thus the geographically largest lake in the Czech Republic. The dam is 296 metres long, is 25 metres high and was built from 1952 to 1959. It is intended to protect the region against flooding, but in particular the downstream towns of České Budějovice and Prague. The power plant Lipno I, located below the dam, has an output of 120 MW.

Large parts of the steep slopes of the gorge are covered with gravel crowned with powerful rock formations. The whole area contains unique and valuable flora and fauna and enjoys the highest level of conservation, but is nonetheless still accessible to pedestrians.

The bike path along the navigational canal is no longer in good condition, especially after rain. Pass the sculpture **"Der Wächter"** (The Watchman) and then you will hit an asphalt path, into which one turns left. The only thing reminding us of the border troops who were once here, are a few abandoned buildings that were once used by the military. Before the next crossing, you will see the **1033 bike path**. Pass **Hüttenhöferbach-Schleuse** and **Bärenloch-Bach-Schleuse**. After that the road is not paved. On the left side you will suddenly see a restored church pop up which has a further building that commemorates the razed village of **Glöckelberg**.

Restored church in Glöckelberg

Zadní Zvonková/ Glöckelberg

In 1929, when the village was still called Glöckelberg, it consisted of 1,352 residents who lived in 200 houses. In May 1945 the city was freed by American troops. In subsequent years, due to the continued harassment by the Czechoslovak rulers, the German inhabitants left the village. Their houses were eventually demolished in 1950, because no-one was allowed to live in the border strip.

After the "Velvet Revolution" the Church and the old "Mesnerhaus" were rebuilt. Here you can find the Urzidil Museum. Johannes Urzidil (1896-1970) was a German poet from Prague, who was married to the daughter of a rabbi and managed to escape from the Germans in 1939.

Behind the church cross the road to Přední Zvonková (Vorderglöckelberg) and get to the border crossing at **Rotbach-Schleuse**. 200 m further, on the Austrian **cycle path R 27**, there is a restaurant where you can stop and also get some tourist information.

The condition of the road is considerably better in Austria, even if it is not paved. Pass the sculpture "Schwimmerin" (The Swimmer), the three locks **Kesselbachschleuse**, **Wessenbachschleuse**, **Landsknechtinschleuse** and the sculpture **"Die 7 Raben"** (The 7 Ravens). At Schrollenbachschleuse, turn left onto the R 803, pass **Glöcklschleuse** and an information board that provides information on the cobblestones that you pass every 2 km.

The Iglbach border crossing

Cross the border where an information board honours the engineer who started this beautiful canal construction. Ride past the Rosenhügel/Koranda and the sculpture **"Wasserscheide"** (Watershed) and follow the paved road with the blue sign. On the Czech-Austrian border in Sankt Oswald you can see a work of art relating to the Iron Curtain, namely an unplugged extension lead. Behind the border crossing follow an asphalt road down to Sankt Oswald.

St. Oswald bei Haslach

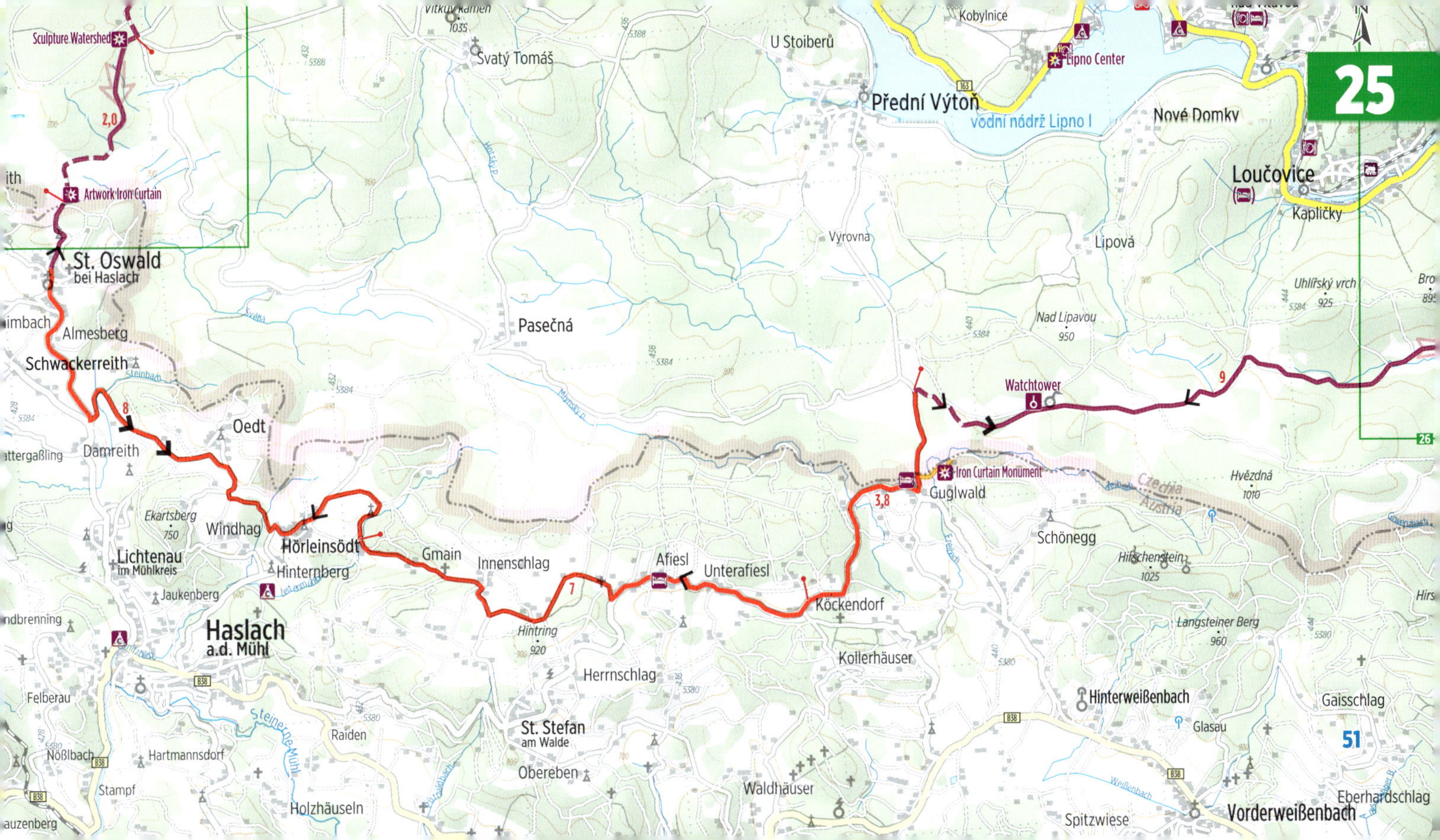
25
Sculpture Watershed
2,0
Artwork Iron Curtain
St. Oswald
bei Haslach
Almesberg
Schwackerreith
Steinbach
Oedt
8
Damreith
Ekartsberg
750
Windhag
Hörleinsödt
Lichtenau
im Mühlkreis
Hinternberg
Jaukenberg
Haslach
a.d. Mühl
Felberau
Nößlbach
Hartmannsdorf
Stampf
Raiden
Holzhäuseln
Steinerne Mühl
Gmain
Innenschlag
7
Hintring
920
Herrnschlag
St. Stefan
am Walde
Obereben
Afiesl
Unterafiesl
Köckendorf
Kollerhäuser
Waldhäuser
3,8
Guglwald
Iron Curtain Monument
Watchtower
9
Schönegg
Hirschenstein
1025
Langsteiner Berg
960
Hinterweißenbach
Glasau
Gaisschlag
Vorderweißenbach
Eberhardschlag
Spitzwiese
Czechia
Austria
Hvězdná
1010
Nad Lipavou
950
Uhlířský vrch
925
Lipová
Loučovice
Kapličky
Nové Domky
Přední Výtoň
vodní nádrž Lipno I
Lipno Center
Kobylnice
U Stoiberů
Svatý Tomáš
Vítkův kámen
1035
Pasečná
Vyrovna
B38
26

Austria's history

Ancestors of the present population in Austria most likely hail from the Baiuvarii and Alemannic tribes, who permanently settled on the territory of the present state after the Roman Empire's gradual decline. From the 8th century the area belonged mostly to the Frankish Empire of Charlemagne. From 1278 the Duchy of Habsburg developed a special status and became a powerful force in the Holy Roman Empire. From the late 15th to the late 17th century what we know as Austria today was under constant attack, often by the Ottoman Empire, which wanted to strive out west from Hungary. But the Ottoman's attempts at expansion suffered serious setbacks after the first attempt in 1529 and also in the second siege of Vienna in 1683. After numerous internal conflicts Franz II founded the Empire of Austria-Hungary in 1804. François I took the title of emperor and at the same time was ruler of the Holy Roman Empire of Germany for two years. However, he had to give this title up under pressure from Napoleon in 1806, which led to the dissolution of the Holy Roman Empire.

The new Empire was a multinational state, strictly ruled by State Chancellor Metternich. After a number of revolutionary upheavals in the late 18th century, the aim of governance was the restoration of the old order, which largely succeeded with the alliance between Prussia and Russia.

The inability to adapt to the profound changes of the 19th century however, led to the Revolution in 1848. The Metternich era was finished. Ultimately, the army prevented the victory of democratic forces but the Emperor still lost power, the state was transformed against his will into a constitutional monarchy and Hungary obtained new rights under a settlement agreement in 1867. Thus an Austro-Hungarian dual monarchy was formally established, which exercised considerable power in Southeast Europe. After the assassination of the Austro-Hungarian heir presumptive to the throne Archduke Franz Ferdinand on 28 June 1914 in Sarajevo, the monarchy was closely involved in the outbreak of World War I due to the mutual assistance pacts, which led to the dissolution of the Habsburg Monarchy after their defeat in 1918.

Sculpture at the border near Dolní Hranična

The new Republic of Austria was its successor, which was organized democratically and brought with it significant social progress. The young republic did not last for long, however: the reigning Nazis viewed Austria as an essential part of their empire and exerted massive pressure until they succeeded in annexing Austria in 1938 with the "Munich Agreement". About a third of the 60,000 SS Einsatzgruppen in the concentration and extermination camps were Austrians. This is another reason why the Allied forces reminded Austria in their "Moscow declaration" of 1st Nov 1943 "that it bears a responsibility in the war for being on Hitler's Germany's side that it cannot escape from." They also expressed the "annexation" of Austria to be "invalid" and the intention to "restore the sovereign state of Austria after the Second World War".

On 27th April 1945 the party chairman of the SPÖ, ÖVP and KPÖ signed a declaration of independence with the Soviet Union, which had not been agreed upon with London and Washington. On 20th December 1945, Karl Renner (SPO) became the first President of the "Second Republic". One of his first acts was to establish the people's courts which led to 43 death sentences of which 30 were carried out. That was a more radical cleanout of serious Nazi criminals than took place in Germany. However, until 1955, the independent, democratic state of Austria was still divided into occupation zones, of which the Soviet was the largest. Unlike Germany, however, it was not split down the middle. After the signing of the State Treaty on 15th May 1955 and the assurance of neutrality towards the western and eastern stock (not in the Treaty) the Republic regained full sovereignty. The

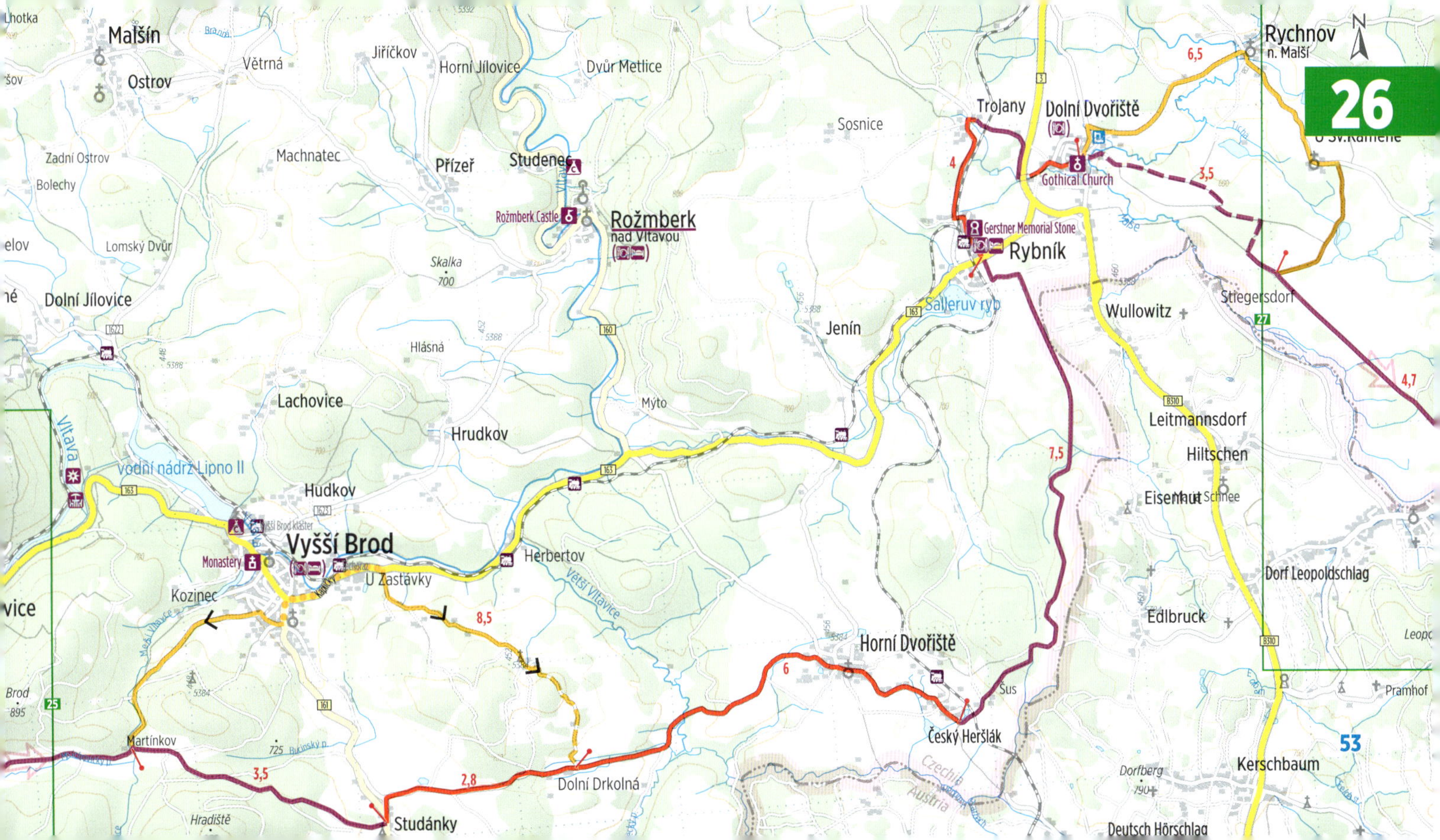
26
Malšín
Ostrov
Lhotka
Větrná
Jiřičkov
Horní Jílovice
Dvůr Metlice
Rychnov
n. Malší
Trojany
Dolní Dvořiště
Sosnice
Zadní Ostrov
Bolechy
Machnatec
Přízeř
Studenec
Rožmberk Castle
Rožmberk
nad Vltavou
Gothical Church
Gerstner Memorial Stone
Rybník
Lomský Dvůr
Skalka
700
Dolní Jílovice
Jenín
Salleruv ryb
Wullowitz
Stiegersdorf
Hlásná
Lachovice
Mýto
Hrudkov
Leitmannsdorf
Hiltschen
Vltava
vodní nádrž Lipno II
Hudkov
Vyšší Brod klášter
Vyšší Brod
Monastery
Herbertov
U Zastávky
Kozinec
Větší Vltavice
Eisenhut
Schnee
Dorf Leopoldschlag
Edlbruck
Horní Dvořiště
Sus
Český Heršlák
Martínkov
Brod
895
Hradiště
Studánky
Dolní Drkolná
Czechia
Austria
Dorfberg
790
Kerschbaum
Deutsch Hörschlag
Pramhof
6,5
4
3,5
4,7
7,5
8,5
6
3,5
2,8
53

Iron Curtain memorial in Guglwald

principle of non-alignment anchored Austria in a "decision on permanent neutrality" and protected it from the Cold War.

But it took 67 years, from the 8th May, 1945 to 8th May 2012 before it finally celebrated its "day of liberation" and the annual wreath-laying ceremonies of the fringe German national fraternities in "Commemoration of the Heroes of the Armed Forces" and in "sadness at the defeat" was abolished. After the fall of the Iron Curtain the country loosened its policy of neutrality and oriented themselves more clearly to the west, not least because of its EU accession in 1995. To date, however, Austria is not a member of NATO - a result of its special role in the Cold War.

From Sankt Oswald (AT) to Vyšší Brod (CZ) 31 km

The "European Iron Curtain Trail" now leads south gently downhill over **Almesberg** until just before Damreith where it meets the **R5 Grenzlandweg** to Guglwald, in which you turn left. It is then quite steep uphill for the next 3 km.

Stay on the main road and continue downhill – and in **Kasbach** do not turn left into Vossweg. Where the road goes right to Haslach, keep left and continue cycling a short distance uphill. Cross the stream in a sharp right turn and stay on the R5. From there it is only a short distance more uphill.

Hörleinsödt

Keep to the right and stay on the signposted R5. After another small slope turn left - the signs are unfortunately hidden. Continue through **Gmain**, Interior **Innenschlag** and **Hintring**.

Afiesl

Wellness Hotel Bergergut, ✆ +43/7216/4451

From the hotel the trail first goes downhill and then gently uphill.

Guglwald

This place seems almost entirely to consist of a hotel complex in pagoda style, with a mix of medieval nostalgia and folklore.

Behind a hotel complex - the trail is only marked from the other side and not to the border crossing, but only to the Vltava River dam - turn left to the border crossing.

EXCURSION A little later, branching off to the right of a footpath, you can find a memorial relating to the history of the Iron Curtain.

ALTERNATIVE It would be nice if this memorial were integrated into the route. That would even be possible on an asphalt road, if you do not turn left at the hotel, but continue straight. What is missing is the connection from the memorial to the road leading to the border.

Iron Curtain monument

Under a concrete roof there are various information boards and original parts of the former restricted zone. The memorial was built in 1999 at the behest of the former Foreign Minister Alois Mock, who, with his Hungarian counterpart Gyula Horn had cut through part of the Iron Curtain on June 27, 1989 near Sopron in an official ceremony.

On the Czech side, turn right at the first opportunity into a dirt road, which is also signposted on the other side. You can see that it belongs to the "Iron Curtain Greenway" from the two yellow arrows with red in the centre. The route takes you uphill for about 2 km and is marked as **1033**.

All of a sudden you will see an old observation tower and the ruins of a chapel with a cross and a sign: "Zum Friedhof – Gedenkmarterl" (To the cemetery – monument). From there it goes downhill towards Kapličky.

EXCURSION If you wish to cycle to Vyšší Brod, 3 km away, remain on bike path 1033, that branches off to the left from Martínkov. You will reach the place after a beautiful descent.

Vyšší Brod

Below the small overflow reservoir, which is called Lipno II, you will find the small town of Vyšší Brod (Hohenfurth).

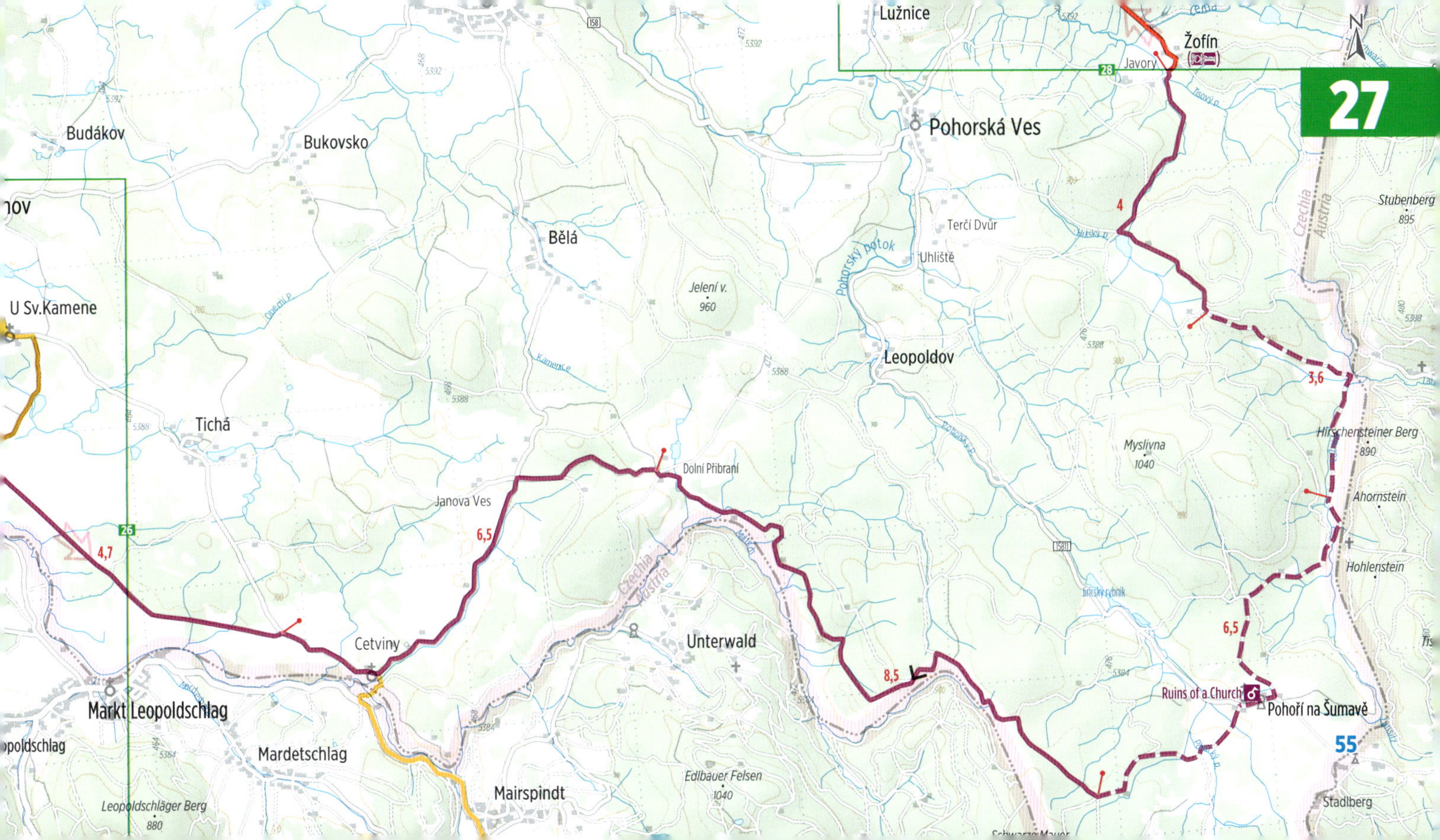

27
Lužnice
Žofín
Javory
28
Pohorská Ves
Budákov
Bukovsko
Bělá
Terčí Dvůr
Uhliště
Pohorský potok
Jelení v.
960
U Sv.Kamene
Leopoldov
Stubenberg
895
Czechia
Austria
4
3,6
Hirschensteiner Berg
890
Myslivna
1040
Ahornstein
Hohlenstein
Tichá
Dolní Přibraní
Janova Ves
6,5
26
4,7
Unterwald
Cetviny
8,5
6,5
Ruins of a Church
Pohoří na Šumavě
55
Markt Leopoldschlag
Mardetschlag
Mairspindt
Edlbauer Felsen
1040
Leopoldschläger Berg
880
Stadlberg

It is known primarily for its monastery. The settlement over a ford on the River Vltava was primarily built to guard the trade route from the mid-13th century. Their fate was closely linked with that of the rich monastery, to which it belonged until 1848. Its economic activities in the early 20th century included the building a power station and the participation in the construction and operation of an electrical train. After the annexation of the Sudetenland, it was not used but after the war it was used again. Weakened by the expulsion of the German Convention members, it could not withstand the hostility of the state, so it was repealed in 1950 again. The building then served as barracks and were later partially abandoned and left to decay. Visitors can now visit the Gothic church, the cloister, the chapter house, the Baroque library and objets d'art from a pen collection.

Direct trains to Rybník can be caught from the local station.

If you want to stay on the "European Iron Curtain Trail" continue straight ahead.

Studánky

Follow the sign 1205 towards Dolní Drkolná.

From Vyšší Brod (CZ) to Gmünd (AT) 102 km

From the centre head towards the station and cycle down past the church. Turn left to get to the station, and then turn right in **Kapličky** in the direction of Horni Dvorište. Keep on bypass **163** (signposted **cycle path 34**) running parallel to Moldova and the railway. Behind a petrol station, turn right towards Horní Dvořiště. The bike trail **Šumavská magistrála** (34) then changes into an asphalt path leading you uphill. At a fork in the road, keep to the left on the gravel and cycle through a woodland and through a meadow.

Dolní Drkolná

Keep to the left until you reach Horní Dvořiště (Oberhaid) after 4km. There you cross the tracks of the first railway in Continental Europe.

Horní Dvořiště

CONNECTION

From the train station you can get direct trains to Linz and one arrives with change in Summerau to Prague.

Gerstner-Memorial

Continental Europe's first railway

This railway was opened in 1832 and was pulled by horses and ran from upper Austrian Linz to Czech Budweis. The train to Czech Budweis was used to transport people and goods. Salt was the main good which was transported, first to Budejovice and from there via ship over the Vltava and Elbe to Prague and Hamburg. In 1872 the horse railway was shut down and replaced by the steam locomotive on an extended track.

In Horní Dvořiště keep to the right, after the triangular village centre, cycle straight past the church and remain on **bike path 34** until you reach **Český Heršlák** where the last station before the Austrian border.

CONNECTION

You can catch direct trains to Linz from here.

Cycle on the former border patrol road, which is paved, uphill and then downhill, and is very close to the border. Cross street 163 and join bike path 34 until you reach Rybník.

Rybník

Pass the train station, from which direct trains go to Prague and Linz.

TIP

Opposite the train station you can find a restaurant with a few rooms.

A memorial stone commemorates Franz Josef Ritter von Gerstner.

Monastery in Vyšší Brod

Josef Ritter von Gerstner

The mathematician and physicist Josef Ritter von Gerstner (1756-1832) was a great proponent of the horse railway. After graduating he worked as a professor at Karls University in Prague. In the 18th century Budweis-Linz was an important route for the transport of salt. Gerstner was hired to find cheap transport routes. Originally a water solution was considered but then due to the high costs he turned his attention towards the horse railway. He also published several scientific works such as the "Treatises on freight wagons and roads".

Even after the crossing the tracks you continue cycling along them.

Trojany

Turn on bike path 34 before crossing a beautiful bridge with the tracks below before reaching Dolní Dvořiště (Unterhaid).

Dolní Dvořiště

- Late gothical church
- Fountain with the statue of St. Nepomuk, on the market square

ALTERNATIVE

The best way would take you via the former border patrol path. Unfortunately, however, one of the bridges across the stream has disappeared. For this, you would cycle right past the church, through the town towards the border. Where the main road branches off to the right you would turn left. If you were able to continue cycling on the relatively good asphalt road over the missing bridge you would reach bike path 34 again.

This being the case, we must turn left past the church, where there is also a restaurant until you hit cycle path 1018, leading to a

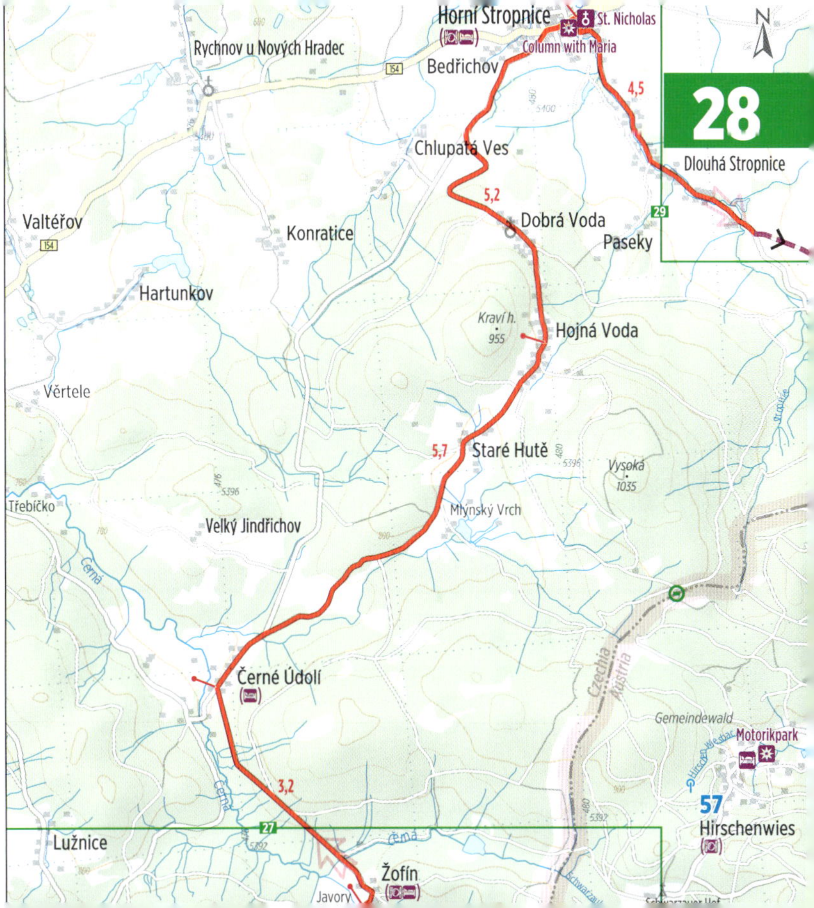

bridge over the stream. This path is actually not recommended because it difficult to navigate, is very rocky and partially extends over meadows until it reaches the former patrol. The repair work for this road would certainly be much more expensive than repairing the fallen bridge over the stream.

ALTERNATIVE If you do not want to choose this path, remain on bike path 34, which leads you via Rychnov to the former patrol path.

On even, paved roads continue on the patrol along the border. On the right side you can see the Austrian town of Leopoldschlag. Where the 1018 branches off to the left, remain on the 34 and cycle downhill to the dissolved municipality Cetviny (Zettwing) directly on the border with Austria, which is marked here by the Maltsch (Malše).

Memorial stone in Cetviny

Cetviny (Zettwing)

The historic Zettwing was an important place on the border between Bohemia and Upper Austria. In 1930, there were 121 houses with 552 inhabitants. After the Munich Agreement (09/30/1938), the majority of the German-populated area was occupied by the Nazis. The Czechs, the antifascist Germans, and the Jews were expelled or forced to flee. After the defeat of the German Reich, the German population was expelled and Romanian, Czechs and Slovaks moved into the abandoned houses. As the place was on the border strip, it was depopulated in 1955-56 and many of the houses destroyed. What was left was used by the border police - including the church tower which served as a watchtower.

In 1995, important members of the public and organisations from the Czech Republic and Austria agreed to the new construction of the 1384 early Gothic Church of the Nativity of the Virgin Mary, which remains one of the oldest churches in the area. The reconstruction was dealt with very carefully and hitherto unknown frescoes were uncovered. The re-opening of the building took place in 2003. It is intended to serve many different purposes for both sides of the border.

EXCURSION Behind the church, turn right onto the "Stone Bridge" (built in 2006) over the Malše towards the upper Austrian Windhaag bei Freistadt.

Stay on the paved number 34 bike path.

Nové Hrady Town Hall

Dolní Příbraní

You turn right and then immediately left in 1193. It is first downhill and then continue on level ground.

Pohoři na Šumavě

Here you can see the ruins of a church, beside which a memorial commemorating the First World War 1914-18 which reads: "The true heroes and the grateful homeland". At the bottom can also be read: "War should never happen again".

At the exit, turn left. After crossing the stream, continue on an unpaved track downhill.

TIP At the next intersection, the sign is missing.

Keep travelling straight – the 1193 sign appears later on - and cycle on the eastern side around the lake, where the road is paved again. At the end of the lake, turn right onto the signposted cycle path 34. You will then enter Žofín.

Žofín

Pension Lesovna, ✆ 7249508-29/30 or 602474257

TIP Here you can dine and stay the night in the high season. There is also a small B&B in nearby Černé Údolí.

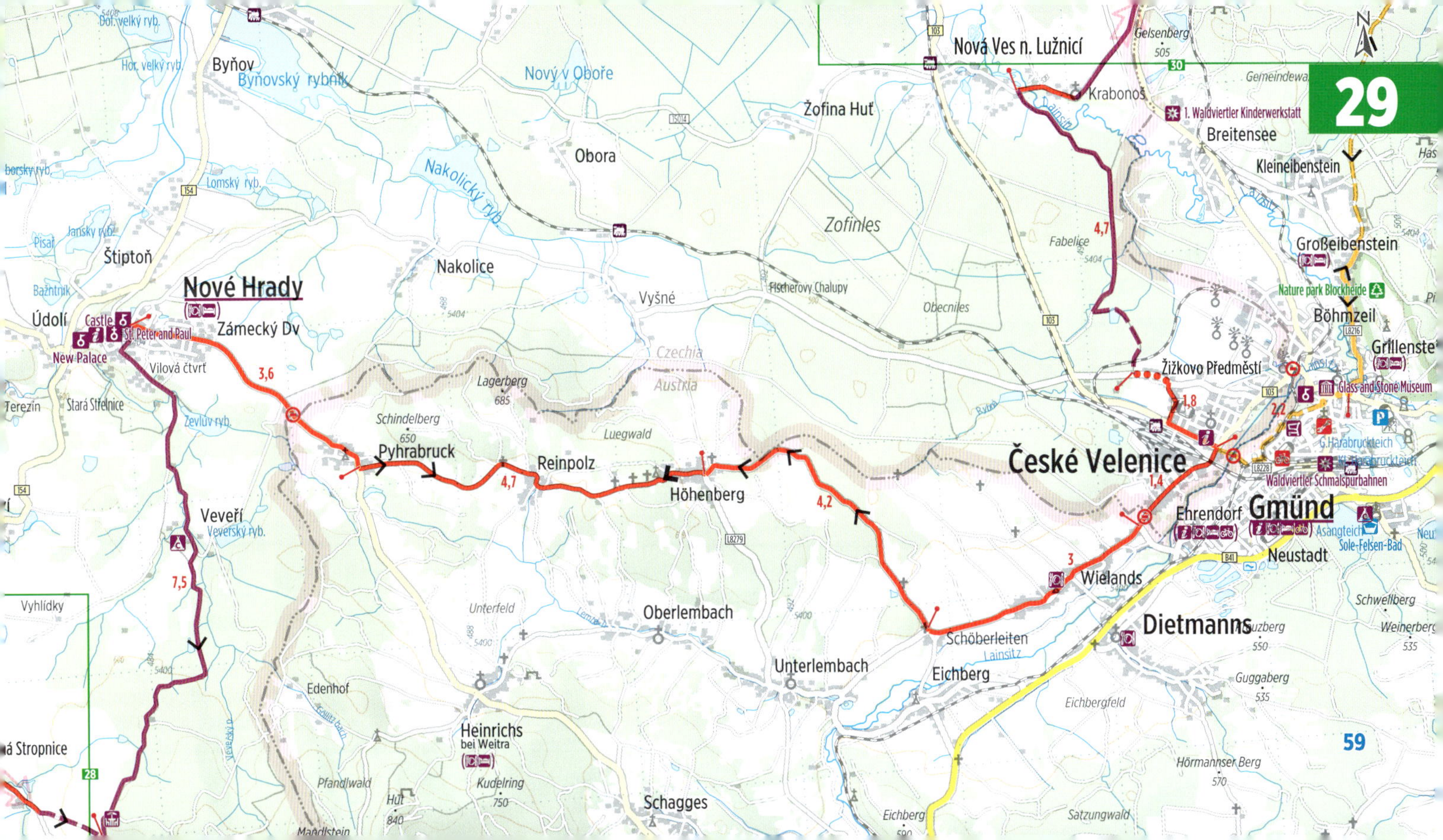

29
Nové Hrady
Castle
St. Peter and Paul
New Palace
Zámecký Dv
Údolí
Štiptoň
Byňov
Byňovský rybník
Nový v Oboře
Obora
Nakolický ryb.
Nakolice
Vyšné
Žofina Huť
Zofinles
Fischerovy Chalupy
Obecniles
Nová Ves n. Lužnicí
Krabonoš
1. Waldviertler Kinderwerkstatt
Breitensee
Kleineibenstein
Großeibenstein
Nature park Blockheide
Böhmzeil
Grillenste
Žižkovo Předměstí
Glass and Stone Museum
České Velenice
Gmünd
G.Harabruckteich
Waldviertler Schmalspurbahnen
Ehrendorf
Asangteich
Sole-Felsen-Bad
Neustadt
Wielands
Dietmanns
Schöberleiten
Eichberg
Unterlembach
Oberlembach
Höhenberg
Reinpolz
Pyhrabruck
Schindelberg 650
Lagerberg 685
Luegwald
Czechia
Austria
Vilová čtvrť
Stará Střelnice
Terezín
Zevlův ryb.
Veveří
Veverský ryb.
Vyhlídky
á Stropnice
Edenhof
Heinrichs bei Weitra
Kudelring 750
Pfandlwald
Hut 840
Schagges
Mandlstein
Unterfeld
Eichbergfeld
Guggaberg 535
Hörmannser Berg 570
Satzungwald
Schwellberg
Weinerberg 535
Fabelice
Gelsenberg 505
3,6
4,7
4,7
4,2
3
1,4
1,8
2,2
7,5
30
28
59

Iron Curtain Trail before Nové Hrady

At the fork behind the settlement, keep straight ahead. Follow a long forest passage until the trees give way to countryside just before Horní Stropnice (Strobnitz).

Horní Stropnice

- **St. Nikolaus,** Roman in origin, with fully restored interiors, renaissance altar, Baroque style side altars and a rococo pulpit.
- **Column with Maria**, marketplace
- **Horní Stropnice**, ✆ +420/386/327222 or. +420/724/589992

The community, which you enter via its long, old village green has been populated since the end of the 12th century. There used to be two mills, a machine factory and an important brewery, and from 1850 it even benefit from tourism.

From the main road, turn right before the church and behind the creek you will see that road 34 is signposted again. On the street with little traffic, ride alongside the stream and leave the road to the left, following the signposted road number 34 uphill on a non-paved path. After the next left bend, the road number 34 is paced again. Continue downhill and after passing a camping site you will reach Nové Hrady (Gratzen). Cycle around the ring-shaped castle which gives the place its name.

VIEW From the castle you get great views over the medieval town at its bottom.

The path continues straight from the castle to the market square.

Nové Hrady

- Baroque **Church of St. Peter and Paul**; the monastery served as accommodation to the border patrol during the Cold War.
- **Castle**. Despite having the biggest castle moat in Bohemia, it still fell prey to various instances of pillaging. It was redeveloped.
- **New palace**, for which the inner-city residency was abandoned in 1810. It boasts a garden which is located between the old town and the new town.
- **Smithy**. The low house is the fourth-last before the castle gate and houses the 300-year-old smithy of family Gossinger (Novohradská kovárna). It was also renovated and is still used to show the ways of the old craftsmanship.
- Imposingly big **market square**. On the Western side you will see the town hall built in renaissance style. It is home to the tourist information. Opposite the town hall you can see the residency of Count Bucquoy, built in early Baroque style (a connection of originally independent manor houses to one complex, today a spa hotel), a Baroque pharmacy and a fountain in late Baroque style.

Marketplace in Gmünd

From the market square you continue opposite the town hall on the Ceska into the direction of Austria. You will pass the Hotel Máj as well as a striking churchyard church and then continue on the quiet road number 34 across the former border crossing.

Pyhrabruck

Just before the sign that you are exiting the village, bear left and continue uphill to the "European stretch". You will pass the **Höhenberg observatory** and a little while later the route takes you downhill in sharp bends on an infrequently travelled road.

Höhenberg

Continue along the **border path** on an even road towards **Schöberleiten**, where you turn left towards Gmünd. The border path is not signposted as a forest path. Continue through **Wielands** and then take the road to Gmünd which you then leave and continue straight towards the border crossing after the bend to **Ehrendorf**.

EXCURSION Those wishing to cycle to Gmünd, turn right behind the tracks of the narrow gauge railway.

Cross the border river Lainsitz on a bridge which is only accessible by pedestrians and cyclists. Turn left into the cycle path and then continue parallel to the railway tracks, later also on the other side. After crossing the tracks again, turn left into the main road which will lead you to the centre.

Gmünd

Country/area code: +43/2852

Tourism office, Schremser Str. 6, ✆ 525060

Glass and Stone Museum, Stadtpl. 34, ✆ 52506-38, open: May-Sept., Mo-Fr 9am-12pm and 1-5pm, Sa, Su/Hol 9am-12pm

Town square with the **Old Town Hall** from the former renaissance era – on the first floor you will find a museum of the town history. Opposite you will find the architectural highlights of the town, two Sgraffito houses (16th Century). The left façade boasts a lavish diamond coating (unique in Austria), the other is decorated with stories from antique myths. Both are crowned by battlements.

Nature park Blockheide, Eibenstein-Gmünd, ✆ 52506-38, accessible all year (free)

If you are interested in special geological formations, you should do a detour to Blockheide via the stream Braunaubach which runs east of the old town. Blockheide is special for its massive granite blocks which are precariously balanced on top of each other. They were formed under ground and then lifted to the surface. The ascent to the viewing tower takes you through exhibition rooms underground which show the exhibition "Birth of the wobbly stones". From the local train station, you can take a direct train to České Budějovice (Budweis) and Vienna.

From Gmünd (AT) to Slavonice (CZ) *81 km*

From the market square continue straight, then turn right at the first opportunity into the signposted bike path and continue straight again until the narrow gauge railway. There you turn left, continue along the narrow gauge railway on alternating sides of the tracks where the path is not paved but still easy to travel on.

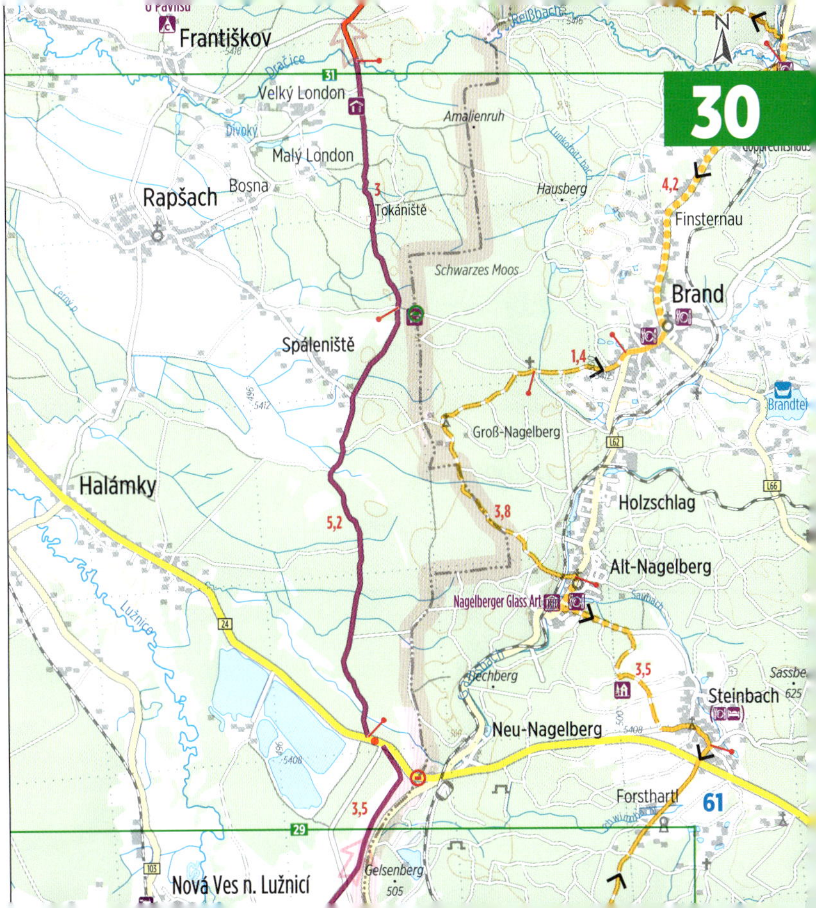

Church of Chlum u Třeboně

Waldviertler Schmalspurbahnen

The "Waldviertler Schmalspurbahnen" narrow gauge railways are a network of three inter-connected railway lines with a track width of 760 millimetres that connect the north-western Waldviertel with Litschau, Heidenreichstein and Groß Gerungs.

For the passenger traffic, steam locomotives were used from 1904. The traffic developed in accordance with expectations and resulted in the region obtaining the connection to the economic development of the time. The region was not only rich in wood, which ensured continued freight traffic, but the local textile and glass industry was also able to develop competitively thanks to the new method of transport.

After the First World War, Gmünd was divided. Many of the railway facilities as well as the first few kilometres of the northern tracks were now located in Czechoslovakia. The Czech part of Gmünd was renamed České Velenice.

The passenger traffic on various side routes was stopped in Waldviertel in 1986, also on the northern parts of the narrow gauge railway. The freight traffic was at first kept to its full extent and was the final railway in Austria where steam locomotives were regularly used. Those trains were not used for nostalgic or touristic value but a regular service that was only stopped in 1996. The entire traffic between Litschau and Gmünd was stopped in 2001. Today, all parts of this route are exclusively used for tourism.

Where the main road branches off to the left, turn right and cycle along the railway. You will reach the Czech České Velenice via a bridge across the border river Lainsitz which may only be used by pedestrians and cyclists. České Velenice used to be called Gmünd-Bahnhof and Unterwielands.

České Velenice

What we see today as an independent town with 3,400 inhabitants, was founded in 1870 on the routes to the village of Wielands which is located south-west of České Velenice as a railway maintenance works for the Emperor-Franz-Josef-Train (between Vienna and Prague) and as a station for the Austrian town of Gmünd, that is located just opposite on the other side of the river Lainsitz. The small settlement quickly turned into a new part of the town. After the dissolution of the Austro-Hungarian monarchy the newly established Czechoslovakia was given further border areas which turned the Lainsitz river into a border river and the station in Gmünd into a Czech town. The biggest employer in the region is still the railway but the establishment of a cross-border industrial park was intended to revive the area.

The huge station building which was built from 1869-71 boasts a restaurant in which you will find around eight coat of arms on every wall and many decorative elements. This coat of arms hall documents the importance of the station for the Franz-Joseph-Bahn before 1918.

A little way outside the town you will find the churchyard whose brick wall formed part of the Iron Curtain for 40 years.

You will get to a road which you cross on the right and then continue cycling straight. Unfortunately, a sign is missing here. Opposite the big station you turn right into the **path number 341**. At the village exit sign, turn right onto a non-

Border crossing near Nová Bystřice

paved path which is still easy to travel and cross the railway tracks. The path is well signposted and leads to the former border patrol path which is paved. Follow this along the river.

Nová Ves nad Lužnicí

You will meet a road here into which you turn right and which will take you across the river Lainsitz. At the village exit and behind the church, you follow the road branching off to the left. Just before the border the route is signposted. Turn left you on the Austrian side you will see a highly frequented road. Continue along that road to the left for about 150 metres. Then you can leave it again towards the right.

The road number 341 crosses Halámecký potok via a nice bridge and you continue along the border until **Nová Hut'**. Just before you get to it, turn right onto road number **1010** and continue on a non-paved but still easy-to-travel path until you reach the border. Once you get there, you will pass a tower. It is not known if it was a watch tower or if it was put up to watch animals. Behind the tower, turn left towards the lake. Behind the lake, the route is paved again and you continue straight until you reach road number 1014.

EXCURSION If you would like to cycle to Chlum u Třeboně, turn left and continue on the southern side of the lake.

Chlum u Třeboně

Guesthouse Horáček, +420/384/797468 or +420/602/658028)

The history of this border town between the Czech Republic and Austria with around 2,100 inhabitants can be traced back to 1399. Situated in a valley it is surrounded by ponds,

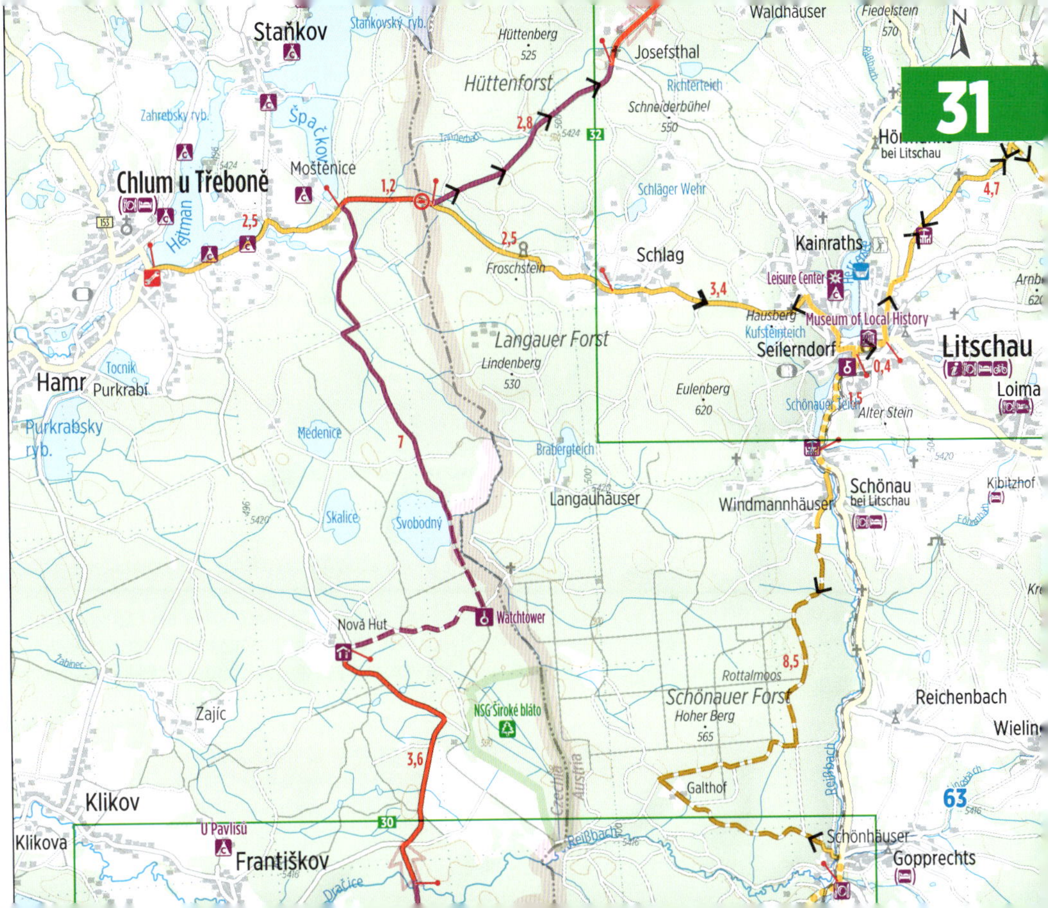

is of some touristic importance and serves well as a temporary base due to its various camping sites and other accommodation possibilities. Behind the church you will see a statue which commemorates the World Wars.

The main route turns to the right and follows the sign 1014 until the border crossing. Afterwards, turn left before the house towards Josefsthal and Haugschlag.

EXCURSION Those wishing to cycle to Litschau continue on the road and after about 11 kilometres they will reach the most northern town in Austria.

Litschau

- **Guest service**, Stadtpl. 17, ✆ +43/2865/5385
- **Museum of Local History**, Stadtpl. 63, ✆ 02865/5385, open: June-Sept., Sa, Su 10am-12pm, July, Aug. also Wed 3-5pm and upon request
- **Church of St. Michael**, late-gothic 3-nave hallchurch (14th + 15th C., baroqueised in 1685) with wall frescoes
- **Palace** with distinctive 13th century keep, privately owned and not publicly accessible
- **City wall** with town gate (1685), pillory (1688)
- **Beach bath at Herrensee**, Strandbadstr. 19

The church marks the centre of the long town square which is lined by old farmers houses from the 19th century. On the final stop of the narrow gauge railway which is operated as a museum during the summer months, the town offers various shopping and eating possibilities. The stream Reiß-bach is dammed here and in the north forms the beautiful and wavy pond named Herrenteich.

The northernmost point of Austria

Josefsthal

Continue straight on the only infrequently travelled road and then slightly uphill into the direction of Haugschlag. At the next branch in the road, continue left on the paved freight path which is signposted to Rottal, the most northern village in Austria. At the hunting lodge bear right and then turn left in a sharp right bend which is signposted towards Peršlák. Just before the paved part comes to an end, you will pass a slightly unconventional house on your right.

EXCURSION If you would like to continue to the most northern point in Austria, turn left here and then follow the walking path number 608 which is not too bad to travel on. However, please note that the route to the border stream between the Czech Republic and Austria will lead you more steeply downhill.

From this house, continue the route which is now not paved anymore and cycle downhill to the border where a wooden bridge was built by Hotel Peršlák. The bridge will lead you across the small border stream. The route is slightly sandy and you turn right at **Lesni Hotel Peršlák** (✆ +420/384/386505) into the old patrol path which is signposted "Iron Curtain Greenway" **1007** and also marked as a cross-country ski trail.

Follow the signposted route – note that strangely enough the sign now indicates 1022 – slightly uphill, then cross bike path number 32 on the right and continue straight. After a left bend, continue for a short stretch on a paved path without any holes. At the point where you exit the forest, you will get to a wide opening where you will also see a golf course. The church of Nová Bystřice can already be seen from this point and to get there you can cycle nicely downhill.

Nová Bystřice

- **Information centre**, Mírové náměstí 54, ✆ +420/384/386909

Pass the big church. At the exit turn right and follow the 1007 straight. Behind **Artolec** leave the 1007 and turn right into the **1008** towards Hirschenschlag – a road that is restricted for motorised vehicles. Cycle past abandoned military buildings, continue straight and pass the border crossing for pedestrians and cyclists. Shortly after the border, before the first two houses, turn left and head towards a **lookout tower**.

The lookout tower was setup on 3 April 1989, shortly before the fall of the Iron Curtain there. In 1995 a commemorative plaque was placed on a stone. It has a wonderful view over the border.

The route is flanked by maps, text and picture panels of the "Path of the 20th Century" presented in three languages.

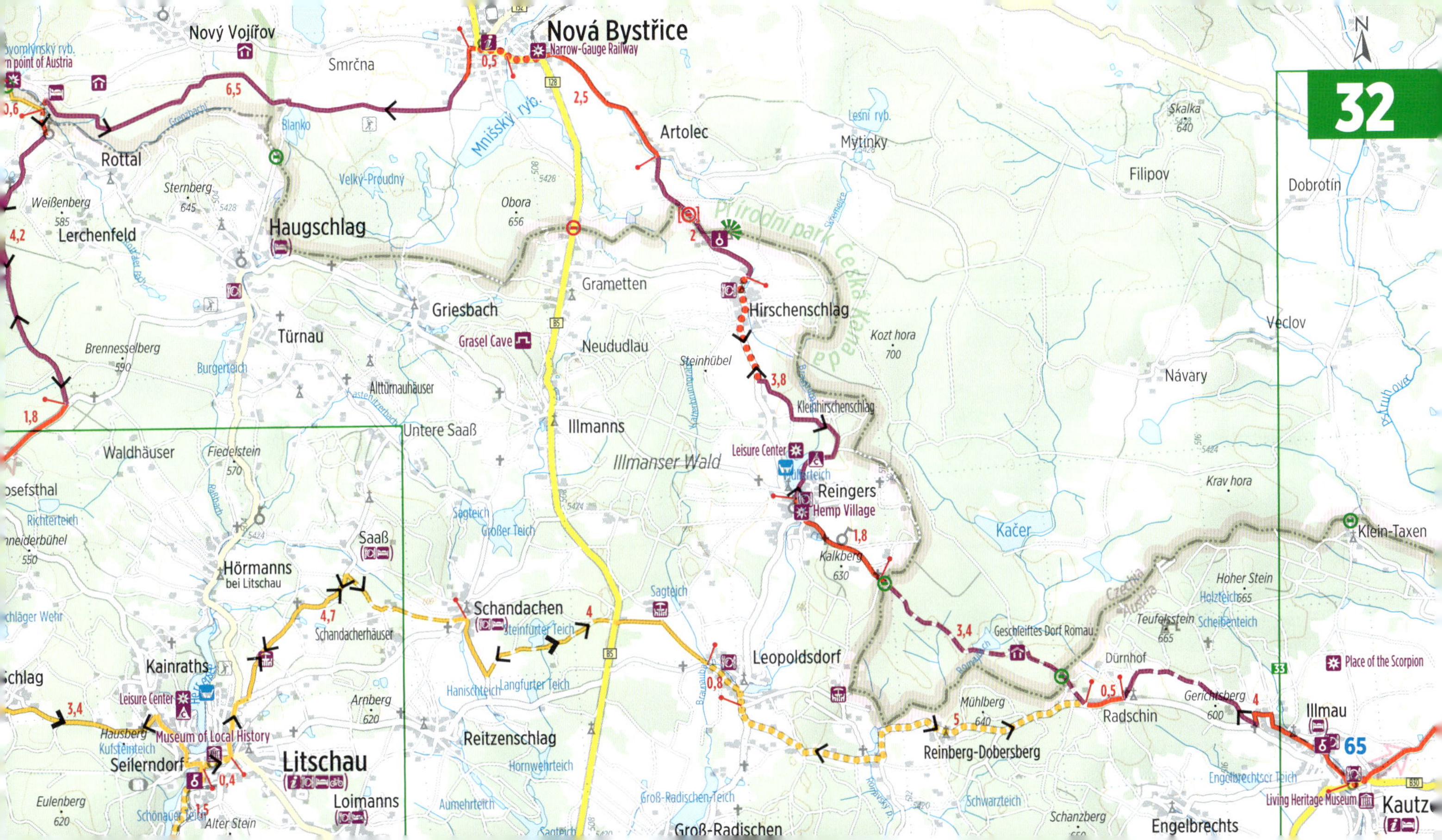

32
Nová Bystřice
Narrow-Gauge Railway
Nový Vojířov
Smrčna
Artolec
Mytinky
Filipov
Dobrotín
Rottal
Sternberg
Weißenberg
Lerchenfeld
Haugschlag
Velký-Proudný
Obora
Mnišský ryb.
Blanko
Přírodní park Česká Kanada
Grametten
Griesbach
Hirschenschlag
Türnau
Grasel Cave
Neududlau
Steinhübel
Kozt hora
Veclov
Návary
Brennesselberg
Burgerteich
Alttürnauhäuser
Kleinhirschenschlag
Untere Saaß
Illmanns
Illmanser Wald
Leisure Center
Reingers
Hemp Village
Waldhäuser
Fiedelstein
Krav hora
Kačer
Klein-Taxen
Richterteich
Kalkberg
Saaß
Hörmanns bei Litschau
Schandachen
Steinfurter Teich
Sagteich
Großer Teich
Schandacherhäuser
Leopoldsdorf
Hoher Stein
Holzteich
Teufelsstein
Scheibenteich
Geschleiftes Dorf Romau
Czechia
Austria
Dürnhof
Place of the Scorpion
Kainraths
Leisure Center
Hanischteich
Langfurter Teich
Arnberg
Mühlberg
Gerichtsberg
Radschin
Illmau
Hausberg
Kufsteinteich
Museum of Local History
Seilerndorf
Litschau
Reitzenschlag
Reinberg-Dobersberg
Hornwehrteich
Loimanns
Eulenberg
Schönauer Teich
Alter Stein
Aumehrteich
Groß-Radischen-Teich
Schwarzteich
Schanzberg
Engelbrechtser Teich
Living Heritage Museum
Engelbrechts
Groß-Radischen
Kautz

On the board behind the watchtower you can see the following inscription: "Already on 4th December 1989 a visa for nationals of Czechoslovakia was no longer required at the border. The new freedom to travel was used first at the Neubriestritz border crossing by 15 people. In the days after, however, the floodgates opened. A toy distribution company at the border crossing in Grametten testified to the joy of the opening of the borders. Soon, delegations of politicians began visiting the respective neighbouring communities and newly established language courses were well-attended. Also shopping tourism flourished, many Czechs found products in Austria that were hard to find in their home country. Some Austrians took advantage of the low prices on the other side and bought things in bulk. Sadly, on the horizon a point of contention was looming with the construction of the Temelín nuclear power plant."

The region was hit hard by the developments of the 20th century. Nová Bystřice was lost to the German Reich as part of the Munich Agreement in 1938 and again awarded to Czechoslovakia after the second World War. Each event led to expulsions of its residents.

Hirschenschlag

We come across the scarcely travelled road which you follow downhill. Turn left a little later left onto the signposted Grenzlandweg 8 to the forest and cycle past a lake.

Reingers

Gasthaus Uitz, ✆ +43/2863/8207 or +43/664/2722584

The village has a cross with the inscription: "Remember the victims of expulsion from Neubiestritz, its surroundings and in Moravia in 1945".

Where the road makes a right turn behind the church, you can find a newly built and scarcely travelled road. Turn left onto the signposted 1007 and head towards the Kalkberg / Romau border crossing. After the border the road is not paved, but still in passable condition. Continue straight down to the lake, cross the stream and cycle along the lake.

Romau (Romava)

At the last census in 1939 the village had 259 inhabitants. After 1945, the Germans were relocated. The Chapel of the Holy Cross, which was located here, originated from the 2nd half of the 19th century. Just like the whole village, it was completely destroyed.

Slavonice

Turn right. After the border, in Austria, take an asphalt road downhill to Radschin, where you turn left into the signposted Waldviertel bike path. At the next branch, turn left into the signposted Grenzlandweg trail. After the first bend to the right the road is not paved, but easily navigable and it goes downhill. Just before the road turn left into Kneippweg. Continue through Illmau – it is possible to stay the night at the church - and follow the sign Grenzlandradweg 8. You will soon come across another place to stay on the main street of Kautzen, into which you turn left.

Kautzen

Living Heritage Museum in the former post office on Waidhofner-str. 9, ✆ +43/2864/2442, OT: mid-April-Oct. and during Advent, Sun / holidays 9-12 and 14-16

Castle Illmau. First mentioned in 1337, it originally served as a border fortress. Today the renaissance building dates from the 16th century. Between 1914 and 1917 it served as a detention centre. Today it is privately owned.

Harrer, ✆ +43/2864/2372

Kautzen won some awards due to its efforts to strive towards village renewable energy sources (European Village Renewal Award, European Solar Prize, lower Austria environmental prize).

Continue past the church, keep left and follow the bicycle trail on the road.

Großtaxen

Cycle over the stream Taxenbach, follow the sign to **Brunn** and cycle straight to the border. Where the scarcely travelled

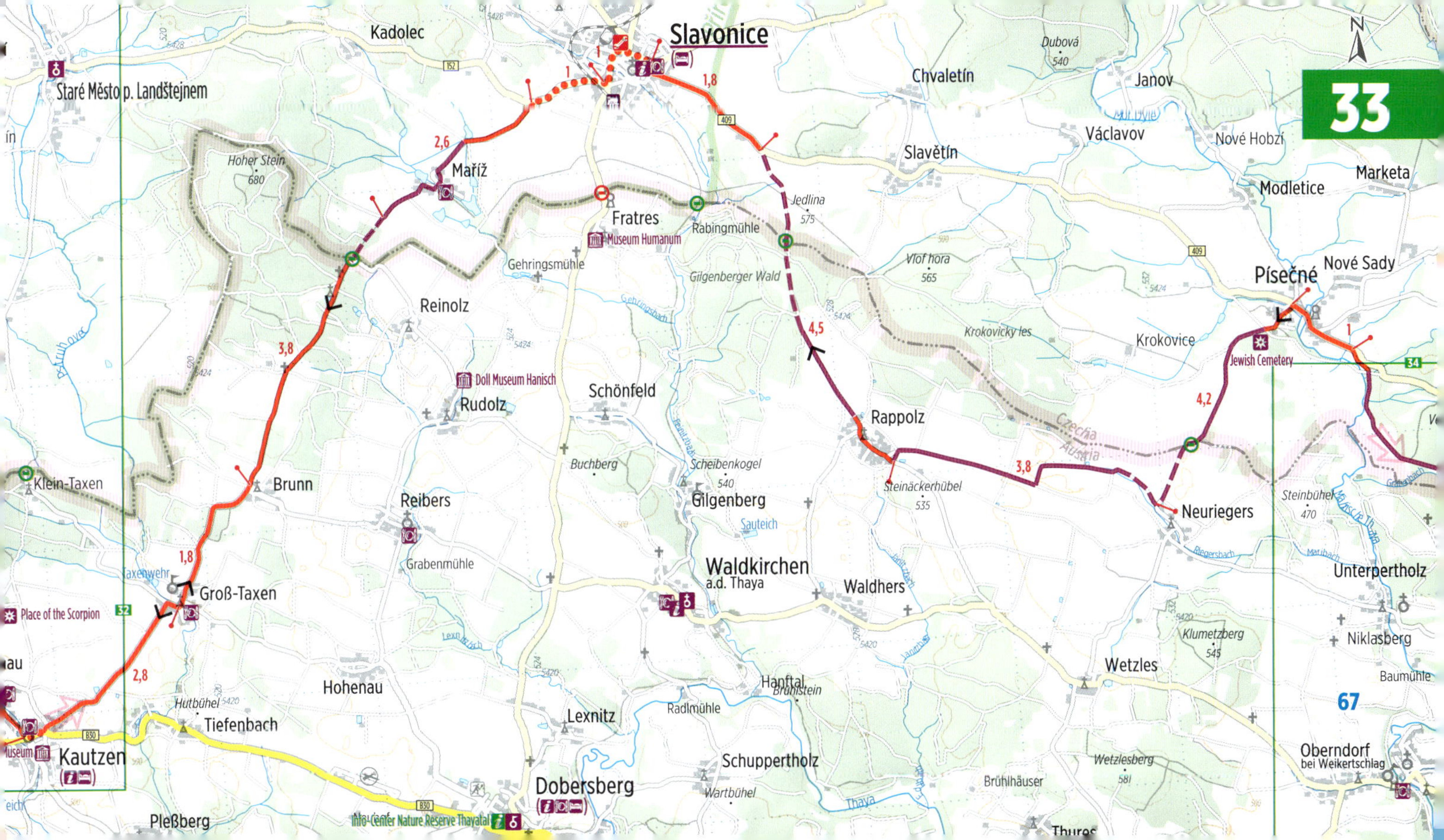

33
Slavonice
Kadolec
Staré Město p. Landštejnem
Chvaletín
Dubová
540
Janov
Václavov
Nové Hobzí
Slavětín
Marketa
Modletice
Mařiž
Hoher Stein
680
Fratres
Museum Humanum
Rabingmühle
Jedlina
575
Vlof hora
565
Gilgenberger Wald
Gehringsmühle
Reinolz
Písečné
Nové Sady
Krokovicky les
Krokovice
Jewish Cemetery
Doll Museum Hanisch
Rudolz
Schönfeld
Rappolz
Czechia
Austria
Buchberg
Scheibenkogel
540
Steinäckerhübel
535
Gilgenberg
Sauteich
Neuriegers
Steinbühel
470
Klein-Taxen
Brunn
Reibers
Grabenmühle
Waldkirchen
a.d. Thaya
Waldhers
Unterpertholz
Groß-Taxen
Taxenwehr
Place of the Scorpion
Niklasberg
Klumetzberg
545
Wetzles
Baumühle
67
Hohenau
Hanftal
Brühlstein
Radlmühle
Hutbühel
Tiefenbach
Lexnitz
Kautzen
Museum
Schuppertholz
Wetzlesberg
581
Brühlhäuser
Oberndorf
bei Weikertschlag
Dobersberg
Wartbühel
Thaya
Pleßberg
Info-Center Nature Reserve Thayatal
Thures
2,6
1,8
3,8
4,5
4,2
3,8
1,8
2,8
1
1
1
152
409
409
B30
B30
32
34

road takes a sharp right turn after Reinolz and Rudolz, turn left into a dirt road. Continue on a path surrounded by birch trees until you encounter a tarmacked former patrol road, which is also labelled **"Greenway Prague-Vienna"** and as **bike path 1003**. Behind the ponds you'll find a rarely travelled road. Turn right into the busy road to Nová Bystřice and Slavonice. It is signposted as **bike path 32**. Cross the track and pass the Train Station where you can take direct trains to Dačice and Kostelec u Jihlavy.

Slavonice

- Hotel Arkáda, ✆ +420/602/349677
- Cyklo-Sport-Servis, ✆ +420/728/828837 or +420/606/133522

Because of their border near the town, Slavonice, with just under 3,000 inhabitants, has an extremely colourful past. It once belonged to Austria and once to the Czech Republic. Due to its exposed location Slavonice was quickly reinforced and has a well-preserved medieval town centre. The city received - now simply just a point of interest - a drainage system, which served as a defensive line. The town has a beautiful square with impressive facades. It also has a very strong cultural scene and a railway station which is well connected to the rest of the Czech railway network.

Thayatalbahn

The single-track branch line from Schwarzenau over Waidhofen to Slavonice was opened in 1903 and disrupted in 1945 by the Iron Curtain. After this happened, the revitalization of the Lower Austrian transport concept was given the highest priority, because the region is highly dependent on the timber industry. The population is fighting the number of heavy lorries on the road. The citizens' initiative "New Thaya Valley Railway" supports the immediate re-commissioning of the railway.

From Slavonice to Znojmo 78 km

From the market square, cycle on **bike path 48**, which is sign-posted "Greenway Prague-Vienna", through the south-eastern gate. Outside the city, the road is not very busy, turn right three times, and then turn into a path with a white square and red dot.

TIP Once you cross the border, the way to Rappolz is unfortunately not signposted.

The paving-slabbed path turns into a field road and then behind the border into a paved road

Rappolz

Ride straight through the village past a small church. Behind the exit sign, turn left into the paved road, which is not signposted. Keep going straight - later the road is not paved. Then turn left, cross the stream and the main street of **Neuriegers** and continue straight. On the left side is a barn and on the right the first building of the village. After a short stretch the asphalt road stops but the path remains reasonably good. After an S shaped bend, continue along the border towards Czech Republic. Where the 1002 turns

Jewish cemetery

left, continue straight on. At the next intersection with two paved field roads, turn right and follow the small sign to the Jewish cemetery.

Jewish Cemetery

In this rather dilapidated cemetery of Písečné, the most recent grave is from 1931. From 1727 to 1920 the Jewish community had a synagogue, a school with just one class and this Jewish cemetery. The entire Jewish population was almost exclusively killed in the Holocaust. The aforementioned buildings were later demolished by the Czechoslovak authorities.

Continue through the city downhill. At the left turn at the entrance, on the right hand side of an asphalt road, there is a small monument.

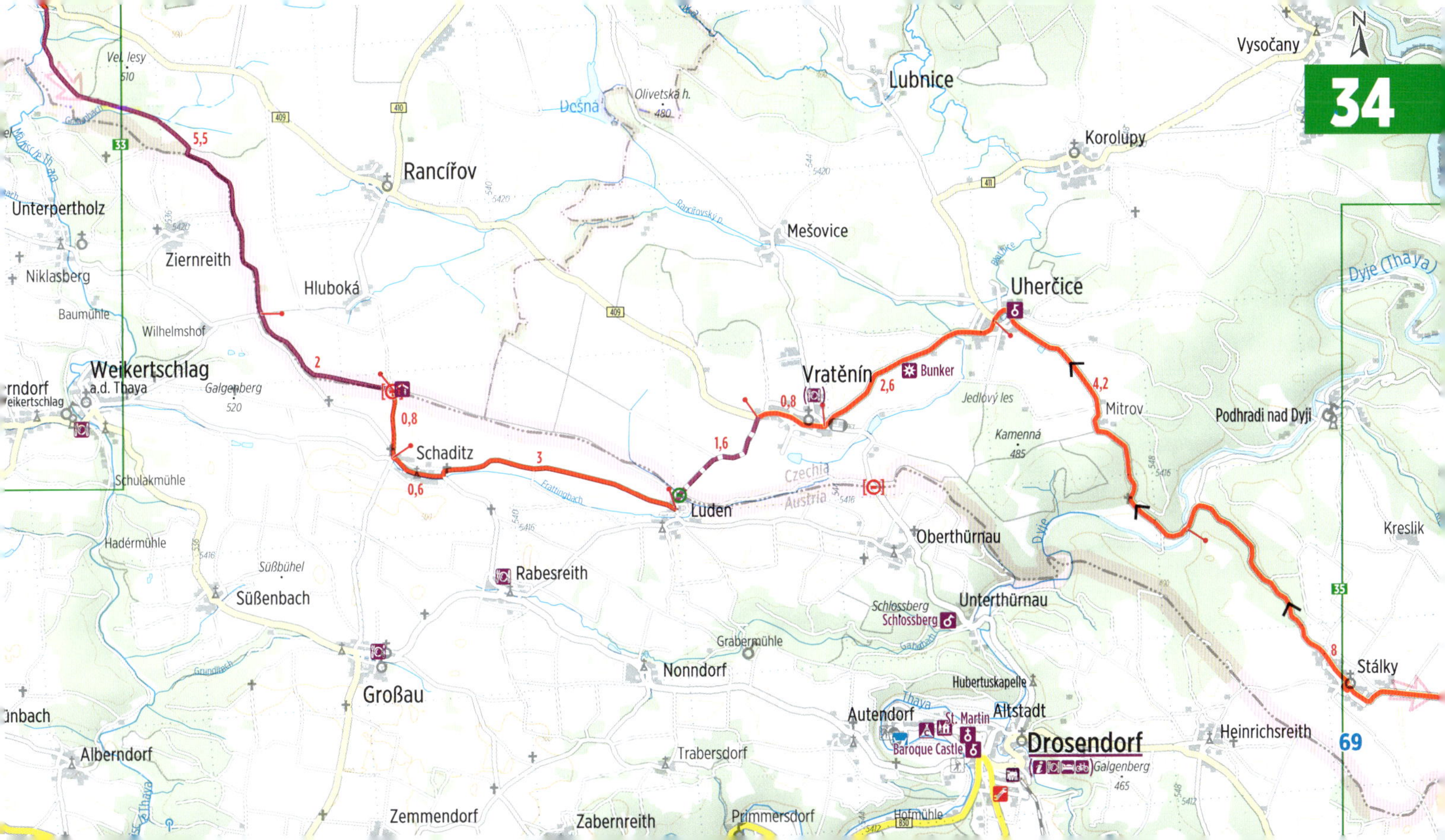

34
Vysočany
Lubnice
Olivetská h.
480
Dešná
Korolupy
Rancířov
Vel. lesy
510
Unterpertholz
Ziernreith
Niklasberg
Hluboká
Baumühle
Wilhelmshof
Mešovice
Uherčice
Dyje (Thaya)
Weikertschlag
a.d. Thaya
Galgenberg
520
Vratěnín
Bunker
Jedlový les
Mitrov
Podhradí nad Dyjí
Kamenná
485
Schaditz
Schulakmühle
Czechia
Austria
Luden
Oberthürnau
Kreslik
Hadérmühle
Süßbühel
Süßenbach
Rabesreith
Schlossberg
Unterthürnau
Grabermühle
Großau
Nonndorf
Hubertuskapelle
Stálky
Autendorf
St. Martin
Altstadt
Baroque Castle
Drosendorf
Galgenberg
465
Heinrichsreith
Alberndorf
Trabersdorf
Zemmendorf
Zabernreith
Primmersdorf
Hofmühle
5,5
2
0,8
0,6
3
1,6
0,8
2,6
4,2
8
33
35
69

Písečné

Cycle through the village, cross the stream and turn right into the road marked **cycle path 48** to Rančířov. Cross the **Thaya** for the first time.

Thaya

The Thaya (Dyje) is a tributary of Morava and is fed from two sources (Schweiggers and Telč), which unite in Raab and open at Hohenau in the Morava. Its course is marked at a length of 235 kilometres through very unconventional curves. Whether the river writhes in pain or in joy, remains a mystery. It frequently crosses the border between Austria and the Czech Republic. For long stretches, it actually forms the border between those two countries. In the middle of the river it measures around 100 metres and is home to numerous castles and palaces on its riverbanks. The Thaya is crossed by a railway bridge (inaugurated 1871), which was made into a technically historical monument in 1998.

Behind the Thaya bridge, turn right into **bike path 48** (sign-posted to Vratěnín). A little while later turn right again into **cycle path 1001** (paved patrol road) and continue along the Thaya to the Austrian border. After an S-shaped bend, keep close to the border. You will see border signs flanking you as you cycle through some fields. The patrol has some weaknesses, and the signs will be replaced by boundary stones. The road on the west side belongs to Austria. Stay on the patrol road, cycling along the border until you hit a busy little street, into which you turn right and cross the border.

Schaditz

Keep to the left into the direction of Luden. At the entrance to the village, follow the sign on the rarely travelled road.

Luden

Just behind the entrance sign, turn left. "Warning: National Border" is written just before the border. A bridge, which almost certainly used to be there, is missing, but you can easily carry your bike over the creek to get to the other side. Continue on a fairly passable dirt road until you come across the main road, into which you turn right.

Vratěnín

The town, with its 300 inhabitants, has seen better days. In the Middle Ages the city was home to an aristocratic ruler and was home to hostels and later had the main postal station on the postal route from Vienna to Prague. The new Kaiserstraße (imperial road) bypassed them, however, so that some of the expensive facilities fell into disrepair or had to be changed such as the former transformer (now a restaurant), the post office (now the town tall) or the palace. Nonetheless, huge efforts were made to make the village more attractive again and in 1996 they won the title "Village of the Year". Newly planted rows of fruit trees line the roads that lead to many of the surrounding areas.

Bunker near Vratěnín

The **State Road 409** is signposted **cycle path 48** and "Greenway Prague-Vienna". Go through the village and turn left after the church.

Bunkers at Vratěnín

These bunkers were not only east of the Morava and built in South Moravia, but also at the borders with Germany and Poland, and were intended to be like a ring circling the external border of the first Czechoslovak Republic. They were a product of the defence concept envisaged by the Czechoslovakian General Staff in 1935/36. They were primarily intended to counter the threat of attack by the German Reich military. The fortifications were built under the direction of French officers – in 1925 the Czechoslovak Republic concluded a military alliance with France. Because they were similar to the positions that the French had built against the German Reich, they are often referred to as Czech Maginot Line. Of course, the Czechs did not believe they would be sufficient on their own to stop the German troops. It was intended that the bunkers and trenches would delay the arrival of the Nazis so that France and Great Bri-

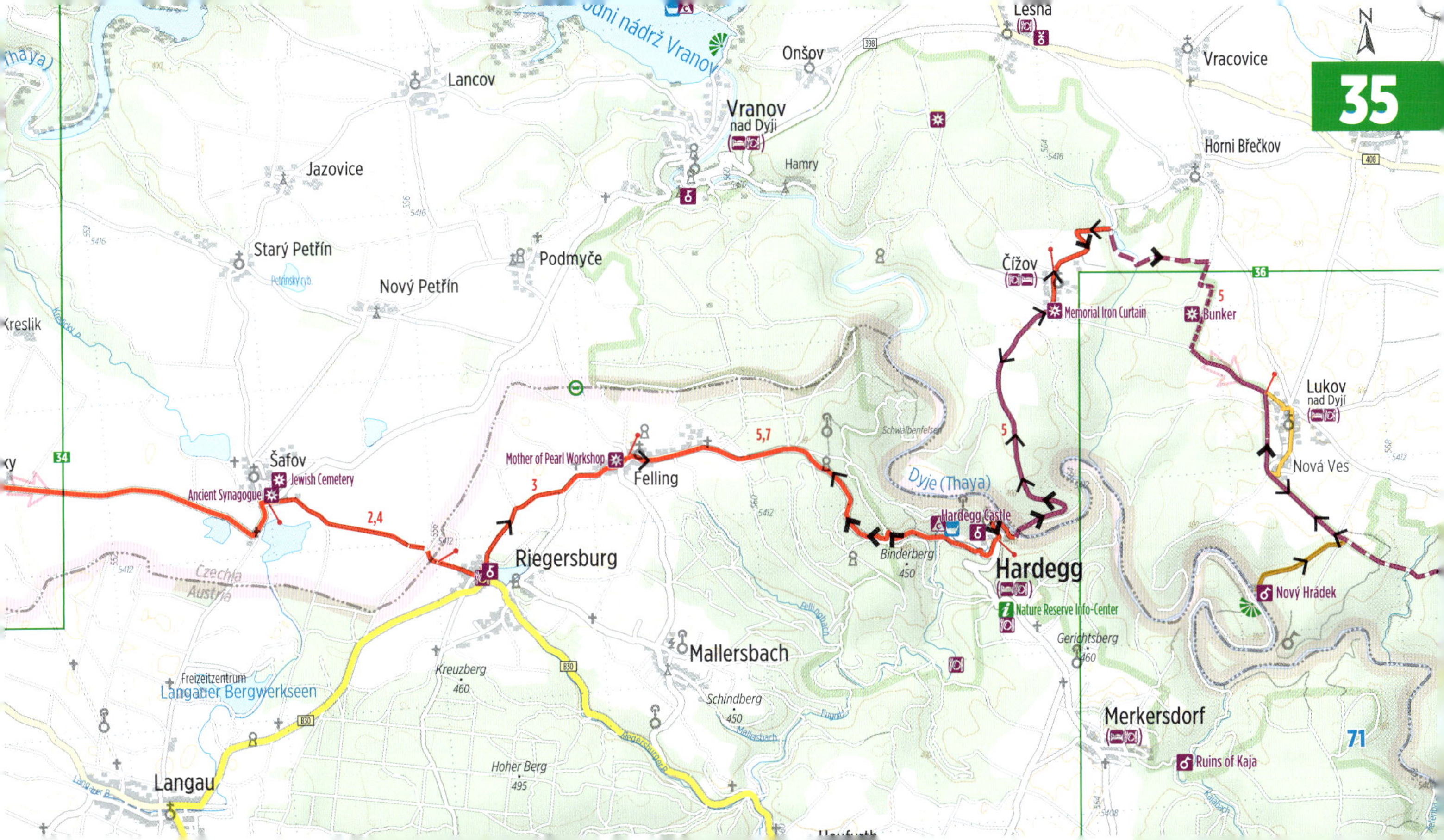

35
Vranov nad Dyjí
Lancov
Onšov
Lesná
Vracovice
Horní Břečkov
Hamry
Jazovice
Starý Petřín
Podmyče
Nový Petřín
Čížov
Memorial Iron Curtain
Bunker
Lukov nad Dyjí
Nová Ves
Nový Hrádek
Šafov
Jewish Cemetery
Ancient Synagogue
Mother of Pearl Workshop
Felling
Riegersburg
Hardegg Castle
Hardegg
Nature Reserve Info-Center
Binderberg
450
Dyje (Thaya)
Czechia
Austria
Mallersbach
Kreuzberg
460
Schindberg
450
Hoher Berg
495
Freizeitzentrum
Langauer Bergwerkseen
Langau
Merkersdorf
Ruins of Kaja
Gerichtsberg
460
Schwalbenfelsen
2,4
3
5,7
5
34
36
71
B30
398
408

tain could begin a counteroffensive. The construction of the bunker was started in 1936. The walls were 200 cm thick, and the frontage was 225 cm thick. They were heavily camouflaged.

Uherčice

Here is a magnificent, multi-winged Renaissance chateau, which was used in 1945 as a barracks and women's prison. It threatened to become derelict but was declared a cultural monument in 2002 and as such is regularly renovated.

On a large right bend pass the palace, cycle along the river, remaining on the "Greenway Prague-Vienna" and always continue straight, and do not get confused by the crossings. A large part of the route is nicely downhill.

Mitrov

Cross the Thaya (Dyje) and turn right behind the bridge into the signposted "Greenway Prague-Vienna", which is only marked by its logo, because according to Czech law a signpost must not show two numbers for different paths. The route takes you gently uphill following the path of a stream.

Stálky

The long village with the architectural concept of a right-angled village green which stretches through the entire village has an ancient steeple which looks as if it were built for fortification purposes and the village is similar in style to the next destination our trail.

Just before the lake turn left.

Šafov

The architectural concept of a right-angled village green is also found here, but the houses are even more compact and crowded together here. That should perhaps come as little surprise because this village with its 170 inhabitants was once considered a town-like settlement. As such, it has a very special story. After the prosperous market town had suffered severely during the Thirty Years War, Vienna and Lower Austria came up with the idea to expel the Jews. The owner of Vranov (Frain), decided to move 85 Jewish families to Šafov, which was under his jurisdiction. Very soon the newly arrived Jews dominated the linen, leather, wool and other raw materials trade for miles around. After the emancipation of the Jews in 1848 and the free movement which came with it, combined with the railway, allowed for the direct supply of factories and markets. In 1938, 68 of the former 650 Jewish residents left. From the remaining ones who stayed, around half could not be saved from the Nazi terror. The Czechs themselves had to leave after the German invasion and the Germans had to leave after the war. In 1843, Šafov had exactly 1251 inhabitants and in 1994 only 169. The large building with the green roof, which you see on the right once you enter the town, is the former synagogue dating back to 1785. The Jewish cemetery is in good condition and is diagonally opposite.

Ludwig Winder

Ludwig Winder (1889-1946) was born in Schaffa (Šafov) and was one of the most widely read authors of the first Czechoslovak Republic. In 1934 he received 1934 a state prize. Some of his books have only been published in Czech and in German. He became famous for his novels "Jewish organ" and "The Crown Prince", which, incidentally, was banned in Austria. His play "The woman without qualities" prompted Robert Musil to produce his 1,000-page rebuttal "The Man Without Qualities". After the Nazi invasion, Ludwig Winter fled with his wife and eldest daughter to London. The youngest daughter and his relatives who stayed behind were killed by the Nazis. Beppo Beyerl describes him in his book "Warning: National Border" as follows: "Ludwig Winder had the misfortune of being caught between a rock and a hard place. For the Czechs, he was a German, so forget about him. And for representatives of the Sudeten Germans, he was a leftist and, moreover, a Jew, so forget him twice."

Before the entrance to the city of Šafov turn right into the little-used unpaved road just before the border.

Riegersburg

Museum Barockschloss Riegersburg, ✆ +43/2916/400, OT: April – middle Nov., Mo-Sun 9-17, July and Aug., 9-19.

Turn left, past the palace, which also has a garden cafe, and cycle past the lake toward Felling. Turn left into a rarely-used road.

Felling

Austria's only mother of pearl workshop, ✆ +43 / +43/2916/203. Manufacture of buttons and jewellery with over 100 years of tradition.

The trail goes first uphill and then you will be rewarded with a simply fabulous downhill ride. Once at the bottom you get to also enjoy a wonderful view of the castle. Continue on the main road to the castle. At the point where it bends very sharply to the right, keep half way to the right following the signs to Čížov whilst remaining on the **Kamp-Thaya-March bike route**. Once you reach cafe turn right following the signposts to Čížov.

TIP Both paths lead over the Thaya bridge; the right path is shorter, but the left takes you through the centre.

Hardegg

Area code: 02949

Nationalparkzentrum Thayatal, ✆ 7005, OT: Apr-Sep, Tue-Sun, holidays 10-18, March, October-December, Thurs-Sun / holidays 10-16.

Parish church with ossuary. Karner, one of the few Romanesque ossuaries (1160) in Lower Austria is nestled in a Baroque church.

Hardegg Castle, the Maximilian of Mexico Museum and the Heritage Museum, ✆ 8225, OT: April 15th Nov. Mon-Sun 9-17, August 9-18. The border between Austria and Moravia has run through the

Hardegg castle

middle of the Thaya for centuries which was one reason for the construction of the castle in the 12th century. With a circumference of 600m, the largest castle in Lower Austria is one of the most impressive Baroque buildings in Austria. On a cliff above the river, it looks very impressive in amongst the lovely valley landscape and the towering caste keep can be seen far from far away in the valley. The romantic chapel, the keep, the kitchen, the armoury and the Emperor Maximilian of Mexico exhibition are particularly worth seeing.

Clock tower, just at the entrance. Here is also the entrance to the castle.

With just 87 inhabitants, Hardegg is the smallest town in Austria.

Once you are in town, keep to the right and cycle along Thaya until you get to the bridge, where there is an old inn.

The bridge over Hardegg

With the famous bridge over the Thaya big politics in the smallest town in Austria was ever present. One half of the bridge, which was demolished, belonged to the former Czechoslovakia, the other, which was provisionally maintained, belonged to Austria. The new bridge was built in 1990 as part of the Thayatal National Park and is only open to pedestrians and cyclists. The national park begins after the bridge.

National Park Thayatal

The Thaya National Park, together with the Czech Národní park Podyjí, is 45 square kilometres large. The flora and fauna close to the boundary could develop almost completely undisturbed over the last few decades. Therefore, many thought-to-be long-lost species such as elk and wild cat are still to be found in this region.

After the bridge the route takes you steeply uphill.

Čížov

Iron Curtain memorial. Opposite the former customs house, you can see an old observation tower and tank traps on the old patrol route. A board provides you with additional information. A replica of the Iron Curtain was built here. Even a gateway for the border police was created so that soldiers could control both sides.

Bed and Breakfast Marka, ✆ +420/737/312188, at the end of the village

TIP Unfortunately, the patrol path is not 100% fit for travelling on, so you have to return to the road after visiting.

Pass a cemetery and a church, before getting to restaurant that is only open from May to November. Follow the road, cycle a bit downhill and turn right once you reach a bridge in the direction of Lukov. The road is unpaved but in good condition. Cycle along the stream, which later turns into a lake. After having crossed a stream, the path rises again. Once you leave the forest, turn right at the end of the road towards Lukov. At the next junction keep left – a sign is missing, but you can see a sign written on the tree. After a right turn you continue down a beautiful path through the woods to a bunker until you hit the patrol path. It would be nice if this patrol path were attached to the memorial. Unfortunately, a bridge is missing for this. Then turn left on the patrol path until you reach Lukov, whose church is easy to find. Before Lukov turn right to Nová Ves.

ALTERNATIVE If you want visit or stay the night at Lukov, go straight through the village, turn right at the restaurant and cycle past the church, where there is also a restaurant. Cycle through Lukov and Nová Ves until you hit the patrol path again, into which you turn left.

Cycle through the National Park along on a paved patrol road.

Nová Ves

Here you turn half left.

EXCURSION At the next crossroads a path goes 2 km right to the ruins of Novy Hradek, a beautiful viewpoint over the Thaya.

At this junction, ride straight ahead and follow the signposted bike path 48 which later ceases to be paved and bends around to the left at the end and onto the paved patrol road. Cross a river – the cycle path 48 is also the 5000 – turn right at the end, shortly afterwards left again and remain on the patrol path until you reach Thaya. Cross the river and turn left at the next possibility and cycle along the 48 to Šatov.

EXCURSION If you want to cycle to Znojmo, turn left before Šatov onto Cyclepath 500.

Znojmo

Městský úřad, Obroková 10, ✆ +420/515/222552

Znojmo Theater

- **South Moravian Museum**, Přemyslovců 6. In the crypt of the former Minorite convent is the grave of King Premysl Otakar II.
- **Late Gothic hall church of St. Nicholas**, Mikulášské nám. The three naves (14C.) are located at the top of a high bank. Despite a Baroque reconstruction (pulpit in the form of a globe) Gothic frescoes are still present.
- **Baroque St. Michael's Church**, on the northern tip of the old town. Its tower was rebuilt after a collapse on the choir side, and is separated by a road.
- **Louka monastery / Bruck**, Loucká. The Collegiate Church of the otherwise somewhat dilapidated monastery (founded 11909 is well worth seeing. The magnificent Baroque building was designed by Lukas von Hildebrandt and Anton Maulpertsch.
- The **castle** replaces the late 12th century unfashionable castle of Hradiště. The inner castle, separated by a moat in the 13th century, was later rebuilt into a Baroque castle. Among the oldest parts is the rotunda of St. Catherine, which is considered the most valuable cultural heritage piece in the city. It contains unique murals, a series of paintings of biblical motifs, interwoven with a gallery of Přemyslid rulers.
- **Town Hall Tower**
- **Underground cellar corridors**, Slepičí trh. An extensive network of cellars permeates the underground spaces of the city. In total they stretch for around 27 km across 3 floors, and you can see about 1 km if you visit.
- Numerous **houses from the Renaissance**

Znojmo with its well-preserved medieval town centre is situated on a rocky plateau above the river. The school near

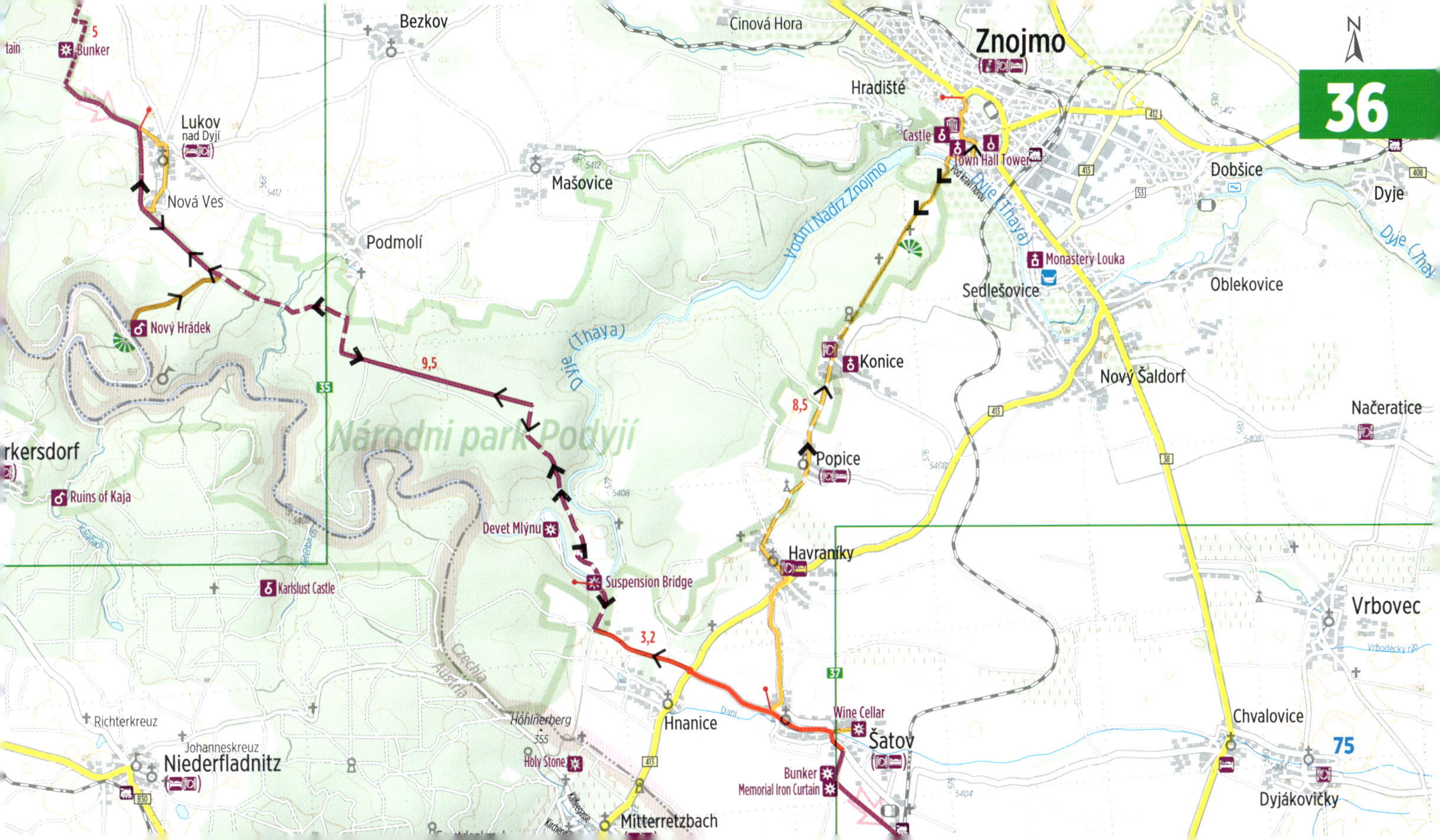

36
Znojmo
Bezkov
Cínová Hora
Hradiště
Castle
Town Hall Tower
Dobšice
Dyje
Mašovice
Lukov
nad Dyjí
Nová Ves
Bunker
Podmolí
Vodní Nádrž Znojmo
Dyje (Thaya)
Monastery Louka
Sedlešovice
Oblekovice
Nový Hrádek
Konice
Nový Šaldorf
Načeratice
9,5
8,5
Národní park Podyjí
Popice
rkersdorf
Ruins of Kaja
Devět Mlýnů
Havraníky
Suspension Bridge
Karlslust Castle
Vrbovec
3,2
Czechia
Austria
Richterkreuz
Johanneskreuz
Niederfladnitz
Höhlnerberg
Holy Stone
Hnanice
Wine Cellar
Šatov
Bunker
Memorial Iron Curtain
Chvalovice
75
Dyjákovičky
Mitterretzbach
35
37

the train station, counts one of the most popular entertainers, the Austrian singer Peter Alexander (1926-2011) as one of its former pupils. Due to various pranks, the Humanist School Döbling had him expelled. Since his mother was from Budweis, he could change after Znojmo and do his emergency A-Levels in 1944.

In Horní Česká there is a bicycle-friendly B&B (✆ +420/775/202010. The railway station provides direct trains to Vienna and Břeclav.

From Znojmo (CZ) to Laa on the Thaya (AT) 45 km

From the station in Znojmo the trail continues to the left. On the right side of **Dr. M. Horákové** is a beautiful bike path running in both directions. At the end of it turn right into **Vídeňská tř.** and at the next possibility left into **Dyjská**. The road winds downhill to Thaya, signposted **126** and provides a scenic view of the railway bridge. On the corner to the left of the bike path 126, the trail continues right into **Koželužská** along the Thaya to the bridge (car museum and a restaurant with terrace). On the right side you'll see a large dam.

TIP The signage here leaves something to be desired.

After crossing the Thaya, follow the signs towards Unterretzbach, turn left after the bridge and immediately turn right and continue cycling uphill. The road is only paved for a short distance and then turns into a quite tricky-to-navigate road. Here you have a wonderful view of the city. Ignore the narrow field path for mountain bikers and remain on the rather broad, if not that good road. At the triangle intersection, turn right. Once at the top, you can see a memorial stone with an information board.

Memorial stone for Anton Vrbka

Anton Vrbka

The teacher and local historian was a lover of Znojmo and its history. Because of his contribution to the history museum, a memorial stone was erected here upon his retirement in 1925. Later he refused to give the Nazis pieces from its museum, which were planned to be given to Adolf Hitler. Due to the Czechoslovak border troops abusing the memorial stone by using it for target practice after 1945, it was smashed. In 2005 it was finally rebuilt. When one thinks about it, it seems rather strange that the Czechoslovak Communists had such little respect for a courageous person like Anton Vrbka (1860-1939) who showed such courage against the Nazis.

Just behind the memorial stone we come to the signposted road to Znojmo, where you turn left to signposted Konice. The flat road is easy to navigate and you can already see the vineyards of some very famous wine. At the next triangle intersection, continue straight. A panel provides - unfortunately only in Czech - information about the vineyard in the Thaya loop in Sobes.

Konice

Do not turn left downhill to the church but go straight on the quiet, paved road signposted to Havraníky.

Popice

Continue straight and cycle on the signposted cycle path towards Unterretzbach. Initially the road is still paved, then it continues a little bit to the right and becomes a bit more arduous but still possible over some rocks. A panel indicates a serpent, called in Czech "užovka Stromová". Turn left just before you reach a Statue. You pass a chapel.

Hermitage of Our Lady of Sorrows

Here, on the Kaitlinger Heide, available in German and Czech: "Dear child, where are you going, do you not know that I am your mother? I love you so dearly, therefore standstill and greet me." In 1993, this chapel was fully renovated.

The road continues to improve. At the next intersection, go straight, the path is signposted through the vineyards with a symbol. In the opposite direction the path marker is more detailed.

Havraníky

At the junction triangle turn left into the paved road towards Šatov. The right path leads you to Sobes and its famous vineyards. On the main road, on which a Bed and Breakfast with a restaurant can be found, turn right until you meet the main road, into which you turn left.

Memorial Iron Curtain Trail in Šatov

Šatov

The place has a chequered history. In the 1930s, the Czech population was expelled and after the Munich Agreement a board announced: "On December 4, 1938, the inhabitants of the market Schattau committed themselves 100 percent to Adolf Hitler their leader and liberator." The only thing that survived the immediate post-war period was one wine cellar. The railway station offers direct connections to Vienna and Znojmo.

EXCURSION If you follow the arrow left, the trail continues on an asphalt road towards a church and shortly before turn left into a dirt road that will lead you to a wine cellar with paintings.

Wine cellar Malovaný sklep

Maximillian Appeltauer (1904-1972) painted the sandstone walls in the cellar from 1930 to 1968. When he came back from the war with just one hand in 1945, he continued to paint with dissolved lime colour pigments. Here you can see some fine examples of naive folk art, landscapes and in one of the five booths some nude paintings.

From the wine cellar, take the gravel road back, turn left and stay on the signposted

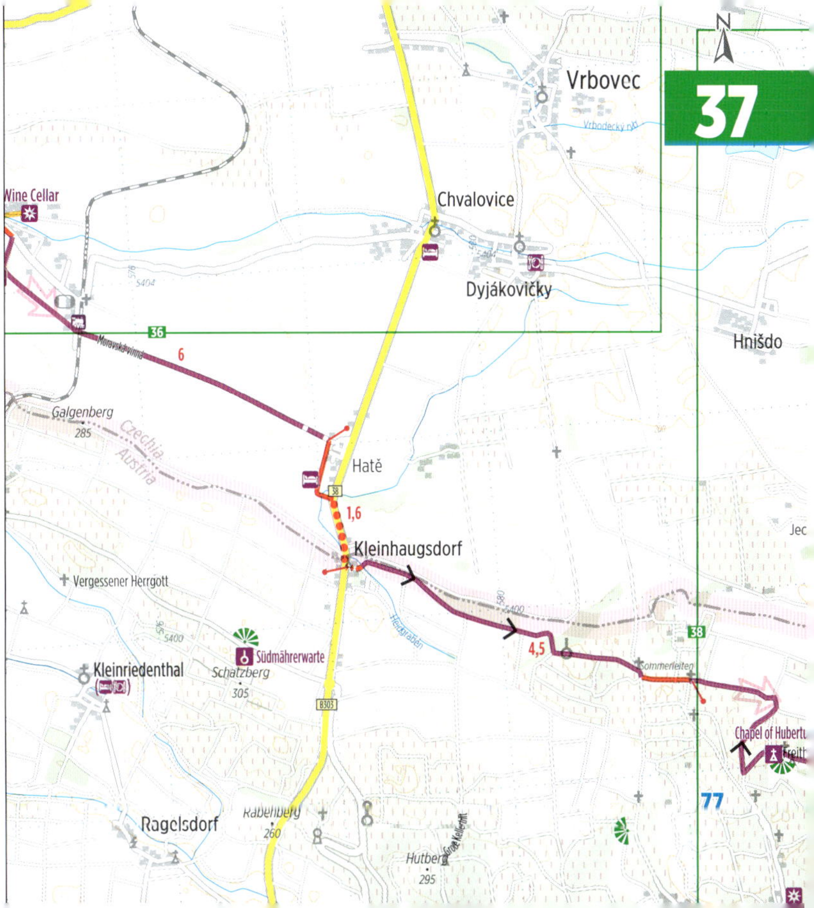

path. At the end of the path, you can see the electricity tower. Turn left over the Daníž. On **bike path 48** a restaurant with accommodation can be seen on the left, where cyclists are welcome. Straight ahead is signposted cycle path (48) Prague-Vienna. On the "European Iron Curtain Trail", turn right to the bunker.

The Šatov bunker

This bunker, which has been painted with funky colours, made history at a time when Czechoslovakia was the only democracy to be found in Central Europe in the 1930s. Due to Hitler threats that he would destroy the Hussite Czechs and bomb Prague from the air, a closed chain of bunkers was created, of which many still exist today, on the border to Germany. After the "annexation" of Austria to the German Reich, expected a massive attack in the direction of Znojmo (Znojmo) was expected which is why the fortifications had to strengthened in this area. The idea was to hold up the German troops just long enough until their French and British allies could come to their aid. These measures turned out to be in vain. The majority of the Sudeten Germans wanted " to go home to the Reich" and terrorized the Czech minority in the populated German majority areas.

In September 29, 1938 Britain and France - the representatives of Czechoslovakia were not allowed to be present - as well as Germany and Italy, signed the "Munich Agreement", referred to by Czech historians as "Munich Dictate". It was declared in a 1973 "Prague Agreement" by the Federal Republic of Germany as "void". After the "Munich Agreement" the German Wehrmacht marched into the Czechoslovakian border areas, the democratic Sudeten Germans, Jews and Czechs were all expelled to the "rump Czechoslovakia". Hitler personally inspected the bunker of Šatov and promptly issued some propaganda photos of the "victorious leader". Many of the population who were still undecided joined the NSDAP or the SS. Ten years later the bunker again played a role: After the forced agricultural collectivisation many of the old boundary field mounds were removed. The first communist state president, Klement Gottwald, walked the few steps from the main road went to the bunker and demonstratively levelled the borderline. For 30 years the path was named after him. A few years ago the bunker was painted with bright colours. Simultaneously, the barbed wire of the Iron Curtain was put up again and tank traps set up. It is quite astounding that the bunker which was directed towards the enemy and the Iron Curtain which locked up its own population now exist next to one another again in the form of a commemoration.

The Šatov bunker

Ride past the bunker, turn left and stay on the paved patrol road. Cross the railway tracks, keep to the left and continue cycling on the **Moravská vínna** straight, which is not paved after the next branch. At the end turn right and pass a huge shopping mall and the Hotel Savannah. After a left turn you come across a busy road that if you continue straight leads to the now deserted border crossing.

Hatě

Directly behind the border crossing turn left into the cobbled street that is paved nicely with tiles. The road on the Austrian side runs directly along the border, and you can see the old patrol on the Czech side. In between you can see the sign "Grenze" (border). It would be nice if there were a photo of a time when these two paths were separated by the Iron Curtain. This part of the trail along the border was incidentally funded by the EU. Follow cycle path 8 slightly uphill to Laa on the Thaya. Once at the top continue on a dirt road to the right, which leads back to another dirt road on the left. Here you can see an observation tower. At the next intersection, close to a large tree, the signposted **cycle path 8** branches off to the right. At the next corner, continue straight downhill. A little later **bike path 8** turns sharply left to the Hubertus chapel and the Cross of Liberty.

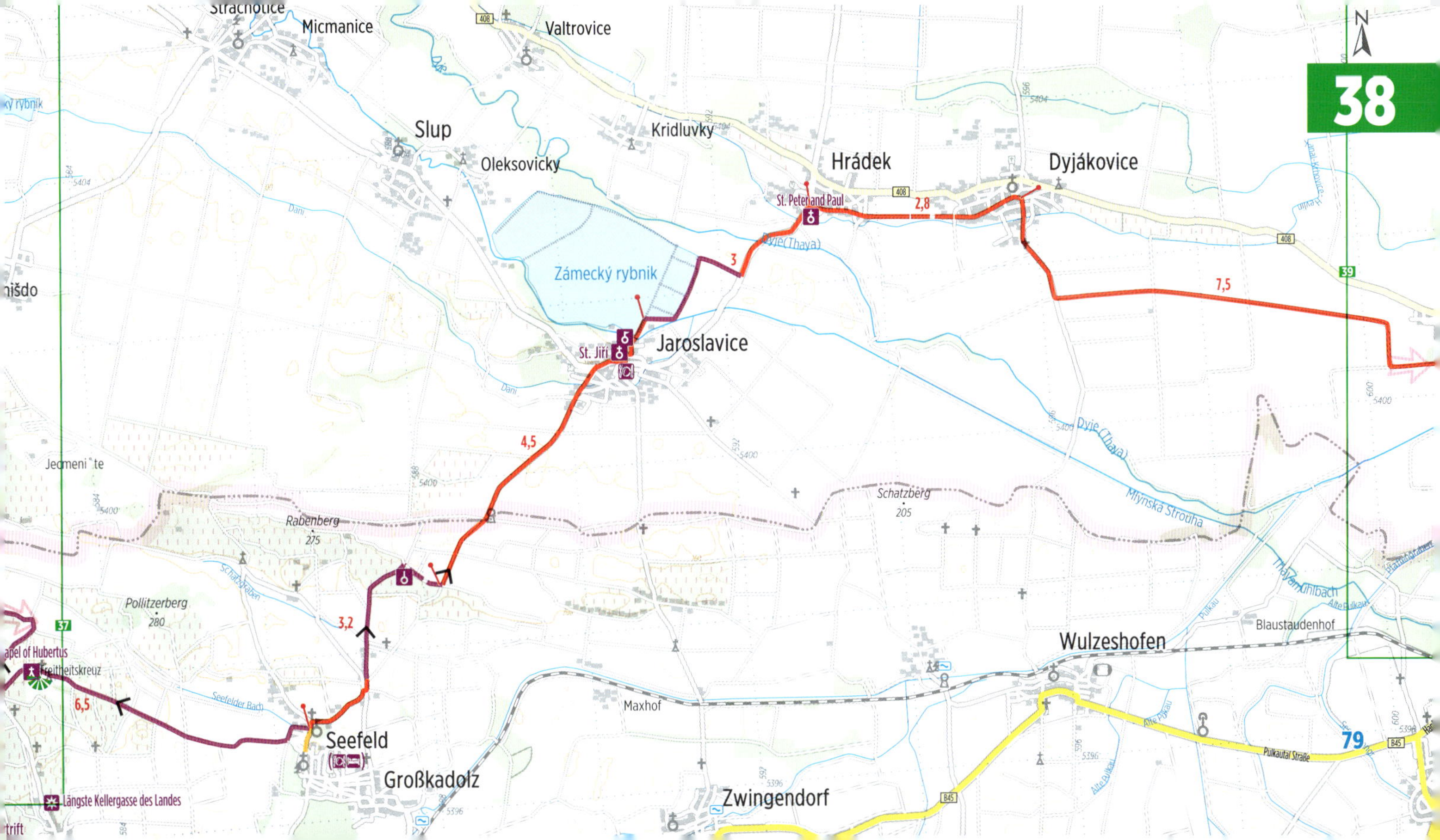
38
Strachotice
Micmanice
Valtrovice
Slup
Oleksovicky
Kridluvky
Hrádek
Dyjákovice
St. Peter and Paul
2,8
3
7,5
Zámecký rybnik
St. Jiří
Jaroslavice
Dyje (Thaya)
Dani
4,5
Jemeni te
Schatzberg
205
Rabenberg
275
Mlýnská Strouha
Pollitzerberg
280
3,2
Chapel of Hubertus
Freiheitskreuz
6,5
Seefelder Bach
Seefeld
Großkadolz
Maxhof
Zwingendorf
Wulzeshofen
Blaustaudenhof
Thayamühlbach
Pulkau
Alte Pulkau
Pulkautal Straße
79
B45
408
39
37
Längste Kellergasse des Landes
nišdo
trift

Cross of Liberty and Hubertus chapel

Cross of Liberty and Hubertus chapel

On the flag it is written: "Never forget the home where your cradle stood! You'll never find a second homeland abroad." Signed by Öller. And on a monument: "In memory of the meeting of the barley fields of South Moravia in 1976. Those who were expelled from their homes in 1945". On the cross, the year 1955 reminds us of the year the Soviet troops withdrew: "Austria is free! Thank God!"

Continue straight along the path, on the left side of the chapel and through the vineyards. Follow bike path 8 downhill on the paved road towards Seefeld. At the intersection of 81 to Hadres, continue straight to Seefeld, the entrance to which is conspicuous for a guesthouse with a welcoming bicycling on it. At this point turn left and continue cycling along the castle wall around the Castle.

CENTRE If you want to enjoy some refreshments in the centre, turn right.

Seefeld

Seefelderhof, ✆ +43/2943/ 3929

Gästehaus Maresi, ✆ +43/664/4006044

Seefeld has about 1,000 inhabitants and was first mentioned in 1108 as a market. The castle is still owned by the Hardegg family. Seefeld-Kadolz won a prize in 1992 for being the most youth friendly city in lower Austria.

Behind Seefeld, turn right into the sign-posted bike path 8. Continue straight on the dirt road, cross the stream and continue cycling uphill. At the observation tower, turn right into a field road, that meets the signposted road to Jaroslavice, into which you turn left. At the border there is a stone with the inscription: "Friendship Place. Namesdi Přátelství. Seefeld-Kadolz Jaroslavice. 13.05.2006". Cross bike trail 5007 and continue straight to Jaroslavice. Once you get there cross the stream and turn right into the sign-posted **bike path 48** main road. There you can see a signpost to Hevlín.

Jaroslavice

Imposing, neoclassical **St. Jiří Church**

The **Renaissance castle** (1730-36) is hidden behind some overgrown trees. The four-wing building is in need of refurbishment and is adorned in one corner with an elegant portico on strong supporting vaults. At the back there is a castle pond.

Turn left at the church, follow bike path 48 and cycle around the castle, which is quite dilapidated, until you reach a large and beautiful lake (Zámecký rybník). Cycle along the shore and then once you reach the back of the lake turn right. The road is asphalted but in poor condition. On a street with little traffic, turn left. First cross the Thaya, then a stream and then you will see from afar a church at the entrance to Hrádek (Erdberg).

Hrádek

St. Peter and Paul, a Baroque church blazoned with colourful frescoes, surrounded by the defensive walls of a castle that no longer exists. On the same site, an old Roman rotunda can be found. In front of the church there is a war memorial for the 1st World War.

Behind the church, turn right into the signposted cycle path 48. At the end of the village, the condition of the street unfortunately gets worse and worse before turning into a fortified field road over which passes a vineyard. Continue straight along the shore of a small stream.

Dyjákovice

Outside the church the signposted path takes you right. After a left and then a right hand bend you leave Dyjákovice. Before you reach the Thaya, bike path 48 takes you left into the signposted road to Hevlín (Höflein upon Thaya). Cycle through the fields towards Hevlín with the spire of the church tower in your sight. Before Hevlín turn right and

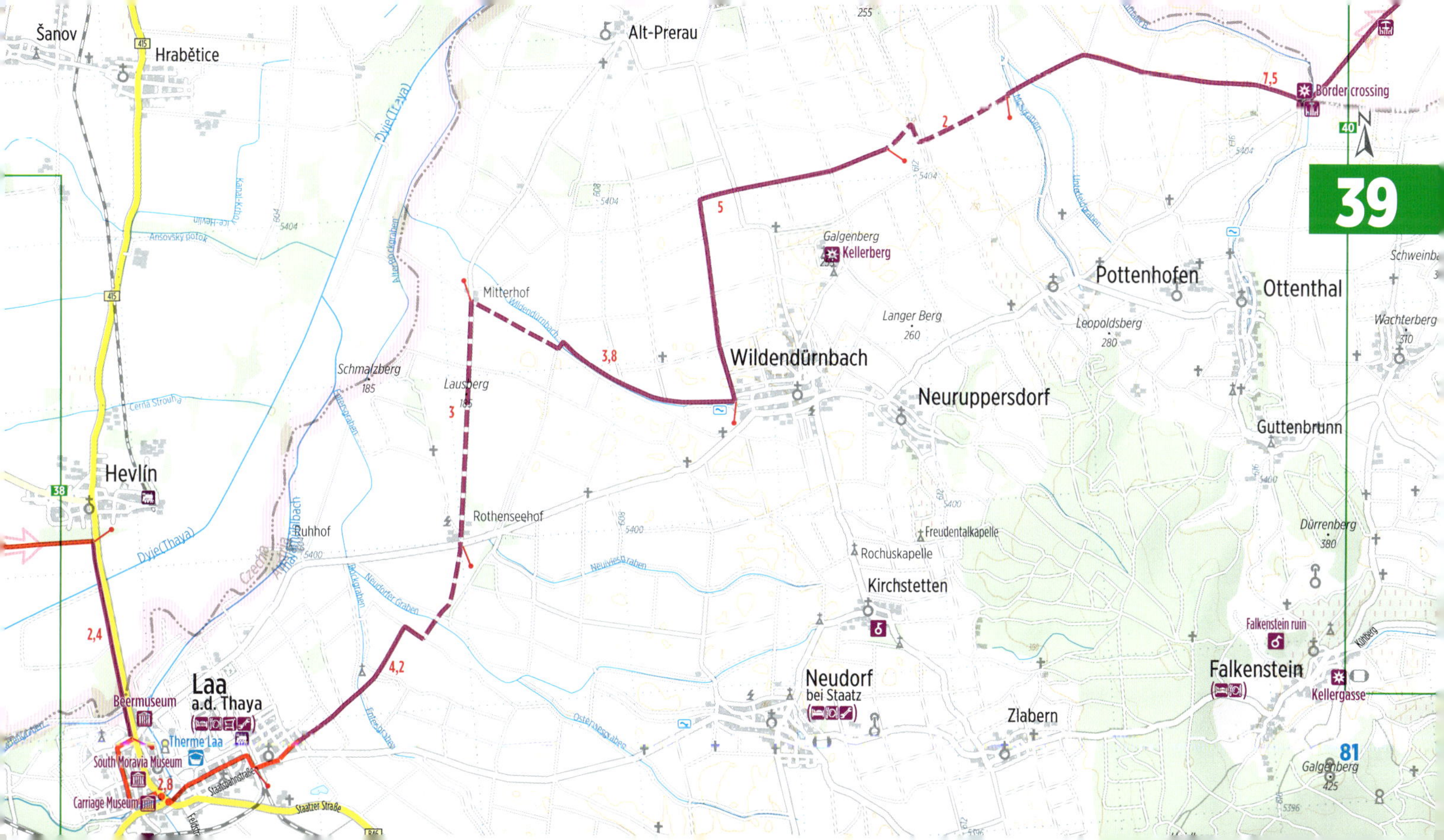
39
Šanov
Hrabětice
Alt-Prerau
Border crossing
7,5
2
5
Galgenberg
Kellerberg
Mitterhof
3,8
Wildendürnbach
Pottenhofen
Ottenthal
Leopoldsberg
280
Langer Berg
260
Neuruppersdorf
Guttenbrunn
Wachterberg
310
Schmalzberg
185
Lausberg
3
Hevlín
Rothenseehof
Ruhhof
Dyje (Thaya)
Freudentalkapelle
Rochuskapelle
Kirchstetten
Dürrenberg
380
Falkenstein ruin
Falkenstein
Kellergasse
2,4
4,2
Laa
a.d. Thaya
Beermuseum
Therme Laa
South Moravia Museum
2,8
Carriage Museum
Staatzer Straße
Neudorf
bei Staatz
Zlabern
Galgenberg
425
81
38
40
415

Laa an der Thaya Town Hall

soon after left, until you meet the road to Laa, into which you turn right. There you can use the separate bike path that crosses the Thaya, the border and the Pfaffengraben and travel straight towards the town hall.

Laa an der Thaya

- **Tourism association for Land um Laa**, Stadtpl. 17, ✆ 250.129
- **St. Veit church**, late Romanesque basilica with Baroque interior.
- **Town square**, used in the past for military purposes. Due to the square's size, it was intended during time of war to serve as a meeting point for army units and refugees from surrounding area. The square is dominated by an eclectic town hall. Due to its magnificent pillars (1575), the old town hall seems almost cozy.
- **Therme/spa Laa**, Thermenpl. 1, ✆ 84700260, OT: Mon-Sun 9-22
- **Guesthouse "Zur Goldenen Rose"**, city maps. 8, "Hotel zum Brüdertor", Stadtfeldg. 3, ✆ +43/2522/8286
- **Toms Radhaus (Toms wheelhouse)**, Nordbahnstr. 19c, ✆ 84846, OT: Mon-Fri 9-12 and 15-18, Sat 9-12 pm.

The northern corner of the church square meets the tip of the Castle Square, which stretches the entire length of the left side of the housing complex and was intended as a staging area for troops. From there we reach the castle, which was originally surrounded by water and set up as a shelter.

The round Churn tower and residential buildings were added at a later date. There are also two cemeteries - on the south side there is an Austrian cemetery, and on the north a Soviet cemetery containing about a thousand fallen soldiers who perished in the last few days of the war. There is also a central monument. The city was founded in 1230 with warlike intentions although its military actions never amounted to much. This was made even worse when she lost most of its hinterland with the founding of Czechoslovakia in 1918. Since the opening of the border, a lot has changed: the population has increased and the number of visitors has increase, especially since the opening of the spa. An electrified train now travels directly to Vienna - more than two decades after the opening of the border but still not over the border into the Czech Republic.

East railway of Laa

The double-track electrified railway line originally ran from Vienna to Laa on the Thaya to Brno in the Czech Republic. After the end of World War II it was interrupted by the Iron Curtain and after more than 20 years is still not back in service. Infrastructure in the form of tracks and a bridge still exists and leads over the mill stream and the Thaya to Hevlín. The route from Hevlín to Hrušovany nad Jevišovkou has also been shut down.

From Laa an der Thaya to Hohenau an der March — 65 km

Cycle from the main road in an easterly direction into **Rathausgasse**, turn right at the path through the park to get to the **Marketplace**. At the end of the street, turn left into the **Pfarrgasse** and then immediately right into **Thermenweg**. After crossing a stream, turn right until you reach **Anton-Bruckner-Straße**, into which you turn left. At the end of this street, at the station, turn right into the street

Border crossing Ottenthal-Mikulov

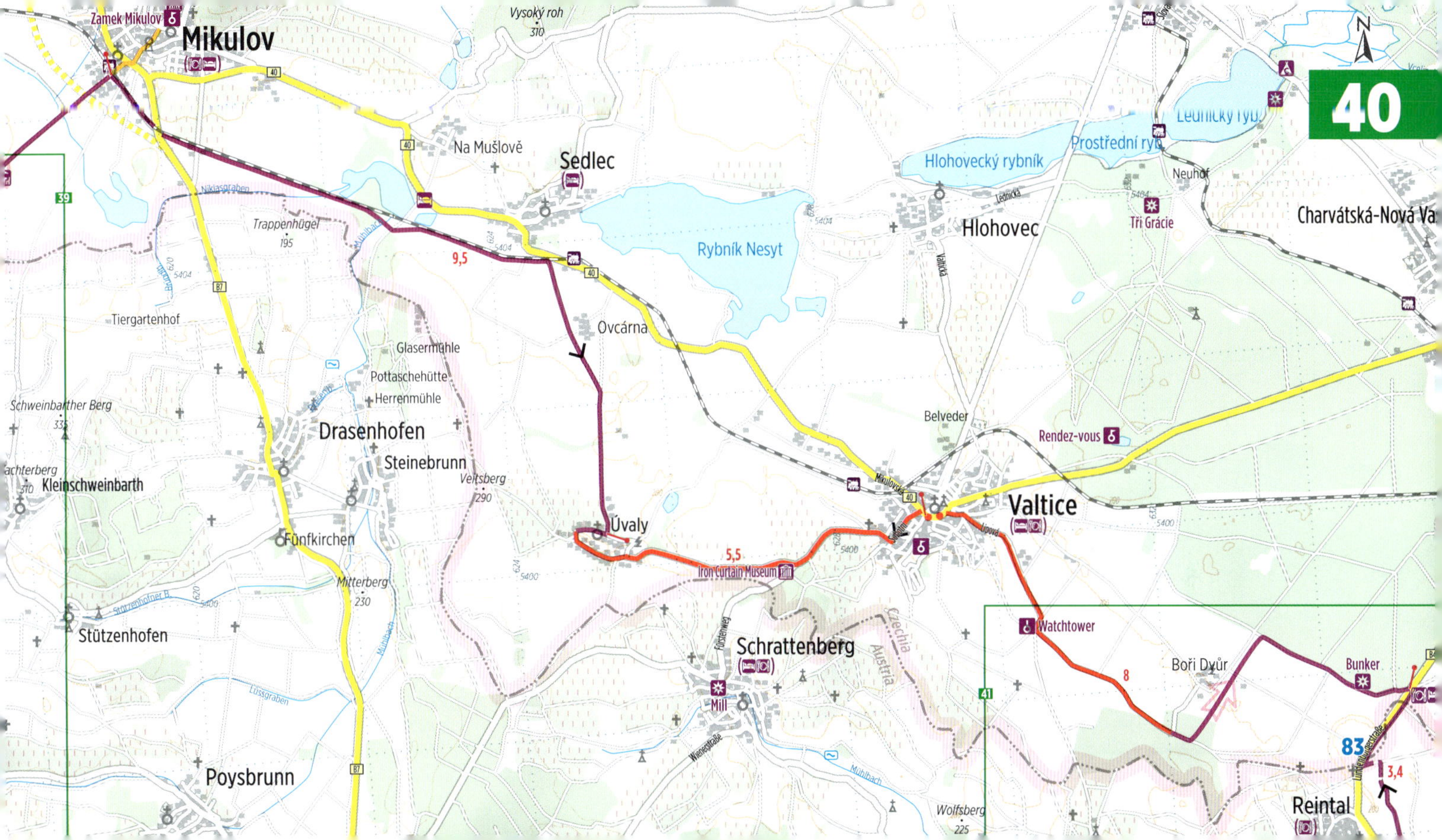

40
Mikulov
Zamek Mikulov
Vysoký roh
310
Na Mušlově
Sedlec
Rybník Nesyt
Hlohovecký rybník
Prostřední rybník
Lednický rybník
Neuhof
Tři Grácie
Hlohovec
Charvátská-Nová Ves
Trappenhügel
195
9,5
Tiergartenhof
Ovcárna
Glasermühle
Pottaschehütte
Herrenmühle
Schweinbarther Berg
335
Drasenhofen
Steinebrunn
Veitsberg
290
Belveder
Rendez-vous
Valtice
Kleinschweinbarth
Fünfkirchen
Úvaly
5,5
Iron Curtain Museum
Mitterberg
230
Stützenhofen
Watchtower
Schrattenberg
Czechia
Austria
Boři Dvůr
8
Bunker
Mill
41
83
3,4
Poysbrunn
Wolfsberg
225
Reintal
39

Am Ostbahnhof, then turn left at the next opportunity and cross the tracks. At this point you will see the signposted number **8 cycle path**. Follow the signs, turn left into the **Johann-Kuba-Gasse** that merges into the **Kellerweg** and later **Güterweg**. Cross two streams and continue straight ahead. Before Neudorfer Graben turn right and then immediately turn left. Behind the ditch, the path is not paved.

TIP Signposts are missing here – you can only see the red sign on a tree.

Rothenseehof

Cycle on the unpaved but well-maintained road straight to **Mitterhof**. Before you reach its first buildings branch off to the right. Cross the old railway track and cycle along the northern side of the river on an asphalt access road..

Dietrichsteinská Trobka in Mikulov

Wildendürnbach

Kellergasse, am Kellerberg

Directly behind the entrance sign, turn left into the signposted cycle path 8. Where the asphalt on this road ends, turn right onto another asphalted path. Cross the street in the direction of Alt-Prerau and continue straight on an unpaved road. Behind Basteingraben the path will lead you around a sharp bend and then you can continue straight on a better path. Cross Mühlgraben, a road and the Unterfeldgraben and follow cycle path 8. At a pentagon keep half right and continue cycling to the border. Just before the border turn right and immediately left again. Cycle on the bridge over the Ottenthal stream to the Czech Republic.

Border crossing at Ottenthal-Mikulov

In 2006, with support from the EU, a resting place was created by the sculptor Josef Zahradník complete with sundial, places to part your bicycle, tables and benches. Some concrete blocks were also installed there. A little while later, the same artist designed another resting place.

Cycle straight ahead and you will reach the Mikulov railway station (direct trains to Břeclav and Znojmo available).

Railway from Znojmo to Břeclav

The course of this railway line played a role in the St. Germain 1st World War peace negotiations because after the founding of the first Czechoslovak Republic a section led through Austrian territory. Therefore, the victorious Allies moved the border to the south.

CENTRE The road which leads you to the centre of Mikulov begins behind the railway crossing.

Mikulov

Castle. This building, which now houses a regional museum, is definitely worth seeing. Most of the castle was destroyed on April 20, 1945 by a fire and restored in the 1950s.

Where the holy mountain Svatý Kopeček together with Rosalie chapel drops abruptly into the foothills, the town spreads out with its ancient lanes and squares. The visible white rocks with silver translucent cracks and the unique flora and fauna ensure that Mikulov belongs to the most interesting and beautiful towns of Moravia. Many events such as the Cultural Summer and the Wine Festival also make the place worth visiting and there are many restaurants and types of accommodation available. The history of Jewish life is also interesting. The first synagogue was built here around 1550 and since 1653 the city has been the seat of the Moravian Rabbinate. In 1868 there were 12 synagogues. In 1938 the Jewish community comprised 500 members, almost all of which were murdered by the Nazis. The Jewish cemetery was founded in the 15th century and still exists today. The oldest grave stone - from nearly 4,000 in the style of Renaissance, Baroque and Classicism - dates from the 1600s. Unfortunately, the beautiful town hall in the market square also played a role in Nazi history when on 27 October 1938, after the German invasion, the population down below cheered Adolf Hitler who addressed the crowds from the town hall balcony. The results of Šatov, when Hitler took the opportunity to be photographed in front of a bunker for propaganda purposes, were also replicated here. When the photo was published in the newspapers, 450 men appeared that same evening to volunteer in the SA. But there were also opponents of the Nazis.

The republican defence

At the cemetery one can find the Mahrischl family tomb. Bedřich Mahrischl (1912-1977) belonged to republican military who fought together with the Czechs against the Nazis. They protected the Czech houses in Mikulov against encroachments by the fanatical Henlein. Henlein was the leader of the Sudeten German party, a grammar school teacher and also a district leader of Sudetenland after the invasion. Bedřich Mahrischl survived the occupation – the rest of his peers were either shot, beaten to death or hung. After the war, the German-speaking population was expelled from Mikulov to Austria - but Bedřich Mahrischl could remain.

The **"Greenway Prague-Vienna"**, leads along the tracks and crosses the busy B. 7

Two UNESCO areas

Between Mikulov and Valtice one finds a large variety of mainly white wines being grown with Welschriesling, Grüner Veltliner and Pinot Noir the most common varieties. The National Wine Centre is located in Valtice in the palace cellar.

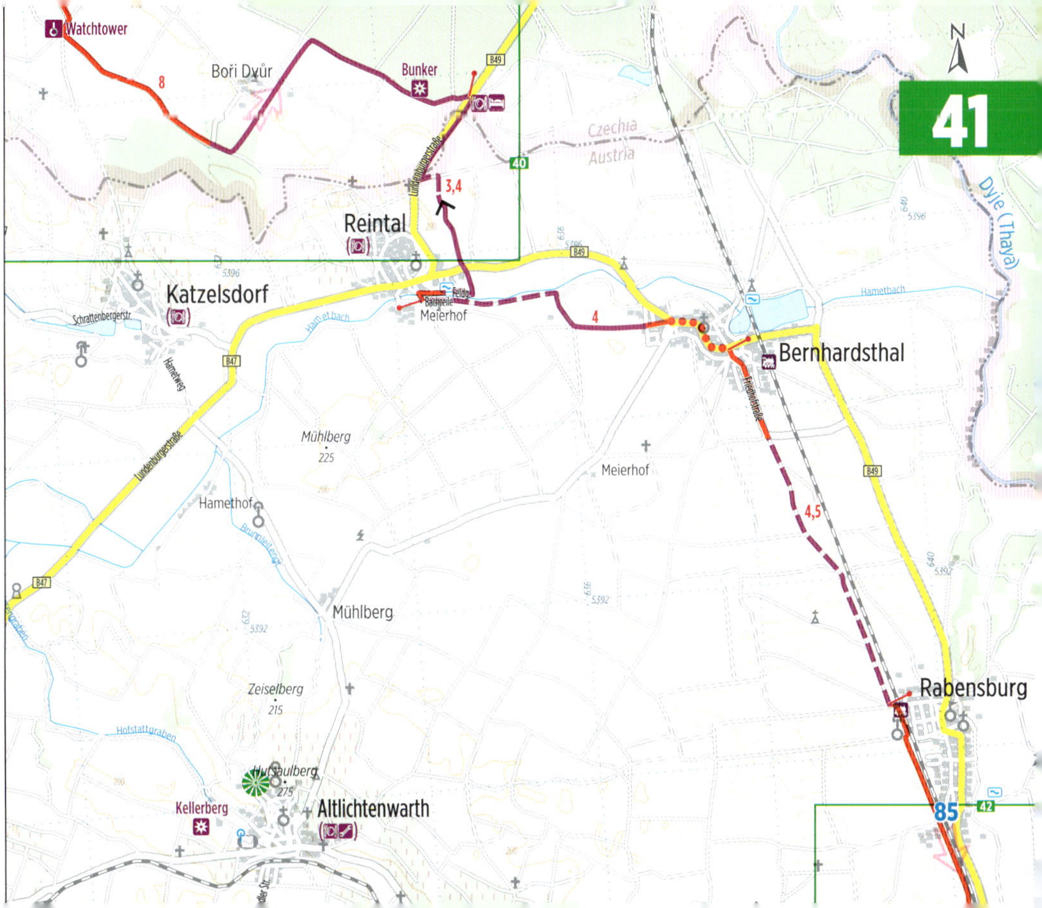

There is also a technical school for Czech wine. With Pálava in Mikulov and their European garden and the Lednice-Valtice park two World Cultural and Natural Heritage Areas collide.

The close juxtaposition of two UNESCO sites is unique in the world.

Ride over Niklasgraben, cross the Mühlbach and continue until you reach **Sedlec**. When you reach the junction (signposted to Valtice and Reintal) turn right onto **cycle path 411** and after a short journey uphill you will meet another road into which one turns right.

Úvaly

The trail takes you right towards the church and then cycle past the village. Continue along cycle path 411, cycling very close to the border. At the former border crossing you will meet not only the road to Valtice and Schrattenberg, but also the "The Iron Curtain Museum".

The Iron Curtain Museum

Museum (Muzeum železné opony), ✆ +420/519/340130, ÖZ:May, June, Fr-Su, July, Aug., Mo-Su, 10-17 Uhr

The museum was opened on 1 May 2011 in the former Czech border post. In addition to a large number of uniforms, weapons and equipment, photos and documents are also on display. A reconstruction of the Iron Curtain and a real cell is also very interesting. One also finds a list of victims who were shot whilst attempting to illegally cross the border - in some cases even on Austrian soil.

Behind the museum, cycle on the 411 down the main road until you reach the huge church and some nice restaurants.

Valtice

TIC Valtice, Náměsti Svobody č. 4, ✆ +420/519/352978

This renovated **palace** is one of the most beautiful Baroque palaces in the Czech Republic and was included in 1996 in the UNESCO World Heritage List. The vault contains a significant wine cellar where award winning wines ("Salon") are offered for tasting and purchasing.

The town of just 4,000 inhabitants belonged to Lower Austria until 1919. She was awarded after WW1 to Czechoslovakia but not due to ethnic reasons but mostly due to its location – the Mikulov Břeclav train line runs through the municipality (Nikolsburg-Lundenburg). After the Munich Agreement in 1938, the town belonged once again to the German Reich, and then after the war changed hands again to Czechoslovakia. The last inhabitants of the German Moravian population were expelled in 1946. The town square and the parish church are also worth seeing.

Behind the church, at Restaurant Haus Qankara on the main road turn right. At the exit, on the right side, you can see an authentic watchtower, which is now equipped with satellite dishes and probably belongs to a barracks. Here, turn left. Where the 411 bends left, continue straight ahead, along the border and a little later turn left again into an access road. At the end of this turn right. After an intersection you will see a bunker in the middle of the road which was built in the 1930s. A short while later you will come across the road to Reintal, into which you turn right. This was formerly the customs house, and today you can find a hotel and a restaurant. Behind the border

Bridge over the Morava river near Hohenau

Bunker near Hohenau

building cross the street, because the bike path on the left side is a little lower down. Just over the border in Austria follow the signposted **Euro Velo Route 9** to the left - the path is not paved, but is in good condition. Shortly after a right bend the path is paved again and it goes downhill. Cross the B 49 keeping left and after a right bend, continue along the Hametbach. After the bridge, turn right into the **Bachzeile**, and cycle again along the Hametbach. After a right turn you come across the **Kobelweg**, into which one turns left. At the **B 49**, turn right to reach your destination.

Bernhardsthal

Turn right into **Hauptstraße**, then right again into **Friedhofstraße**, which later turns into a dirt road along the railway tracks.

Rabensburg

Here the path is paved again. Reach the entrance of Hohenau and then turn right into **Adamstalstraße**. After a sharp left turn into **Weststraße** continue until you reach **Hausbrunnerstraße**, into which you turn left. On the main street cross the railway line.

STATION On the south side is the train station, where you can catch direct trains to Vienna, Břeclav and Gänserndorf.

Follow the signs to March. Before the big building with the tower, turn right and go straight ahead through the **Kirchengasse** towards the church.

Hohenau an der March

- **Parish Church**. The church is Romanesque in origin and around 1700 was redesigned in Baroque style and refurbished. Of particular artistic value is the late Baroque Barbara Altar.
- **belfry**
- **Kellergasse**
- The little **bird paradise** that has formed on the vast, relatively warm cooling water pond belonging to the old sugar factory - which even

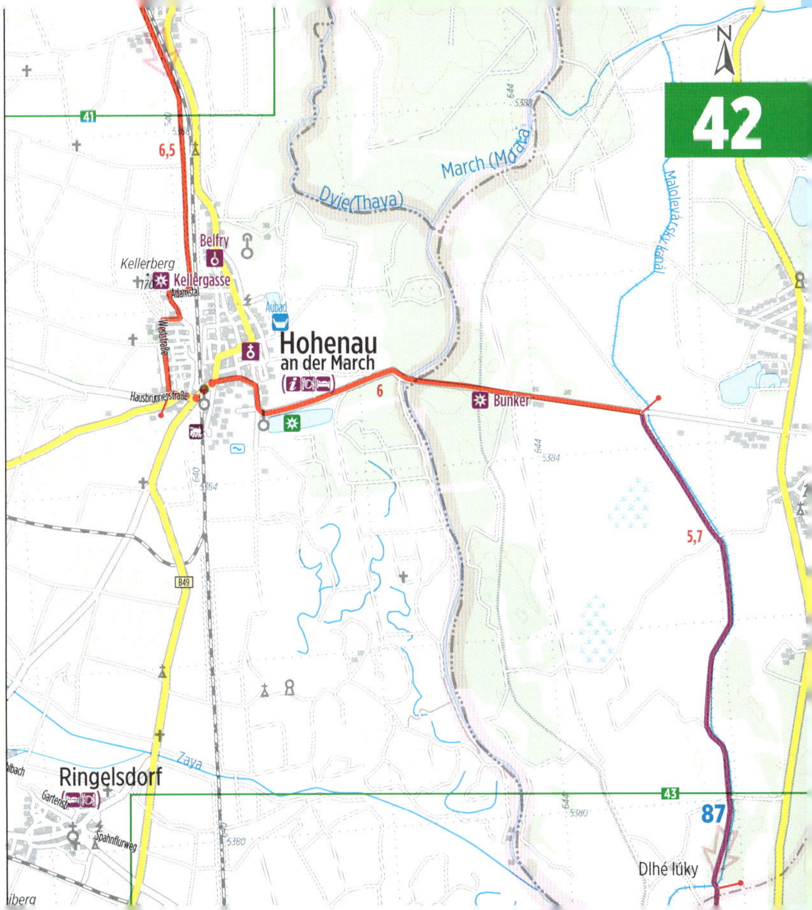

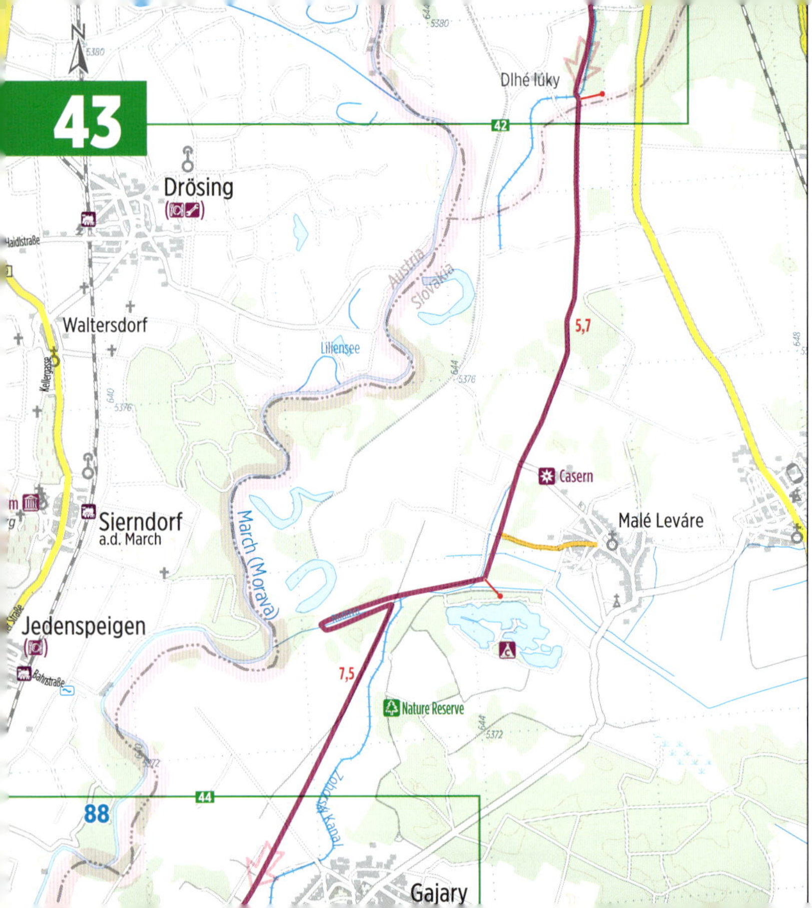

had its own research station - is now sadly endangered due to the factory's closure.

B&B Stadlbauer, ✆ +43/664/3075914, ✆ +43/2535/2415

In this sparsely populated region and strategically only slightly advantageous transport route, no economic recovery occurred after the opening of the borders. And, since the closure of the 140-year old sugar factory in 2006, the economic situation is even less favourable. Even from the newly opened bridge over the river Morova, the only one north of the Danube, the region does not expect too much, with just a single-lane lifting bridge.

From Hohenau an der March (AT) to Bratislava (SK) 80 km

Continue on this street until you come to the border crossing signposted **Forsthausgasse**, into which one turns left and continue past a lookout tower and a big former cooling pond. Cross the river Morova via a blue bridge, which is the only bridge which crosses the border river.

TIP However, the crossing is prone to flooding and entry is restricted even with light flooding. If you do not want to cycle for 28 km on the Austrian side and try a spot of fishing in the Morova with the assistance of a ferry can take a detour and travel over 50 km north to Břeclav (Lundenburg) where you can have a very nice time, because the city, with its varied history, is well worth a visit.

Morava river

For more than 1,000 years, the river Morava river was the natural border between the "Germans" and the "Slavs" and is now the border river separating Slovakia and the

Czech Republic (50 kilometres) and Austria (91 kilometres). The river is a left tributary of the Danube, and is accompanied at a low point on both sides with a dam to protect against floods. The Morava flows from the Snieznik Mountains and reaches an altitude of 1,194 metres at the border between Poland and the Czech Republic and after 358 kilometres flows into Devin (Slovakia) in the Danube. Several kilometres further north, at the confluence of the Thaya and March, there is the tri-border region of the Czech Republic, Austria and Slovakia. The Bridge at Hohenau is - alongside the Schlosshof bridge for pedestrians and cyclists (opened 2012) - the only bridge between Austria and Slovakia north of the Danube. Right up until the end of World War II there were several bridges that were blown up by the German Wehrmacht as they retreated. The Stein bridge between Schlosshof and Devin was blown up by Czechoslovak Communists after the war. It was rebuilt as a cyclist bridge and came into operation in 2012. The bilingually-signposted cycle path is called in Slovak "Moravská cyklistická cesta" and in English "Iron Curtain Greenway". Two old tank traps remind us of the Iron Curtain.

The history of Slovakia

The Celts, in the Slovakia we know today, were replaced in the first century by the Germanic Quadi. Slovakia was back then a Germanic region on the border of the Roman Empire (1st-5th. Century), where numerous Roman Quadi wars took place. In 500 the Slavic ancestors of today's Slovaks arrived. In the 7th century, Slovakia was part of the main area of the Empire of Samo and in the 8th century the Nitra principality was formed here, which in 833 became part of Great Moravia. In the 11th century the territory of Slovakia was part of the Kingdom of Hungary, which was since 1526 part of the Habsburg monarchy, since 1804 the Empire of Austria and since 1867 Austria-Hungary. After the First World War, the First Czechoslovak Republic was created in 1918. This existed until 1938, when with the Munich Agreement, the areas with a German population majority (Sudetenland) were handed over to the German Reich. The southern part of Slovakia and Carpathian Ukraine fell to Hungary and the Těšín area was occupied by Poland.

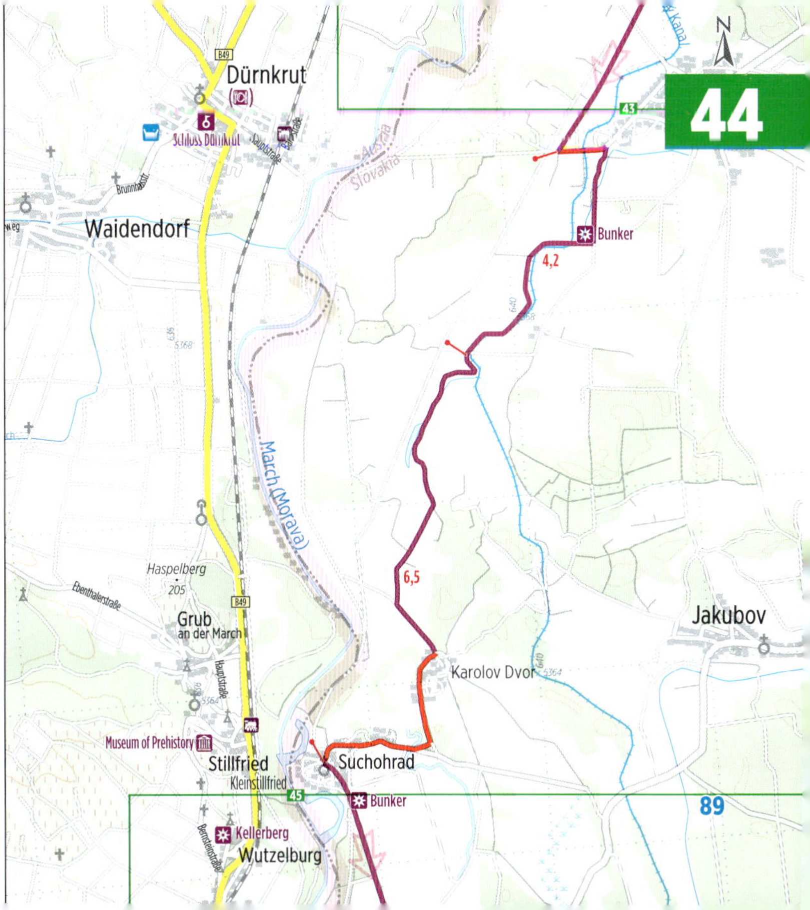

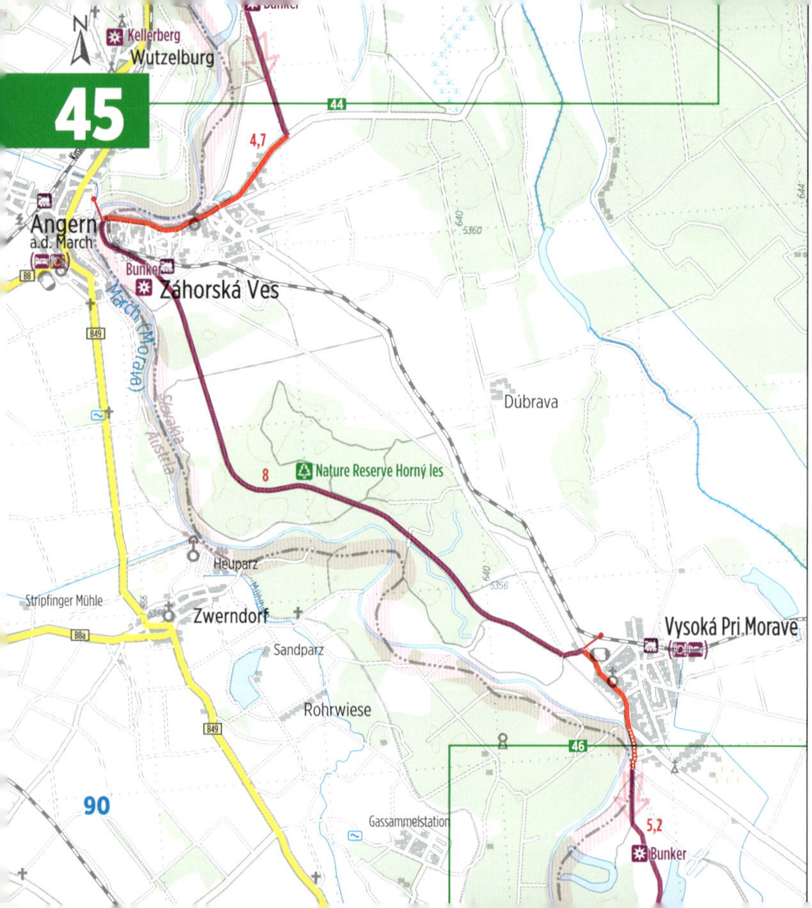

Cycle path on the dam next to the Morava river

Slovakia was seemingly independent under the rule of the fascist Jozef Tiso from 1939 to 1945, but was in fact merely a satellite state of Nazi Germany. After the Second World War it was again part of Czechoslovakia. The "Prague Spring" in 1968 under Alexander Dubček, represented an attempt to create "socialism with a human face". He was crushed by the military intervention of the Warsaw Pact states, for Herbert Marcuse, the "greatest tragedy since the Second World War" and for Jean-Paul Sartre, a "war crime". The reformist government was then replaced by a party line.

But the resistance had been only temporarily broken: A civil rights movement called "Charter 77" under the leadership of the writer Vaclav Havel (1936-2011) turned even more against the regime. When Mikhail Gorbachev relieved the pressure through his policies of glasnost (transparency) and perestroika (reconstruction), the resistance increased their protests. On 24 November 1989, the "Velvet Revolution" forced the Communist government to resign. On December 28 Alexander Dubček was elected President of Parliament and a day later, Václav Havel was elected the fourth president of Czechoslovakia, which was renamed the Czechoslovak Federative Republik on April 23. The first free elections were held on 5 July 1990, confirmed by the Havel in office.

The negotiations between the Czech Prime Minister Vaclav Klaus, who won the elections in the Czech part of the country, and his colleague from the Slovak part, Vladimir Meciar, led to the division of Czechoslovakia into two independent states - the Czech Republic and the Slovak Republic - on 1 January 1993.

The Czech Republic became a member of NATO in 1990 and on 1 May 2004 a member of the European Union. Slovakia has been a member of NATO and the European Union since 2004.

On the road to Moravský Svätý Ján at a river dike, you will see an informative map on the Iron Curtain Greenway and on the right is the first bunker.

TIP It is planned to relocate the European Iron Curtain Trail on the dam.

Continue along the road – signposted the **Euro Velo Route 13** complete with the symbol. The route then takes you right where you follow a canal signposted Malé Leváre. Cross the Malolevársky Canal in **Dlhé Lúky** and at the bridge you can also receive some information about beavers. The route takes you along an even, paved path leading you through corn, wheat and cabbage fields and is sometimes lined with trees.

The scenery is inspiring and quiet, and it is not unusual to see herons and storks flying over the heads of cyclists from here to Malé Leváre. More than 200 species spend the winter, breed and hunt here or pass through this bird paradise near a floodplain forest along the Morava. Occasionally you will see a few bunkers belonging to the Czech Horni Vltavice Czechoslovak Wall, whose expansion was abandoned in 1939.

TIP Between Drösing and Velke Leváre a cable ferry ran for 300 years with a pub on both banks.

Cross the formerly joined gravel path behind the turnoff that leads left to Velke Leváre. A little later you pass the old border troops barracks, which currently houses the largest military dog school in Slovakia.

CENTRE Later, turn left towards the centre of Malé Leváre.

Malé Leváre

Ride straight and follow the signs for Gajary. The path on the embankment parallel to the canal to the west, into which you turn right, has some weak areas. Cross the Rudava canal and you will see some concrete triangles that were previously used as tank traps. A lake and a campsite are nearby.

After the bridge the road is very good again.

TIP Signs are not allowed in the nature reserve, so the "C" for the Iron Curtain Trail (Euro Velo 13) has been painted on some trees.

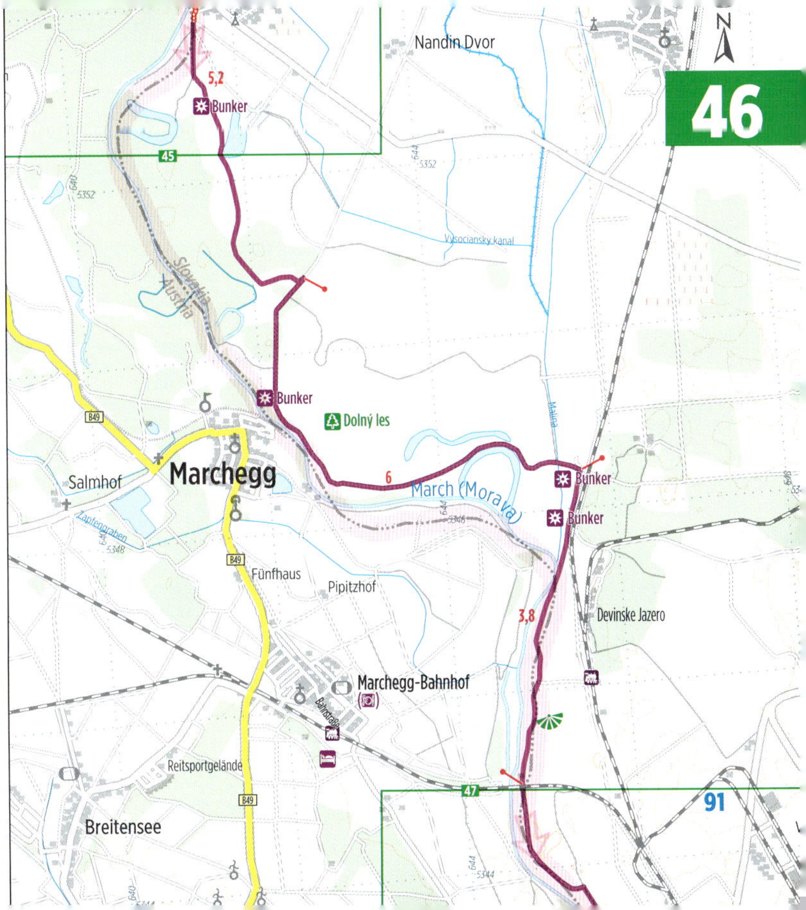

Shortly after Gajary there are several oil pumps. South of Gajary, turn left and stay on the street for a while before turning off to the right. At the next corner, on the right side, you can see another bunker. Cycle on a long stretch along the lake, later through canola fields that are beautifully yellow when in bloom in the spring time.

Karolov Dvor

The village was built around the courtyard of a noble family called Pálffy. The estate was converted in the 1950s into a cooperative, however, remains of the stately possessions are still recognisable.

Back on the road, cycle through the town. At the next bend, follow the signposted "C" right to Suchohrad, where you turn left and reach the centre.

Suchohrad

After 1948, the community was denied potential opportunities to develop because new buildings and settlements were not allowed. Visitors needed a special permit for the territory and border guards controlled access roads. Under these circumstances, by 1989, the population dropped by half.

At the church, turn right into a narrow asphalt road towards the dam. Stay on the dam and next to the road you will see the Suchohrad bunker. The road is in excellent condition. Soon you will be able to see the Church of Záhorská Ves. Turn left after the last bollard for cars and continue until you meet a road on which the Euro Velo 13 is signposted. Turn right and head towards the centre of Záhorská Ves.

Záhorská Ves

The significantly larger municipality of Záhorská Ves, the westernmost place in Slovakia, also suffered from the border regime. History has left its mark here - as well as on other places of the region – as evidenced by the frequently changing place names, where the Hungarian, Czech, Slovak and German language all played a role. A "place without development prospects" because the community lost its industry and with it three fifths of the population. Before the war, the city was connected by a wooden bridge over the Morava as well as by through another bridge to the Austrian railway network. In May 1945, Nazi troops destroyed both bridges. Since then, these two towns have had a "bridgeless coexistence" (Beppo Beyerl). Although Záhorská Ves was only a stone's throw from the well-connected Austrian Angern, it took until 2001 to establish a yaw cable ferry. In the main street there is a war memorial. The opera singer Lucia Popp (1939-1993) was born in Záhorská Ves and died in Vienna. She probably felt more like someone from Bratislava because the sentence: "Every real Bratislavian has an aunt in Vienna" came from her.

In Záhorská Ves the signposted route suggests you turn left, but ignore it and continue cycling straight on the road ahead and at the old customs station turn right towards the dam. At this point turn left, and if you look to the right you will see the ferry to Angern and a little bit later on you will see a bunker. From the dam, take the signposted and asphalted former patrol road. This route will take you through corn and wheat fields, to the edge of the Horný les (upper forest) nature reserve.

Horný les nature reserve (upper forest)

This lowland forest area of 543 hectares consists of hardwoods and softwoods, sand dunes and tributaries from the river Morava. The protected area is part of the Záhorie nature reserve, which also includes the following national nature reserves: Abrod (comprising 92.37 hectares since 1964), Červený rybník (118.91 hectares since 1966), Dolný les (186.26 hectares since 1981) and Zelienka (82.52 hectares since 1980) as well as the nature reserves Bogdalický vrch (33.2 hectares since 1993) and Šmolzie (45.59 hectares since 1993).

With the Vysoká pri Morave church steeple in sight, cycle past a gas storage plant and very close to the dam. Turn right into the street and pass the church - left from the church you can find a restaurant and a place to stay the night.

Vysoká pri Morave

Here the barbed wire of the Iron Curtain severed the gardens. Unlike its northern neighbour, Vysoká pri Morave is still growing. New enterprises have settled here, and many tourists from Bratislava come here. There is an abundance of cultural activities and festivals here.

You should now be by the river and thus directly on the border. The road goes left, but stay on the signposted and asphalted road on the dam. You will encounter a bunker and a large conveyor system. Cross the assembly line on a bridge.

VIEW Ahead of you is a mountain, which is one of the "Small Carpathians". Also, you should be able to see Bratislava.

Ride along the top of the dam until you encounter a field road just before **Marchegg**, into which you turn right and cycle very close to the river. Soon you will see the sign "Warning: National Border", the river and then a bunker. If you are lucky, you will even see a stork's nest. At the next branch in the road, just before the railroad, turn right towards Devinska Nova Ves. You will pass first one bunker and then a second one, and then the route takes you a little bit downhill. Cycle along the tracks and on the southeastern edge of the **nature reserve Dolný les** (Lower Forest) the route takes you close to the shore of the river Morava.

Shortly after passing the small settlement of **Devínske Jazero** you can see on the left the huge factory premises of Volkswagen Slovakia - which already belongs to **Devínska Nová Ves** - and on the right the far less modern but still impressive, long stone arch bridge, which facilitates the railway connection between Bratislava and Vienna. Where you emerge from the forest, you can see the confluence of two rivers the March-Rud Morava and Malina. At the next branch in the road continue cycling along the river where you can admire the railway bridge over the Morava. There is a house made from concrete on a small hill, which was once used by the army. Arrive at Devínska Nová Ves.

Devínska Nová Ves (Bratislava)

Church (1581), the oldest historical monument in the city.

The first written record dates back to 1451 and state that Devínska Nová Ves was under the rule of Devin. After the Battle of Mainz, the Croats who fled from the Turks settled here and built the church. Devínska Nová Ves's importance rose, after the Turkish invasion of Bratislava and it became the residence and coronation city of Greater Hungary. During Maria Theresa's time (1740-1780) DNV was particularly important. The shortest route from Vienna to Bratislava led over the Morova bridge, and in the 18th century it was also a strategically important border crossing between Hungary and Austria. The current town hall served as a customs office. The 19th century brought major changes with the opening of the rail link between Vienna and Bratislava (1848), the foundation of the brick factory and

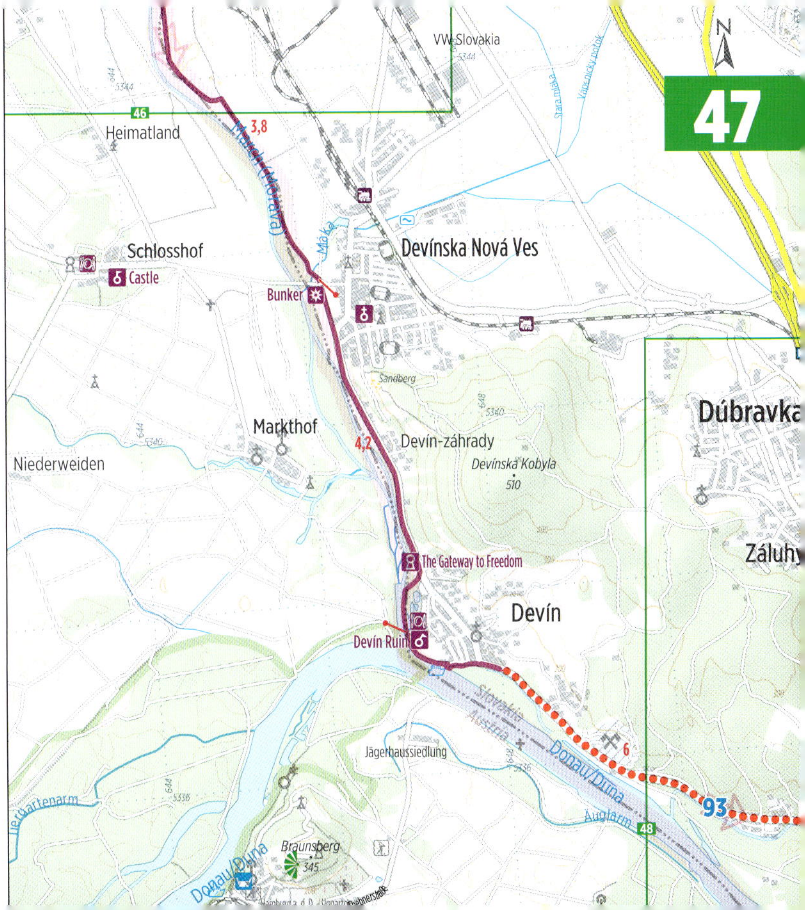

Nový Most Bridge over the Danube

the opening of the quarry. In 1972 Devínska Nová Ves was affiliated with Bratislava and several areas with high-rise buildings popping up forced the area to take on a more city-orientated look. Today, the large VW plant is the most important employer in the region.

In the castle courtyard there is an old bridge, which was inaugurated in 2012 as a bicycle and pedestrian bridge. A referendum took place to vote on the name of the bridge. The city government favoured the name "Freedom Bridge", the population, however, seeing an opportunity for mischief argued for it to be called the "Chuck Norris Bridge", in homage to the American movie hero. Despite 12,599 votes for the Norris name, the Bratislava assembly called the bridge the "Freedom Cycling-Bridge" in memory of people killed attempting to escape communist eastern Europe. A section of the Iron Curtain is also on display here.

Behind the branch in the Austrian Groißenbrunn there is an old bunker and the bicycle and pedestrian bridge. The trail now runs between the road and the river, where you can see the signs to the border. A little bit above you is the road.

Between the dunes on the left and the Morava, the trail leads you behind the town further south, and after 3 km on a wide asphalt road you reach Devín. At the remains of a bridge over the river Morava you can see a memorial built by the confederation of former political prisoners.

The gateway to freedom

The bright white monument 'Gateway to Freedom" has the names of roughly 400 men and women engraved upon it who were killed in Czechoslovakia whilst trying to escape along the Iron Curtain, so that their "sacrifice for freedom can inspire future generations".

Devín (Bratislava)

Devin Castle, sadly in ruins since its destruction by the French in 1809

Devin (Thebes) lies at the confluence of the Danube and Morava (Morava). The castle ruins - the imposing castle rock can be seen for many kilometres - still seems to guard the former Porta Hungarica, the constriction of the Danube at the confluence of March. The current confinement is considered by the Slovaks as a kind of national shrine. It already had in the 9th century during the Great Moravian Empire - eventually the modern states Czech Republic and Slovakia emerged from this - a sense of identity and strategic importance. Settlements on the hill have been traced back to the Neolithic period. The Celts and Germanic tribes were the first to settle there and they were followed by the Romans and then the Slavs. The remains of the Roman fort Gerulata, part of the Limes, which was built to protect the Roman Empire against the barbarians, are the oldest evidence of development in Slovakia. The view from the ruins is spectacular and sometimes on a clear day you can even see the Vienna Woods.

Hinter dem Mahnmal biegt man rechts ab von der Straße und erreicht die Mündung derMarch in die Donau.

Behind the monument, turn right off the road and reach the point where the Morava flows into the Danube.

Follow the **ICT 13** sign on a beautifully landscaped bike path along the Danube River towards Bratislava. Unfortunately, this beautiful bike path comes to end all too soon and you

Slovak National Theater in Bratislava

have to spend the next 5 km on a busy road without a bike path along the **Karlovesky canal**, which cuts out one of the arms of the Danube. Continue under a road bridge and then the route goes away from the road again. The marked path leads to the highway, so before you reach this, turn right towards the Danube riverbanks. Reach the **Lafranconi bridge**, which offers you majestic views of the river and the capital. There is a footpath to the east of the motorway bridge and the west side, underneath the road, there is also bike path.

CENTRE If you wants to travel into the city, cycle on the wide promenade along the river to the next bridge. Here, turn left and continue along the Staromestka ulica and on Pražská and Štefánikova ulica to the central station.

To stay on the "Iron Curtain Europe Cycle Path", take the bike path behind the motorway bridge towards the other riverbank.

Bratislava

Postcode: 81000; Area code: 02

- **Bratislava Culture and Information Centre**, Klobučnícka 2, ✆ 54,433,715, www.bratislava.sk
- **Slovak National Museum** (Slov národné múzeum), castle palace, OT: Tue-Sun 9-17
- **Wine Museum** (Vinohradnícke múzeum), the Old Town Hall, OT: Tue-Fri 10-17, Sat, Sun 11-18. Exhibition by the municipal museum detailing the history of wine in the region.
- **Watch Museum** (Múzeum hodín) Židovská ul 1, OT: Wed-Mo 10-17. The house survived the "land consolidation" of the seventies, which particularly affected the Jewish Quarter, and presents itself as one of the best preserved rococo buildings in Europe.
- **City Gallery of Bratislava**, Pálffy Palace, Panská 19, Mirbach Palace, Fantiškánske námestie 11, OT: Tue-Sun 11-18. Medieval paintings and sculpture, 20th century art and contemporary artists.
- **Slovak National Gallery** (Slov narodna galeria), Rázusovo nábrežie, ✆ 544 320 812, OT: Tue-Sun 10-18. Numerous paintings and sculptures from different eras. Guided tours are available by appointment.
- **St. Martin's** (Dom sv. Martina), Rudnayovo nám. 7. The three-aisled Gothic building from the 14/15. C. Served 1563-1830 as a coronation church of Hungarian kings, initially Baroque style and in the 19th century neo Gothic. Rich interior.
- **Franciscan Church** (Františkánsky kostol) Františkánske námestie 1. consecrated in 1297, the church was rebuilt in the 17th-18th century in the Baroque style.

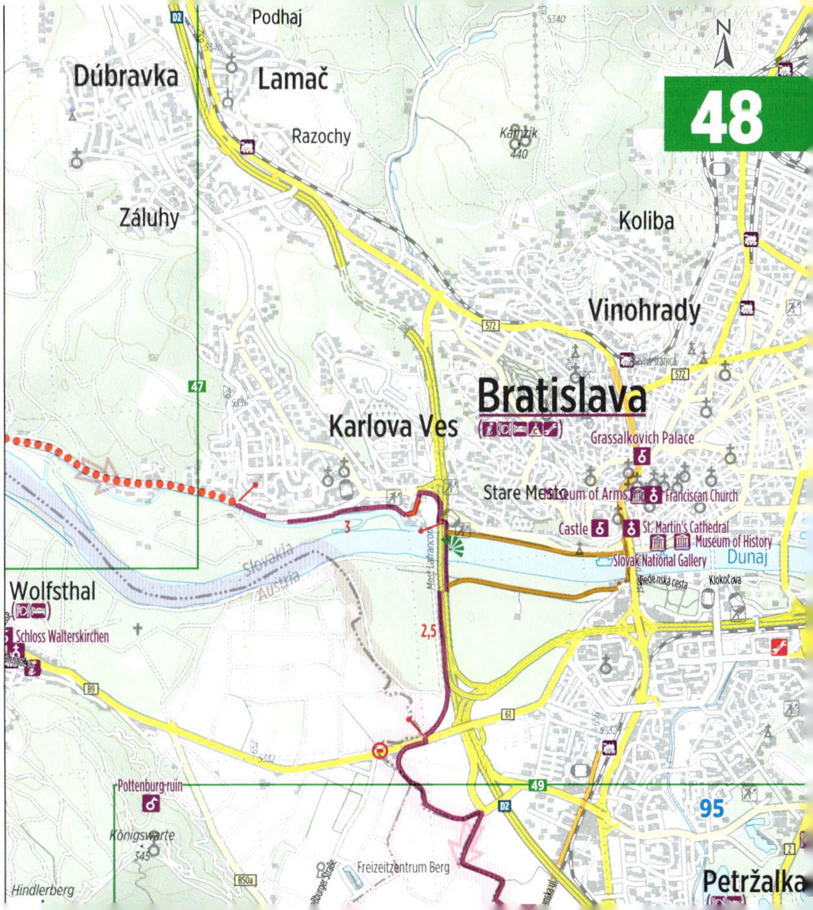

Castle (Hrad). The 12th century castle was rebuilt in 1430 in Gothic style, and is the most important fortress in Hungary. Under Maria Theresia it received the honour of being a representation palace, but the rise of Budapest as Hungary's capital meant it soon lost its importance. Today the seat of the Slovak National Council.

Grassalkovich Palace (1760), seat of the President of Slovakia

Michael's Gate, Michalská ul. The last goal of the fortification, originally a Gothic building from the 14th century, now houses the Museum of Arms.

Old town hall (Stará radnica) Hlavné námestie. Re-modelled Gothic building in Baroque style with a unique courtyard and city tower.

Monument Slavín, in the northwest of the city. A memorial for the fallen Soviet soldiers in 1945 who perished during the liberation of the town. There is also a monument here relating to the communist era which offers lovely views of the surroundings.

chilli's bike, Šustekova 25 (Petržalka), ✆ 622 509

The only capital in the world that borders two states, is the political, economic and cultural centre of Slovakia and with about 427,000 inhabitants, the largest city in the country. Bratislava is often called "Little Big City" and celebrated as "Partyslava" or "BratisLover" and is seemingly always in a demonstratively good mood. Bratislava was under Hungarian rule since the beginning of the 10th century, and served as the capital of Royal Hungaria from 1536 until 1848. During this time it flourished, and the positive effects of this time can still be seen today in its architecture and other ways.

After the administration was moved to what is today Budapest, it turned into the centre of the Slovak national movement. Since 1918, it was the capital of the Slovak part of the state and since 1993 Bratislava has been the capital of independent Slovakia. The region benefits from the proximity to Western European markets and together with Vienna, which is only 69 km away, it is trying to follow the development concept of a Twin City - and generates 25 percent of the country's gross domestic product. The numerous global corporations positioned there are thanks to its strategic location and the high density of universities and research institutes. Anyone who wants to appreciate the most important historical and modern attractions, needs to spend far more than just a day here. The first thing one should see are the protected old buildings on Hlavné námestie (main square). The most striking building here is the old town hall which is made up of three of the oldest-surviving buildings in the city and is decorated with a Baroque tower. It now houses the town museum. Opposite, just in front of Sedlárska ulica (Sattlergasse) and behind the flashy gold-studded Roland Palais is the Maximilian fountain. The right corner is occupied by the white Esterházy palace in the Rococo style and on the left is the famous Café Mayer. The square is often used for concerts, festivals and markets.

The Sedlárska leads to the right (NW) to Michalská ulica which contains several street cafes. 100 metres from here, on the right hand side, you can see the Michalská brána, the only surviving medieval gate. From the observation gallery on the sixth floor, you can get a good view of the old town. Next to the door, with a width of just 1.30 metres, is the narrowest house in Europe. If you turn south, just before a junction, you will find the huge promenade Hviezdoslavovo namestie. In addition to the National Theatre, you can also find the German Embassy here. At the intersection with Panská ulica turn right to get to the gothic St. Martin's cathedral. The significance of this church for the self-confidence of the nation is reflected in the replica of the Hungarian Holy Crown, which adorns the spire instead of a cross. Between 1563 and 1830, the coronations of eleven kings and eight queens from the Habsburg dynasty as monarchs of the Kingdom of Hungary took place here. They were German as well as Austrian.

On the other side of the motorway that leads from the church tower and at the foot of the castle hill, runs the Židovská ulica. The name refers to the Jewish settlers who lived here in the Middle Ages and were under the protection

Michael Cramer and Johann Bernhardt on the Danube, 1984

of the castle. A part of the Jewish cemetery has now been restored and is located underground near the tram tunnel. But the name is also a reference to the Jews who were deported after the "annexation" of Austria and the annexation of Bohemia and Moravia from the first Slovak state by Nazi Germany 1939. Quaint, alleys and steep stairways are present on the castle hill. The Gothic in origin place of refuge with four wings is 85 metres above the Danube. After several reconstructions it was burned down in 1811 by the French and rebuilt in Baroque style after the 2nd World War. Its architecture is less spectacular than the location and the view.

The city is characterised by numerous Baroque palaces, but also has a number of bold and interesting contemporary buildings. The Kostol svatej Alžbety (Elisabeth Church) with its idiosyncratic Hungarian Art Nouveau style in pink and blue pastel colours is a peculiarity of tradition and modernity and is certainly eye-catching. You can find it in Bezručova ulica in the south-eastern part of the old town. It is of course no surprise that in this culturally-rich and well-populated city there is always "something going on" especially in the music scene. The Bratislava Jazz Days, the Wilsonic Festival (Rock, Alternative, Pop) and the Bratislava Music Festival (Classical) are all popular events. The railway station offers direct connections to Vienna, Berlin and Hamburg.

The Danube

The Romans called the river after the Roman river god Danubius and regarded it as the Limes, the border between the Empire and the barbarian world. At 2,888 kilometres, the Danube is second longest river in Europe – the Volga being the first. It rises near Donaueschingen in the Black Forest, crosses the northern Alpine foreland, the Pannonian Plain and the Romanian lowlands and finishes in the Black Sea. Because the exact location of the source is controversial, it is calculated from the outlet. Hundreds of tributaries run into the Danube, springing in the Eastern Alps and the Carpathians and in the Balkans and increasing their volume of water downstream by two-thirds. About 100 million people live along its banks, and it flows through Germany, Austria, Slovakia, Hungary, Croatia, Serbia, Bulgaria, Romania, Moldova and Ukraine and for 1071 kilometres - 37 percent of their length – marks a

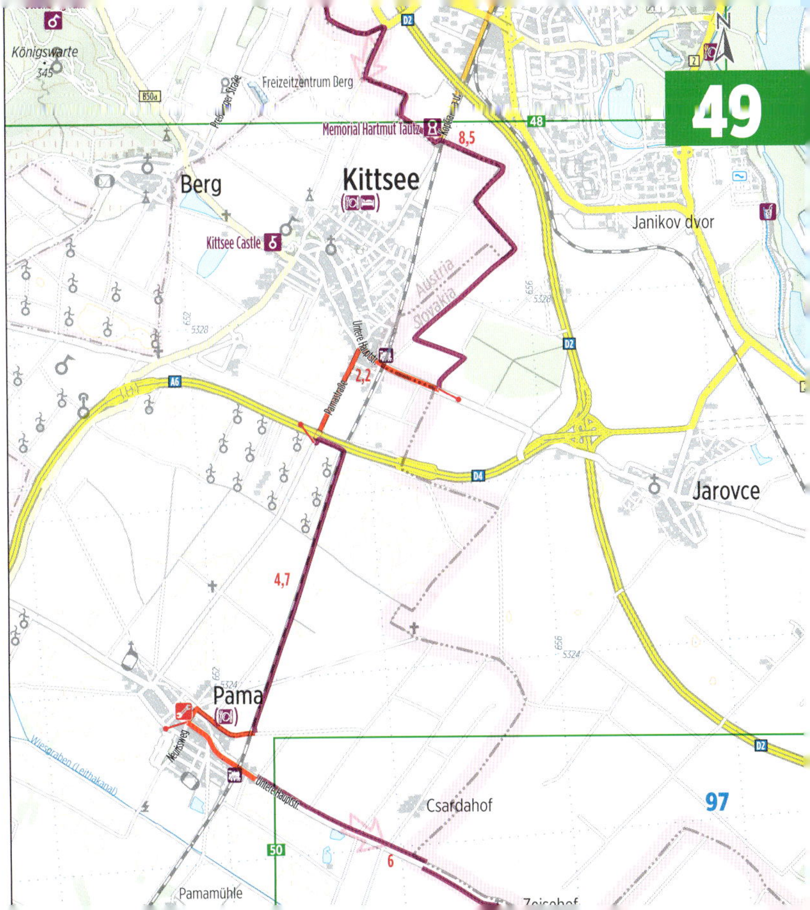

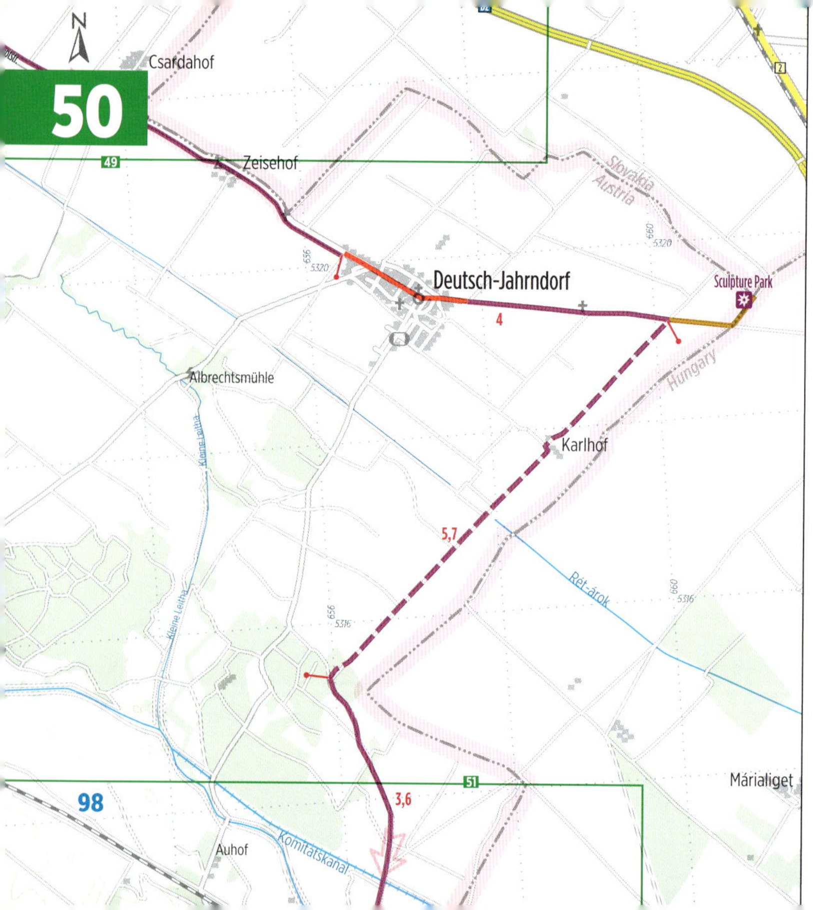

state border. It has often been named a "murderous border river" throughout its history, because the Danube was often filled with blood. The Danube once gave a monarchy its name and has often been described in literature and music. The Johann Strauss waltz "The Blue Danube" was composed in 1867 is famous the world over.

Border remains before Deutsch-Jahrndorf

From Bratislava (SK) to Andau (AT) ***66 km***

From the main station in Bratislava cycle straight along the **Pražská** and **Štefánikova**, then turn right into **Staromestská ulica** and cycle on the Danube bridge **Novy most** to the other shore. Immediately after the bridge, turn right into the signposted cycle path until you reach the motorway. Behind the motorway turn left. Before the major junction, turn right and cycle parallel to state road 61 to the **border crossing Petrzalka-Berg**. Cross the main road just before the boundary and continue on the former border patrol road (which follows the border for the next 5 km) to the southeast of the former customs building. The cycle path, in part bordered by trees, is in excellent condition.

CONNECTION If you turn left on the Bratislava road (Kopčianska ulica), you will get to Bratislava Petržalka station. This is the final station for direct trains from Vienna Central Station.

Bratislava-Petržalka

This district is one of the largest uniformly built housing estates in Europe with 120,000 people in more than 40,000 flats. A sports ground is located outside the station on the west side.

The death march

About 2,000 Jews were gathered in this football field on Maundy Thursday in 1945 and were housed in pathetic accommodation. They had been deported here from Budapest to build the south-eastern border for the Nazis. As the Red Army approached Petržalka, on 29 March at 22.00 hours in front of the former Semperit building, the death march began that led them over Wolfsberg to Altenburg. Shots were fired indiscriminately by the Austrian Nazis into the crowd. During the following march many allegedly sick and elderly people were shot and left in ditches at the side of the road.

After the war, numerous people were put on trial for these crimes. The most important were the six "Engerau trials" of 1945-54, in which 21 SA-men were put on trial. Nine Austrian nationals were convicted and sentenced to death.

If you turn into **Pressburger Straße** (Kopčianska ulica), you will see an information plaque commemorating Hartmut Tautz.

Hartmut Tautz

Due to the fact that he had relatives in West Germany, he was not allowed to study music in the GDR after graduating from high school. Therefore he tried to reach the West via Austria. He traveled via Prague to Bratislava and on the evening of the 8th of August 1986 tried to slip across the border at Petržalka into Austria. The Austrian village of Kittsee seemed so close. He overcame the barbed wire fences and ran through tall corn field towards Kittsee. Upon cutting through the so-called signal wall he triggered an electrical alarm. The Czechoslovak border guards released two specially trained attack dogs, which at the end of the field, only 22 meters away from the border, caught up with him. The dogs tore into him delivering massive injuries. When the border guards arrived at the scene, they made no attempt and giving first aid, and instead frisked and interrogated the refugee. One and a half hours later, he was admitted to the Military Hospital in Bratislava, where he died a few hours later of his injuries. To date, nobody has ever been held accountable for the death of the 18 year old. For this reason, the

Sculpture park Dreiländereck

organisation Platform of European Memory and Conscience has been campaigning hard for justice.

On August the 9th, 2016 - the 30th anniversary of his death - a commemorative plaque was inaugurated for Hartmut Tautz at the point where he was killed. His name is mirrored on the board, because you only see someone fleeing from behind.

Cross the street and the tracks and remain on the former border patrol path. At the next border crossing to Kittsee turn right, cross the tracks – the station is on the right – and you will arrive in the **Untere Hauptstraße** on which you can reach the centre of Kittsee.

Kittsee

Many Croatians fleeing from Turkish invaders settled in this easternmost municipality in Austria in the 16th century. They still maintain their language and culture even to this day. The Ethnographic Museum in the Baroque castle Bathyany, however, closed in 2008. Trains run directly from Kittsee station to the main station and Vienna Bratislava Petržalka.

Emil Švec

On August 2, 1959, a pilot trained by the Czechoslovakian military succeeded in escaping from Czechoslovakia. He had hijacked a "Fieseler Storch", a military propeller aircraft which had been converted for spraying fields. Later he found out that Czechoslovak fighter jets had been launched to shoot him down. However, they did not manage to catch him and he was sentenced in absentia to 15 years in prison for high treason. Emil Švec (1925-2010) was lured into a trap in Kittsee in October 1962, was kidnapped by the STB on Austrian territory, taken to Slovakia and had to serve his sentence in various prisons. During the Prague Spring, he was not amnestied like other political prisoners. He had to wait until 1969 to be pardoned and released. However, three years later, that decision was reversed. He was arrested again and remained imprisoned until 1977. After 1989, the "Flying refugee" tried to receive an official pardon and recognition as a victim of communism. This was, however, repeatedly rejected or bureaucratically held up. When he criticized in a letter of complaint accusing the judiciary to still be dominated by ex-communist cliques, he was sentenced to conditional imprisonment for "insulting a public official". None of the agents involved in the STB abduction had to stand trial.

The "European Iron Curtain Trail" bends behind the tracks immediately left into **Pamastraße**. After crossing the motorway, turn left, crossing the railway tracks and turning right into the signposted cycle path. Ride parallel to the tracks and follow the signs right to Pama, where you turn left into the main road.

Pama

Cycle through the village and then on a separate bicycle path through Zeisehof.

Deutsch-Jahrndorf

Continue through here and stop just before the border. Behind a white monument on the left side, an homage to the Holy Wendelin, turn right into a dirt road in decent condition.

EXCURSION Continue straight on to the border. Directly before the border turn left into a field road and after 400 metres you will reach a sculpture park on the triple border of Austria, Hungary and Slovakia.

Sculpture park Dreiländereck

In 1989 several international artists created sculptures to commemorate the fall of the Iron Curtain. Memorial stones, boundary stones and barbed radicals complete the "International Symposium", which has become a popular tourist attraction for visitors from the three countries. A triangular stone with the national flags of the three countries can be found exactly on the border. Unfortunately, there is no information about the artist and their motivation or any more information about the border triangle. There is only one information board in three languages on the bustards.

Great bustard

Although intensive farming dominates the landscape in this border area, the Great Bustard, the heaviest flightless birds of our planet, could survive. They were still being hunted as trophies until the 1960s. By the end of the 1980s there were only 20 of the birds left. After the opening of the border, brownfields were created with EU funds, giving the males space to puff their plumage during courtship and impress the ladies. Numerous measures were also taken not just in Austria but also in Hungary and Slovakia, leading to over 400 great bustards today, which can be observed from many observation towers around Andau. From the three country border, cycle back and turn into the unpaved but comfortable path.

Cycle along the border where you can observe rabbits and deer until you reach **Karlhof** where you continue cycling straight, keeping to the left hand side. Cross the Lajta canal until you hit a paved access road, into which you turn left. Crosses the Komitats canal and also the Lajta and pass the **Nickelsdorf Train Station** which offers direct trains to Vienna and Bruck / Leitha. Then you will get to the main road no 10, into which you turn right in the direction of Nickelsdorf.

Nickelsdorf

Breuer Bed and Breakfast, ✆ +43/2146/2234

Nickelsdorf has had, just like many other places in the "European Iron Curtain Trail", an eventful history. Like the rest of Burgenland, it belonged, until the conclusion of the Treaties of St. Germain and Trianon (1920), under the name Miklós Halma to Hungary.

Since 2005 Nickelsdorf has hosted "Nova Rock", which has quickly become the largest rock festival in Austria.

Turn left off the main road onto **Lindengasse**, which merges into **Kleylehoferstraße**. On **bike path B 26**, cross the motorway on a bridge, from which you can survey the area used for rock concerts. Shortly after the bridge, you can find a 2004 monument to the Iron Curtain which was unveiled by the two Foreign Ministers Alois Mock and Gyula Horn on June 27, 1989. Unfortunately, an information board is missing for the official opening of the border between Nickelsdorf and Hegyeshalom which took place on 2 May 1989. (For more information on the

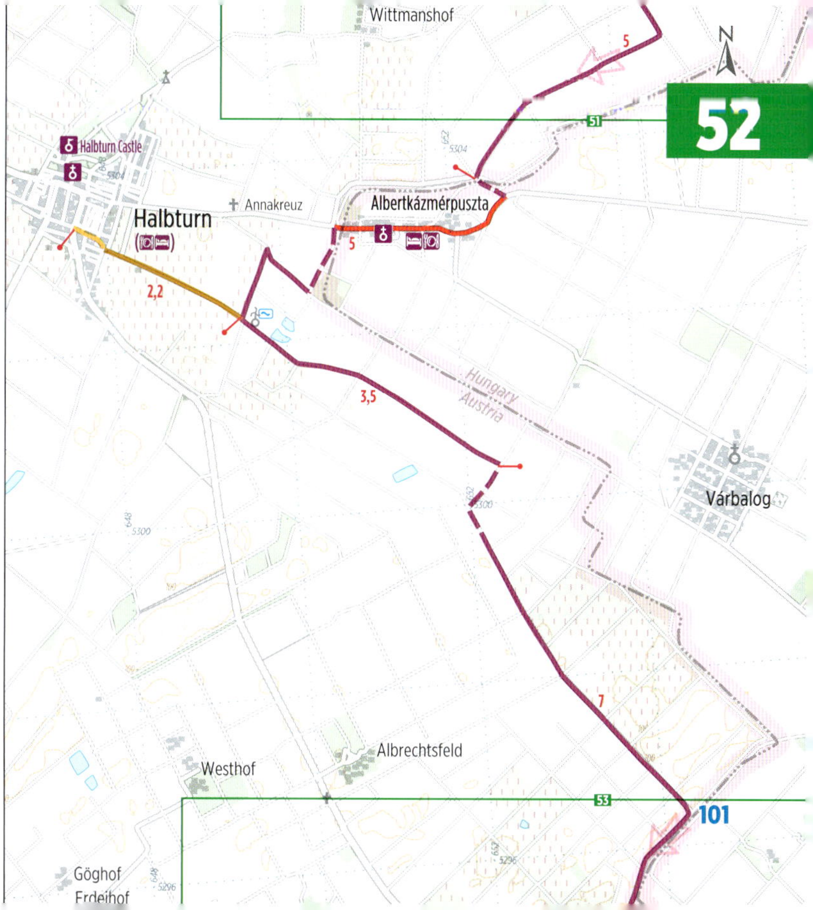

opening of the border turn to page 106: "The dismantling of the Iron Curtain".)

Miklós Radnóti

Miklós Radnóti (1909-1944) was one of the greatest Hungarian poets of the 20th century. After he had been drafted for hard labour on several occasions because of his Jewish ancestry, he was ordered in May 1944 to the Ukrainian Front and then later detained at Camp Bor in Serbia. The resulting poems there - Bori notesz (Notes from Bor) - could illegally be smuggled to Budapest. As Tito's troops were advancing, he was driven through Hungary to the Austrian border along with thousands of Jewish labourers in forced marches. When he collapsed due to exhaustion, he was shot on 9 November 1944 on the way to Hegyeshalom with 21 of his fellow prisoners by the Hungarian guards. The mass grave was exhumed in 1946. His last poems were found in a jacket pocket, written during the death march. They appeared in 1948 in the collection Tajtékos ég (Sky With Clouds).

Before **Kleylehof** turn left into the side road and after 400 metres turn right into the signposted **cycle path B 26**.

Cycle through the countryside which was described by Beppo Beyerl in his book "Warning: National Border, On the trail of the Iron Curtain" as follows: "on the left, the strips of the fields that reach up to the horizon, and on the right, more strips of fields which stretch to the horizon". Many wind turbines, however, can also be seen there.

Church in Albertkázmérpuszta

When you reach the border, leave the B 26 in a right bend, turn left and cross the border into the unpaved field road. After 400 metres turn right into the street.

Albertkázmérpuszta

The **Gothic church** of the Votive Church.

Németh György Guesthouse, ✆ +36/30/4537940

Through the town, on the outskirts, cycle again across the border and turn left into the dirt road which is along the border. After 800 metres turn right into the asphalted access road, then turn left and continue cycling past some grapevines to **bike path B 22**, into which you turn left.

EXCURSION: If you want to cycle to Halbturn, turn off to the right.

Halbturn

Parish, consecrated in1714, expanded in 1725 according to plans by Fischer von Erlach in the Baroque style.

Halbturn, OT: Apr-Oct, possible to stay at the Schlosshotel ✆ +43/2172/82390. The most significant Baroque building of Burgenland was built in 1711 by Lucas v. Hildebrandt and is now privately owned. The vast palace complex is well maintained, has space for exhibitions and occasional venue for concerts.

The paved bike path B 22 leads past a treatment plant with wind turbine, and bends right after 3.5 km and after a left bend leads you straight to the border. There, turn right along the border. Where the sign for the B 22 points straight, turn right onto a paved road and you will reach Andau, without having to use the busy L 206. At the end of this road turn left, follow the road and turn left into **Hauptstraße** until you reach the Church of Andau.

Andau

Church of St. Nicholas, in the middle of the interesting former village green. The church is a combination of Baroque and modern elements, and has two minaret-like, round towers. What looks fine on the outside takes some getting used to on the inside. Outside the church, to the "hero of two world wars" is inscribed on a grave stone.

From Andau (AT) to Hegykő (HU) **50 km**

Behind the church, turn right at the guest house towards Hansaghof into **Ungergasse**, then keep left and go straight into **Hansaggasse**. At the end of this, turn left into the signposted B 22, which turns into the sculpture boulevard and leads to a famous bridge.

Church in Andau

Sculpture boulevard

Between 1992 and 1996, a symposium was organised by Hrdlicka student Franz Gylocs, sculptors were invited from Hungary, Austria and Slovakia. Along the so-called "escape road", the nearly nine-kilometre stretch of Andau, numerous artists created sculptures and installations made of wood and stone and displayed them in an impressive open-air gallery.

Andau bridge

The inconspicuous wooden bridge served the local farmers well on both sides of the diked Einser channel and helped them in reaching far out fields and therefore also both sides of the border. In 1956, during the Hungarian uprising, a wave of refugees arrived. This outlying construction was one of the last opportunities to reach the West. As such, on 4 November 1956, around 70,000 people fled across this bridge. A few days later it was blown up by Hungarian soldiers. In cooperation between Hungarian and Austrian soldiers, a new bridge was built 40 years later. The name "Bridge of Andau" has been heavily featured in literary and cinematic

Bridge of Andau

fields. It was, for example, the centre of the Franz Antel film "The Bockerer" about the revolution in Hungary. A lookout tower is also present at the spot.

Cycle over the bridge and turn on the Hungarian side right into the unpaved but cyclist-friendly and well-maintained path.

History of Hungary

The origins of Hungary can be found a long way away from its present-day territory. The Magyars, the Hungarians' ancestors, left western Siberian and after centuries of migration, eventually settled down in the year 1000 in the Kingdom of Hungary. "Saint Stephen I" (Szent István), who lived from 969-1038, was the first king of Hungary and is now the patron saint of the country. With the defeat at Mohacs (1526) by the Turks, the Christianized empire came under Ottoman rule and was divided. The largest part was incorporated into the Ottoman Empire and the smaller part came under Austrian influence. After the defeat of the Turks at Vienna in the "Battle of the Bald Mountain" (1683) Habsburg troops occupied the entire territory. Independence movements were then repeatedly and bloodily suppressed until in 1867 Hungary was absorbed into the Imperial and Royal (k. U. K.) Dual Monarchy to defuse tensions in the multi-ethnic state. In World War I (1914-18), which England and France won, with support from the USA, the soldiers of the Dual Monarchy fought against Serbia, Russia, Romania and Italy. On 16th November 1918, a democratic republic was proclaimed, with Mihaly Karolyi as the first President. His government was overthrown by the communists under Béla Kun and his Soviet Republic was likewise also overthrown on 1st August 1919. On March 1st, 1920, the Miklós Horthy "Regent" (1868-1957) restored the monarchy. On June 4th 1920, the "Treaty of Trianon" was signed banning the restoration of the Habsburg monarchy and Hungary lost over half of its inhabitants and - like Poland - two-thirds of its territory, including the Burgenland, Croatia, Slovakia and Transylvania. Since then, there is an old joke that "Hungary is the only country in the world, which is surrounded by herself."

In the years between the two World Wars, Hungary increasingly approached the Mussolini-led fascist Italy and also entered into various pacts with the Nazi German Reich. During the reign of "Regent" Miklós Horthy (1920-1944) - a lifelong anti-Semite - the first anti-Jewish law in 20th century Europe was adopted in 1920. This was followed by three other Jewish laws in 1938, 1939 and 1941. The last law - Raoul Hilberg - was even stricter than the Nuremberg Race Laws. In the last years of the war, roughly 600,000 Hungarian Jews were killed, with the support of the fascist Hungarian government. With the help of the Hungarian police, many were deported to Auschwitz, where, of the 1.3 million people who died there, 430,000 were Hungarian Jews. On the 70th anniversary of the liberation of Auschwitz, Viktor Orbán recognised the participation of his country in the Holocaust and called it a "national tragedy". During World War II Hungarian troops actively supported the German campaigns in the Balkans and against the Soviet Union. Finally, the Red Army conquered the Hungarian capital Budapest. The hope of the Western Allies of a democratic constitution quickly faded. In 1949,

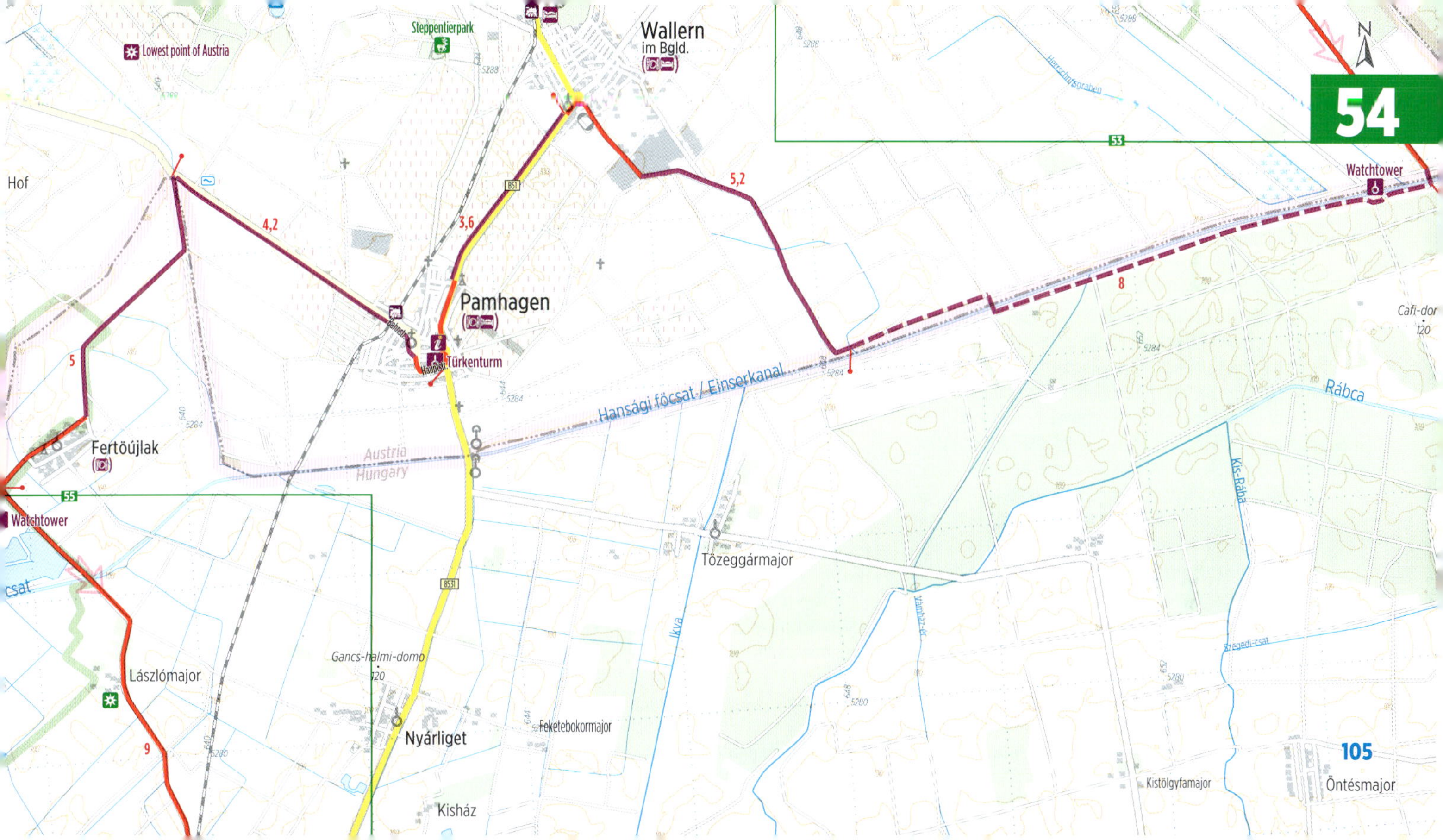

54
Wallern
im Bgld.
Steppentierpark
Lowest point of Austria
Hof
4,2
3,6
5,2
Watchtower
8
Pamhagen
Bahnstr.
Hauptstr.
Türkenturm
5
Fertőújlak
Hansági főcsat / Einserkanal
Rábca
Austria
Hungary
Cafi-dor
120
55
53
Watchtower
csat
Tőzeggármajor
Kis-Rába
Ikva
Lászlómajor
9
Gancs-halmi-domo
120
Nyárliget
Feketebokormajor
Kisház
Kistölgyfamajor
Öntésmajor
B51
B531

Hungary received a constitution based on the Soviet model, and in 1955 was a founding member of the Warsaw Pact.

The "Hungarian Revolution" in 1956, whilst being initially successful, was then ruthlessly put down by Soviet troops. Imre Nagy was tried and executed with many other supporters of the revolution. From 1968, many economic reforms were carried out, which were known as "goulash communism". János Kádár had to resign as a Hungarian party leader in May 1988, and was succeeded by Karoly Grosz. On 23rd November 1988, he was replaced by Miklos Nemeth. Together with Imre Pozsgay, he began a peaceful regime change, and economic reformers took over the helm.

On the 10th and 11th February 1989, the Central Committee (CC) of the Communist Party disagreed publicly with the doctrine of the "counter-revolution of 1956" and called for the introduction of a multiparty system. Work also began on May 2nd, 1989 with the dismantling of the Iron Curtain. On June 16th, 1989, exactly 31 years after the execution of Imre Nagy, more than 200,000 citizens in Budapest remembered the victims of the post-revolution time and praised the former minister president with a special grave of honour. They also buried at the same time - according to the historian Ilko-Sascha Kowalczuk – communism forever. On July 6th, 1989, Imre Nagy was posthumously pardoned by the Supreme Court in Hungary on all counts - the same day Janos Kádár died. On October 23, 1989, the anniversary of the 1956 revolution, the Republic of Hungary was proclaimed as a democratic and parliamentary republic. Hungary joined NATO and the EU in 2004.

The Iron Curtain in Hungary

After the Second World War 291 observation towers were erected on the heavily guarded 356-kilometre border with Austria and the 630-kilometre border to Yugoslavia. In the spring of 1949, work began on the construction of barbed wire fences and the laying of landmines. Austria and Hungary were separated by 1.6 million personnel mines. A defence system was also developed in the 1950s; some bunkers of which are still present today.

The dismantling of the Iron Curtain

Following the Hungarian government's decision to dismantle the Iron Curtain rather than the expensive option of maintaining parts of it, the electronic signal system and the frontier barriers were already dismantled in late February 1989 and on April 18th, 1989 the first piece of the border fence in Györ was removed. Hungarian soldiers officially began the systematic dismantling of the Iron Curtain on the 2nd May 1989 settlement between Hegyeshalom (Hungary) and Nickelsdorf (Austria). Because this received very little public attention, on 27th June 1989, the then Austrian Foreign Minister Alois Mock and his Hungarian counterpart Gyula Horn met and separated the border fence together near Klingenbach in Sopron. On this occasion, the previously remote border fortifications were rebuilt.

Cycle through the **Fertö-Hanság national park**, of which 23,000 m^2 is in Hungary and 10,000 m^2 are in Austria. Continue on the old patrol path along the **Einser canal** (Hansági-föcsatorna) around an ancient watchtower and cross the canal on a bridge. Since 2013 you can reach the Austrian side via the newly built Baron Gustáv mountain bridge on the and there cycle further along the canal. Follow the sign to Wallern.

TIP: The path (signposted to Pamhagen) ends after a few metres in scrubland.

The small asphalted road will later turn into a street.

Wallern

Gartner Bed and Breakfast, ✆ +43/2174/2220

You will now hit the **B 51**, into which you turn left and continue cycling on the separate "Jubilee Route" R 1 to **Pamhagen**. At the roundabout, continue straight to **Stephansplatz** and once there, turn right into the **Hauptstraße**.

Pamhagen

Steiner, ✆ +43/2174/2165. The "Radlwirt" serves Pannonian delicacies.

"Vila Vita", ✆ +43/2175/21800, just outside the town.

Türkenturm. The secluded, square bell tower is 10 m high and has a six-sided pyramid spire. On it a banner of the prophet mounted on a crescent, star and named "Mosco Pasha" with the year "1683". There are several legends regarding the origin of the tower.

55
Watchtower
Austria
Hungary
Hansági főcsat
Lászlómajor
Gancs-
Sarród
Fertőd
Esterházy Palac
Fertőszéplak
All Saints Church
Railway Lightmuseum
Hegykő
Fertőhomok
Hidegség
Kövecses-hegy
Fertőboz
Gloriette
Csucsos-szőlő
Kisboz
Balf
Bad Chapel
Castle church
Kópháza
Kiscenk
Széchenyi-Castle
Cseralja
Bozi-csatorna
Fő utca
Petőfi tér
Kossuth Lajos utca
Joseph Haydn út
Fő út
Bozi út
3,4
1,2
2,2
7,5
5,7
9
54
56
57
85
107

Esterházy Palace in Fertöd

Behind the "Türkenturm" turn right, leave the **Hauptstraße** on the **Kirchenplatz** and cycle in the direction of the church, which you pass on your left. Keep right and continue straight to the **Bahnstraße**, into which one turns left. Cross the tracks – on the right there is a train station, where direct trains to Vienna and Fertöszentmiklós depart. Cycle on the separate **bike path B 10** to the border. Behind the river, turn left into a dirt road which after a few metres is paved.

Fertöújlak

You will get to a road, into which one turns right. Look for a church and a bed and breakfast and at the end of this, turn left and head towards the border. Cycle through a veritable bird paradise and you will even see an old watchtower, which you can use to watch the birds. (Föcsat Hansági). Cross the Einser canal to get to the Laszlo Major bird observatory. Cross the railway again and keep going until you reach the next place on our tour.

Sarród

The way is called **Fö utca**. After a sharp right bend, turn left into **Petofi tér**, which leads us to **Kossuth Lajos utca** and **Sarródi út** to Fertöd.

Fertöd

Esterházy Palace. The "Hungarian Versailles" is one of the largest rococo palaces in Hungary and the World Heritage Site. The fact that the conversion of a small hunting lodge took 46 years, can easily be believed when you consider the scope of the project and the building (the middle part can be visited).

The name originated in 1950 from the Hungarian word fert = swamp, and is inseparable from the Esterházy Palace and for classical music lovers the court composer Joseph Haydn. The park, together with the Hanság, the low moorland south of Lake Neusiedl and Lake Neusiedl itself, are all part of a national park, that together with Austria's Steppen national park, is also a UNESCO World Heritage Site.

Turn right into **Joseph Haydn út**. On a separate cycle path, cross the tracks into the neighbouring community of Fertöszéplak where you travel straight on the road in front of the church which has a speed restriction of 30 km/h.

Fertöszéplak

- twin-tower **All Saints Church**, with internal Baroque Calvary
- **ancestral castle** of the noble family Széchenyi

Godwit at the nature reserve

You will be welcomed here by a string of white pearls, buildings in Hungarian Peasant Baroque style. Some of these beautiful arcaded houses form part of the Folklore Open Air Museum, which is dedicated to ancient working class trade.

EXCURSION To get to the church, turn left uphill into Ady Endre utca.

The main route goes through **Széchenyi utca**, which ends with a signposted right into **Rákóczi**. Then turn left into **Hunjagy utca**. At the end turn right into the main road and follow the signs to Hegykö.

Hegykő

Tornácos Bed and Breakfast, ✆ +36/99/540200, with spa

The cycle path around Lake Neusiedl has been around since the visa-free "late socialist" times and has been popular since then. So it is no wonder that tourists are well catered for. In Hegykö there is a campsite, hot baths, accommodation and planet of restaurants.

From Hegykő to Sopron 52 km

You can reach Fertöboz through **Fertöhomok** and **Hidegség**.

Fertöboz

- **"Gloriette"**, viewing pavillion in round stamp style, 1801, built on a hilltop
- **Panzió Bozi Rozi**, ✆ +36/99/357495

EXCURSION The "Gloriette" is located south of the community and you will reach it after a descent of a few hundred metres.

From Fertoboz, cycle on a moderately busy road towards Balf where the "European Iron Curtain Trail" makes a northward loop.

ALTERNATIVE If you want to cycle directly to Sopron, continue straight ahead.

The main route turns right into **Bozi ut**.

Balf

The three writers from Balf

The three writers of Jewish descent were deported in July 1944 from Budapest to Balf in order to help with the construction of the South Eastern Walls. The literature professor Antal Szerb (1901-1945) was one of the most widely read authors of the 20th century in Hungary. His best known work is "Hungarian literature" which was published in 1934 published and still read today. György Sárközy translated "Joseph and His Brothers" by Thomas Mann and the "Faust" into Hungarian. Gábor Halász was a well-known poet and essayist. Antal Szerb was killed on the 27th of January 1945 in the Balf camp by underage Hungarian paramilitary guards who battered him with their rifle butts. Halász and Sárközi died of starvation a few weeks later.

The route continues through wine-growing areas and the wetlands of the lake, past a high metal watchtower after **Fertörákos** (Kroisbach). The elongated municipality offers a large array of sights and monuments of various different ages.

Fertörákos

- **The church**, a Baroque building with an old defensive tower is surrounded by grave stones and pillars ranging in artistic styles from Baroque to Classicism.
- **Episcopal Palace**. Grand Baroque building with courtyard on older foundations, surrounded by a landscaped garden in French style.
- **Baroque water mill** belonging to the episcopal property, with an idiosyncratic coloured ornamented facade and a sundial. Müller craft items are exhibited in the courtyard.
- **quarry**, currently blocked off due to danger of collapse. Over centuries of activity a gorge with jagged outline and vertical walls was dug into a hill. The south side is hollowed out and supported on mighty pillars provides a spectacular setting for the Cave Theatre, which since 1970 has become known throughout Europe for its musical performances, particularly of Wagner and Liszt. The site was also used as an inherent stronghold. After the annexation of Hungary in 1944, German authorities established transitional and labour camps here, where thousands of Hungarian Jews and political prisoners were murdered. Many were deported to concentration camps in Germany and Poland. The cavern was the main place of execution and you can see the numerous bullet holes in the walls alongside a plaque. Unfortunately, this painful piece of the past is rarely referred to in German travel literature.

A small chapel from 1714 with a seemingly archaic, simple design and exposed stone ashlar can be found approximately 150 metres after the start of the closed building, on the left hand side, close to a new residential building. The site was part of an episcopal hold and was protected by a medieval castle. Two strong walls are still around today. Prior to 1996, there were three white statues. One of them was the Fertőrákos Madonna based on the resettlement monument by sculptor Örsi András. It bears the names of the displaced people who had been banished fifty years before. Continue towards the Episcopal Palace. The tourist office can be found on the square on the right side of the road. The centre of the square is occupied by a monument referring to the referendum in 1921, which resembles a baptismal font. (The area around Sopron remained part of the Hungarian State after this referendum.)

Behind the block of houses to the left there is a small square, which was designed in 1989 to be a small park. There is a monument to the opening of the border consisting of a stone block with barbed rows. It is split by a wedge with the year 1989 written on it. A Baroque watermill can be found in the same area. The simple pillory on the narrow village green stands on the spot where there used to be an underground prison. The route to the church can be found on the right hand side and is accompanied by numerous monuments: Stock Friedrich von Kreuzpeck, the warhorse from the Kroisbach noble family, the fallen in the First World War and lastly the Trinity statue which commemorates the deliverance of Vienna from the Turks. The road then merges into a cross street and leads you to an old quarry.

On the northern hill there is an oversized piece of barbed wire in the sky. These is the monument of Gabriela von Habsburg commemorating the Pan-European Picnic of 1989 which the route also leads to. It carries a ribbon with the Latin motto of the Pan-European Union: In neccessariis unitas in dubiis libertas in omnibus caritas (Unity, when in an emergency – freedom, when in doubt – but above all, love).

From Fertörákos continue on bike path B 10 and turn right.

ALTERNATIVE If you want to cycle to Sopron, at the junction, follow the signposted cycle path left to Mörbisch and you will reach the city after 8 km.

The main route leads towards the border and just before you reach it, you will encounter Mithraeum.

Mithräum

Mithraeum, OT: mid-March to mid-Oct, Tue-Sun 10-17. The early third century Mithraeum is located directly on the present border crossing.

In the Roman Empire around the 4th century AD, Mithraism had developed into a mystery religion, and it was forbidden to report on it. Because it differed to the official Roman state religion, both before and after the introduction of Christianity, it was mostly practiced in secret and because it was exclusive only to men, it was particularly widespread among legionaries. A temple belonging to this cult was accidentally discovered in 1866 among luxuriant undergrowth on a path between Mörbisch am See and Fertörákos. The building which stretched deeply into the ground - the "rock-born" Mithras was worshiped mostly in caves - was restored and now contains three altars as well as a relief, typical of this cult relating to bull-killing. The relief is now astronomically interpreted as the end of an era and the beginning of a powerful new one. On the 20th anniversary of the Pan-European Picnic on 19th August of 2009 the 9th Symphony by Ludwig van Beethoven was played here.

Monument of open doors

Continue to Mörbisch am See, known for its lake festival and being close to Lake Neusiedl.

Mörbisch am See

Lake Neusiedl

The "Sea of the Viennese" located on 80 percent Austrian land and 20 percent on Hungarian territory is one of the few steppe lakes in Europe and in terms of area it is the largest lake in Austria. The runoff ponds are known locally as "Lacke" (puddle). The westernmost steppe lake in Europe at about 320 square kilometres, is at its deepest 1.80 metres and is the biggest of these puddles. It only has a few tiny tributaries and 80 percent of its water comes from rainwater. The reeds, the shallow depth and the mild and windy climate are characteristic of this lake. Some of the best wines grow in this, the hottest and driest area of Austria, not least because the slate and limestone soil is particularly well suited for growing grapes. The lake, which stores the heat and reflects the sun onto the vines also ensures the quality is good. Despite this, before every harvest, half of the grapes are cut away but the lower yield is more than offset by the better quality.

Lake Neusiedl national parks

The lake Neusiedl and Fertö-Hanság national parks, with their unique flora and fauna, have belonged to the UNESCO World Heritage Site since 2001. In relatively close proximity to each other you can find various different habitats: the forest of Leihagebirges, dry grassland, salt and sand habitats, vineyards, road villages, Seerandwiesen, the reeds and the water of the youngest and westernmost steppe lake in Europe. This biological "multinational state" lies between the Alps and Puszta and is home to species from Alpine, Pannonian and Mediterranean landscapes.

The list of species recorded at the national parks include 341 divers, cranes and swallows. Here one can also observe the rare common shelduck and Canada goose godwit, bittern and Great Bustard. Tree frogs, marsh owls and Pochards can be identified by their croaking and other sounds.

In Mörbisch turn left behind the church into **Eschengasse**. At the end of this turn left and then immediately right into **Rosengasse**, which then merges into Triftweg. Ride straight on the paved bike path, until you come to a forest rest area, where you keep to the left until you reach the site of the Pan-European Picnic on the road that if you turn right leads to Sankt Margarethen.

The Pan-European Picnic

On 19 August 1989, the Pan-European Union, which had been in contact with the opposition of the Eastern Bloc, held a peace rally in cooperation with the Hungarian Democratic Forum on the border north of Sopron, which was known as the Pan-European Picnic. During this event, under the auspices of the Emperor's son Otto von Habsburg and the writer György Konrad - the latter under the protective hand of the Hungarian chief reformer and State Minister Pozsgay - the border fence was to be opened for three hours as a symbolic gesture. Participation in this event had been vigorously promoted, also amongst the stranded East German refugees in Budapest who had imagined that the onward journey to the West would not be a problem. Thousands of them came, and, when the gate was finally opened, nearly 700 of them spilled over to the Austrian side without encountering any significant resistance. In the following days, the guarding of the borders was strengthened, but three weeks later, on September 11, they were opened for GDR citizens without any restrictions. In addition to a signposted border trail with information boards and a watchtower, a number of works of art in various forms can be found here, including a well house, a liberty bell and the monument of the open doors.

Monument "Change"

On the 20th anniversary of the Pan-European Picnic on 19 August 2009 a monument by Miklós Melocco called "Change" was inaugurated in the presence of the Hungarian President Sólyom, German Chancellor Merkel and the Austrian Foreign Minister Spindelegger. It consists of 15 life-size figures with a stylized background and the following quotation: "On August 19, 1989, oppressed people opened the door of their prison, to give freedom to other oppressed people." In this commemoration, the then Hungarian Prime Minister Miklós Németh said that the Pan-European Picnic had been to "test Moscow" because the Hungarian government wanted to know if Mikhail Gorbachev dared to stand by his statement in March 1989 that there would be "no second 1956".

"Change" monument

Monument of open doors

On the east side there is also a monument to the open doors, in homage to the 27th of June, when the Hungarian Foreign Minister Gyula Horn and his Austrian counterpart Alois Mock cut through the Iron Curtain in Klingenbach. However, this monument is currently not in the place where this event took place. In Hungary there is a heated debate about whether it should be moved there.

Japanese pagoda

On the other side of the street is a Japanese pagoda, which was funded by a citizen initiative as a sign of joy at the reunification of Europe. As in several places along the border strip in Berlin, cherry trees were also planted here. The Japanese celebrate their traditional Cherry Blossom Festival under cherry trees. No other plant plays such a significant role in the national life of the Japanese. They are considered a national symbol of aesthetic beauty and idealise the soul of Japanese chivalry. Unfortunately, the cherry trees are no longer present. The border trail with information boards and the integration of the watchtower continues on a marked bike path on the Austrian side.

Cycle on paved **bike path B 3**, turn left at the first opportunity, pass the former watchtower and continue until you reach Klingenbach.

Klingenbach

The city became world famous when Alois Mock and Gyula Horn broke through a section of the Iron Curtain.

Alois Mock und Gyula Horn

June the 27th, 1989 was an historic day. Three months before the fall of the Berlin Wall, the Iron Curtain was "officially" cut by the two foreign ministers of Hungary and Austria. On this day the international public learned about the partly open but still guarded border. How did this happen? What was the motivation behind this, especially from the communist government in Hungary?

The reasons can be found in a report by János Székely, who in 1986 became commander in chief of the Hungarian Border Guard, and at the request of the Interior Ministry was asked in October 1987 to review the critical electric systems. To aid him in this task, he called upon the border commanders to issue him with a report on the state of the equipment. In summary, it was found that the electrical signal systems were outdated in almost all respects. The 20-year-old signal systems were dealing with a variety of false reasons - only in the rarest cases was it triggered by an escape attempt, but mostly it was by animals. An additional safety fence was erected but this did not prevent false alarms because it was skipped over by deer. In addition to this, often strong winds were known to trigger the alarm. In total, only ten percent of the alarms were triggered by people.

At the resting spot near Schattendorf

The Hungarian border troops registered on average about 2,000 escape attempts each year, about ten percent of which were from Hungarian citizens. Most of the attempts were made spontaneously by people who wanted to leave their country through a porous border. Many returned the day after their flight, because even then 90 percent of the Hungarian population were in possession of a passport - the "world passport" was introduced in 1988 with which they could come and go easily. The Hungarians were envied. I'll never forget the astonished faces of the GDR participants, as a Hungarian in the early 1980s, told them of a trip organised by the state comprising of a paddle tour on the Danube from Ingolstadt to the Bulgarian Silistra. She continued to tell them of her relationship with her boyfriend in England, whom she visited in London every 14 days and then in turn, he visited her in Budapest. On this canoe trip, participants from the GDR were not allowed to be in West Germany. From their perspective, the Hungarians were already free. Party officials in the border regions also complained about the border installations because they adversely affected tourism. Therefore, for the Hungarian government, there were only two alternatives: The complete renovation of the fence and the soldiers be equipped with advanced monitoring methods or the degradation of the fence. The new installation would have cost 20 million euros – a reduction in the fence 3.5 million. The Ministry of Interior called for the elimination of the border fence, but the final decision was postponed again and again, because the decision affected not only Hungary but all of the Eastern Bloc.

Following the resignation of János Kádár in May 1988, Imre Pozsgai became the new Minister of State on April 18th, 1989. In the Rayka region on the border triangle of Austria, Hungary and Czechoslovakia a first trial demolition of the border fence took place. On May 2nd, the destruction of electronic signalling systems was announced at an international press conference of the border troops. By May 28th half of the equipment had been disposed of - the Hungarian government was finally formally advocating the fence be taken down. At the same time, the military forces were instructed to assist in the disposal, which is why the electrical systems had completely disappeared by September.

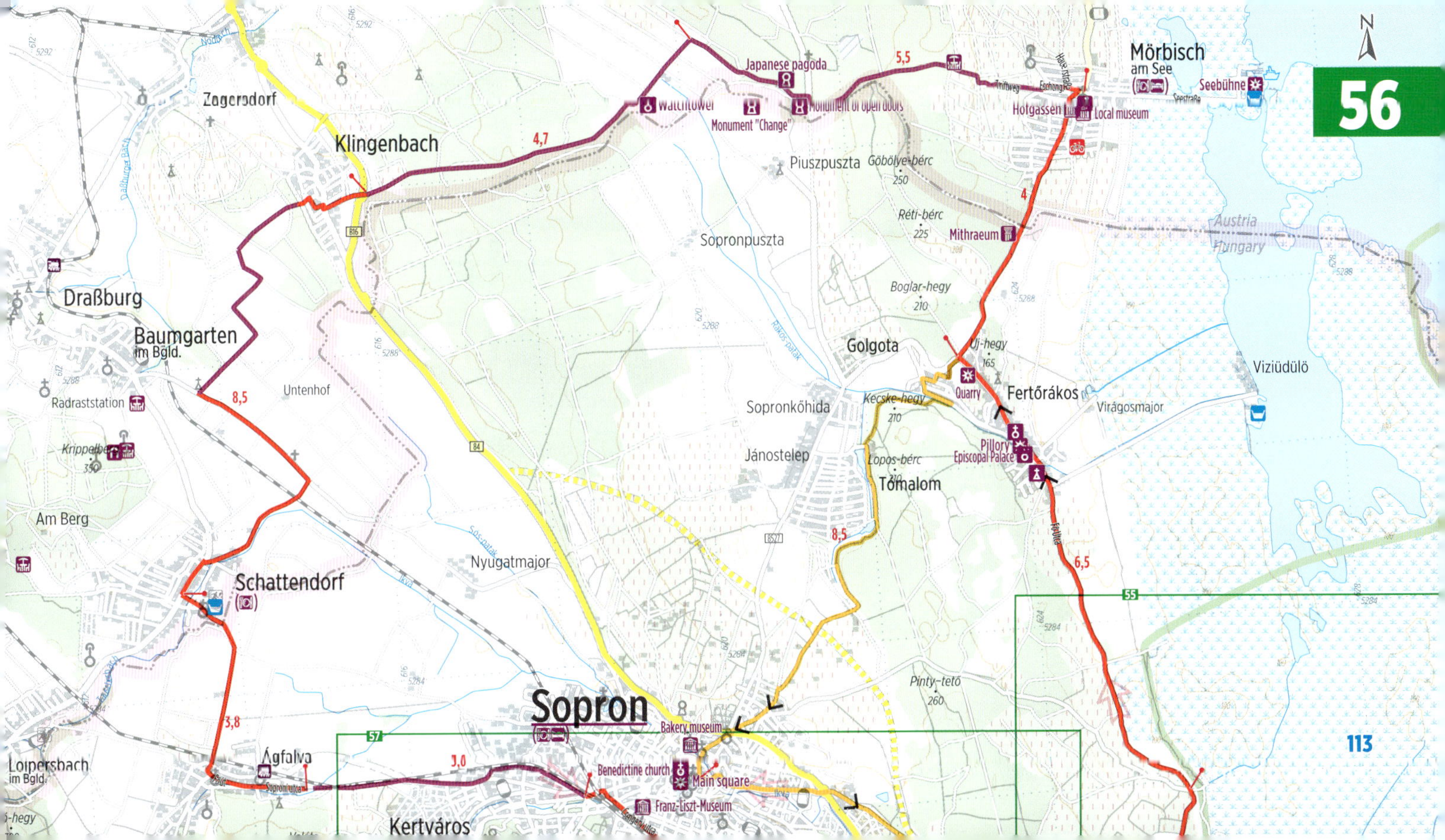

56
Mörbisch
am See
Seebühne
Japanese pagoda
5,5
Watchtower
Monument "Change"
Monument of open doors
Hofgassen
Local museum
Zagersdorf
Klingenbach
4,7
Piuszpuszta
Göbölye-bérc
250
Réti-bérc
225
Mithraeum
4
Austria
Hungary
Sopronpuszta
Draßburg
Baumgarten
im Bgld.
Boglar-hegy
210
Golgota
Uj-hegy
165
Quarry
Fertőrákos
Viziüdülő
Untenhof
8,5
Radraststation
Sopronkőhida
Kecske-hegy
210
Virágosmajor
Krippelberg
350
Jánostelep
Lopos-bérc
Pillory
Episcopal Palace
Tómalom
Am Berg
8,5
6,5
Nyugatmajor
Schattendorf
55
Pinty-tető
260
Sopron
Bakery museum
3,8
57
113
Loipersbach
im Bgld.
Ágfalva
3,0
Benedictine church
Main square
Franz-Liszt-Museum
Kertváros

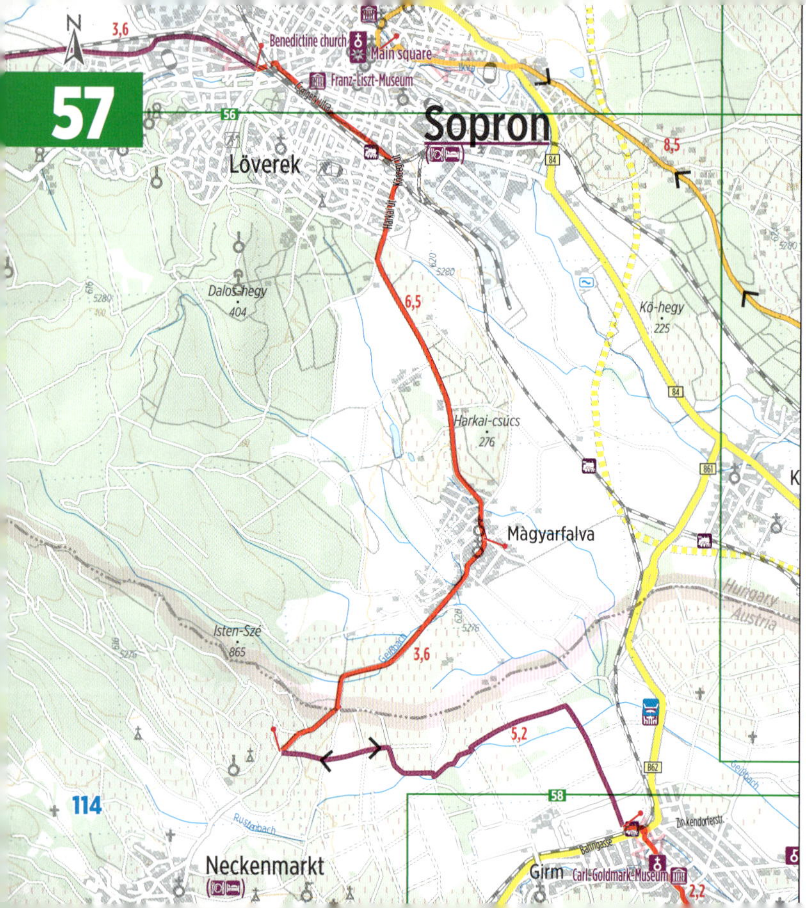

View from an old watchtower near Sopron

On August 19th, the "Pan-European Picnic" took place, which was used by 700 GDR citizens to flee. On September 11th, the border between Hungary and Austria was opened. Due to the fact that 25,000 East Germans took advantage of the opportunity within the next three weeks to escape, the East German government banned travelling to Hungary.

Not only the events of the 27th of June 1989 were important but also their consequences. When the two Ministers Gyula Horn and Alois Mock wanted to cut through the Iron Curtain, they had to be content with cutting the back fence, because the front one had already been dismantled.

Cycle from Klingenbach to Schattendorf.

In Klingenbach cross the B 16 on the **Pusztaweg**, before veering right into **Ödenburgerstraße** and then left into **Grünberg Allee**, which you follow straight. When leaving the town, continue straight on the signposted **EV 13** road and into the **Neuriss** path, from which, after a left bend and then a right bend, turn left into the **Pfarrbreiten** path which leads to **Wiener Neustädter Straße** after a right bend into which you turn left. At the **Untenäcker** path, turn right, cross the tracks and you will get to **Zollhausstraße**, at the end of which you turn left into the **Hauptstraße** in Schattendorf.

Schattendorf

The shots in Schattendorf

The shots in Schattendorf were deemed to signify the beginning of the end for the first Austrian Republic. Austria in 1927 was a country that was marked by conflict between Christian Socialists, Social Democrats, Ger-

man Nationalists and its paramilitary units. Violent clashes between Christian Socialists and Social Democrats were commonplace. On the 30th of January 1927 three nationalist frontline fighters opened fire with their hunting rifles fire on some unarmed socialists. The seven-year-old Josef Grössing from Schattendorf died as did 41-year-old disabled veteran Matthias Csmarits from Klingenbach. Five other people were also injured. The perpetrators came before the court in Vienna on 5th July 1927 and were acquitted by the jury nine days later on the grounds of alleged self-defence.

Socialist workers from the Viennese suburbs marched downtown on 15th of July, the day after the verdict. At the Parliament and at the University mounted policemen with drawn sabres met the demonstrators. There were violent street battles and the Palace of Justice was set on fire. The riots were violently suppressed. Once the dust had settled, 80 lay dead and a further 800 were injured, some very seriously. The gap between the two camps became deeper and deeper and ended with the dissolution of Parliament, the prohibition of social democracy and the resulting civil war in February 1934.

In Schattendorf take the **Koglweg** (B 30) to the church, cycle past the cemetery towards Ágfalva. At the border crossing, there are signs that talk about some of the history in German and in Hungarian. Even parts of the Iron Curtain can be seen there. After crossing the state border, keep right and cross the railroad.

Ágfalva

Turn left into **Fő út**, cycle on a bike path next to the road through the village and at the left bend, turn right into Soproni utca. Cycle over the river Ikva and remain on the southern side of the railway line on the non-signposted and only after 1km paved bike path. Pass underneath the tracks on the Csengery út until you arrive on the eastern side of the railway station in Sopron. From here direct trains travel to Vienna and Budapest.

Sopron

fire tower, a 61-metre-high landmark in Sopron located on the main square. On the upper floors there is an exhibition of local history. The northern gate tower has existed since the 13th century. It received its present shape with the

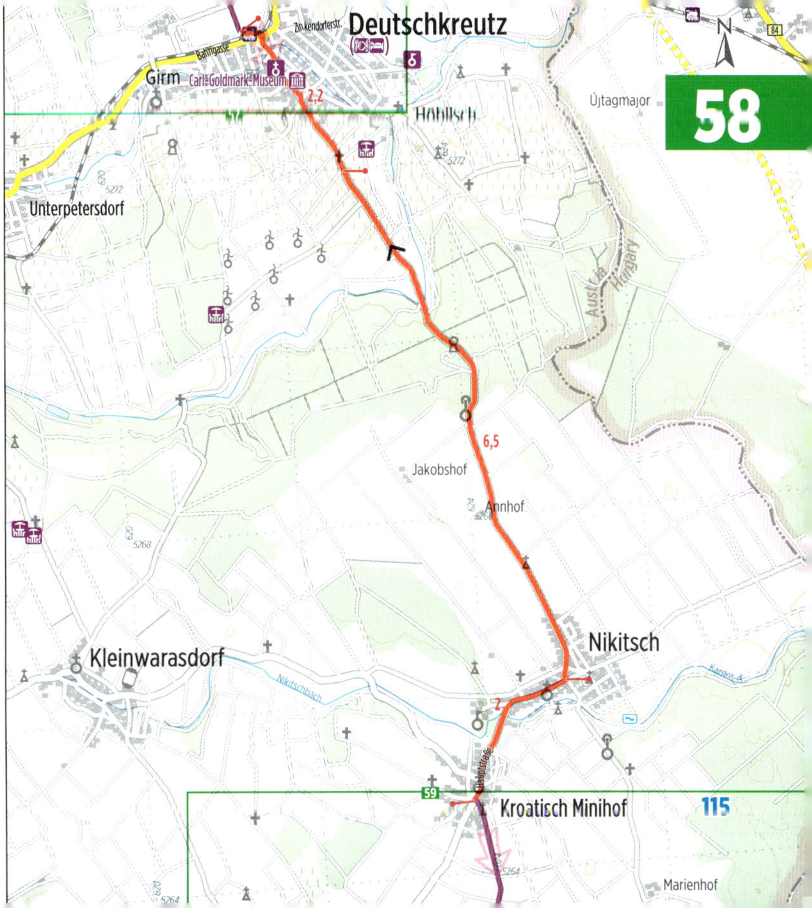

Baroque spire and surrounding bay after a fire. On the south side, the "Gate of Faith 'was built to commemorate the referendum, "civitas fidelissima" (particularly faithful city).

Main Square (Fo ter): tasteful, eclectic town hall (1896), opposite the Storno House, one of the most beautiful buildings in the city with a richly decorated bay window over two floors, at number 2, the Pharmacy Museum, House Number 6 Fabricius-house with stone souvenirs of the Roman period, including a marble tomb and the original altar relief from the Mithraeum of Fertörákos. The south side of the square is dominated by the side-mounted tower Geißkirche which was a crown city of monarchs and venue of inter-parliamentary assemblies. It has several fresco painting masterpieces.

Loyalty Fountain. This symbolises three events of momentous importance: the collection free royal city in 1277 after a brave resistance against Bohemian occupation, the plebiscite of 1921 and the opening of the border 1989.

OJ utca, southeast of the main square. In No. 1 remains of the Roman Forum and no. 22, the Gothic synagogue with mikvah, the ritual bath, restored in 1967 and unique in Central European.

The exposed position with respect to the Western European countries, which was once considered a massive disadvantage, has now been transformed into one of the most important factors for the economic recovery. It was decided in a referendum in 1921 in Hungary by more than 62 percent to officially become a bilingual country. A border station in Bernstein street in the Pannonia province played an important part for the Romans. After a devastating fire in 1676 it was rebuilt in the Baroque style, of which the old town is still influenced. Charming narrow streets, architectural rarities from Gothic to Baroque, numerous monuments, a wine cellar with a village atmosphere, but also musical events and shopping make the place with its 55,000 inhabitants highly attractive for tourists and investors alike. The old town is still surrounded especially in the west and east parts by tall city walls and this can be seen well in Vákerület street. Outside of Budapest, the most historic buildings in Hungary can be found in Sopron, which is why the city is often used as a film set.

From Sopron to Köszeg 51 km

Continue to the south along the tracks and towards **Köszegi út**, into which one turns right and then cross the tracks. Just behind it, turn left and slightly uphill and continue straight into **Harkai ut** which is later called **Soproni út**.

Harka

Cycle through the town and cross the border. A picture of how it looked in the past is displayed on an information board. After the border turn left into the **redwine bike trail (B 40)** and cycle through vineyards parallel to the border. Before the railway line the road leads you over a creek to the south and from there you reach the Deutschkreutz railway station (direct trains to Vienna, Ebenfurth and Sopron). Before the station, turn left, cross the track to your right and the B 62 and from the roundabout on the main road cycle straight on the **L 228** through the town centre.

Deutschkreutz

At the exit, cross the Frauenbrunn stream and cycling on a nice downhill stretch and then on a quiet, hilly but not too steep road.

Nikitsch

Turn right at the intersection in the direction of Lutzmannsburg.

Kroatisch-Minihof

Once you arrive turn left into the **Hauptstraße** (also called Glavna ulica). Keep left at the church and continue cycling to Lutzmannsburg. There you cross the Zagabach, take the next left after the next right leaning bend and keep going until you hit the **Hauptstraße (L 225)**, into which you turn left.

Lutzmannsburg

The old market town was originally located directly on the Rabnitz but was rebuilt in a higher position in the early 19th century after floods. This left only a small settlement next to the Catholic Church, however, it benefited from the increased flat area. The traditional wine-growing region has the highest temperatures and the most hours of sunshine in Austria, but he suffered from the closure of its neighbouring country and lost half of its population due to emigration. A certain amount of stabilisation has now occurred, particularly with the opening of a spa in 1994, which has been extended three times since then. This once largely peasant community is now one of the largest tourist destinations in Burgenland.

The Lutschburger Stuben restaurant, on the edge of town, catches people's attention with a wooden bicycle.

Monument near Lutzmannsburg

There you can also get brochures and maps. To get to the border, cycle over the village green.

TIP It is possible to stay a few nights at the Landgasthof Pacher in Hauptstr. 22 (main street) (✆ +43/2615/87212).

Pass a neoclassical Protestant church, a rarity in Catholic Austria, cycle through the thermal area and behind the Thermenhotel turn left into a road with a few cars sitting on it, although it is closed to motor traffic. Pass the crossing into Hungary, which is only open for cyclists and pedestrians. There you are reminded of the Iron Curtain time of barbed wire and watchtowers by a memorial stone which reads - "I was once a stranger and you welcomed me". A sculpture was built by students in honour of the last refugee who was shot at the Iron Curtain.

Sacred Heart Church in Köszeg

Kurt-Werner Schulz

The 36-year-old Kurt-Werner Schulz wanted to flee with his wife and 6-year-old son Johannes to Austria on the 22nd of August 1989. They had already passed the dilapidated border fence at Répcevis when a border guard wanted to arrest him. His wife and child ran away, Kurt-Werner Schulz struggled with the guard and in the ensuing scuffle was shot at point blank range and killed. From the drag marks on the ground, it was clear that the dead body had been dragged from Austrian territory into Hungary. A border violation by two Hungarian border guards was later confirmed. Whether this was intentional or accidental, could not be fully established.

After 20 years (Die Presse, 14.08.2009) an interview described the then 20-year-old border guard's situation as follows: "He let the woman and child simply run away but he tried to stop the man. Perhaps the greatest misfortune in the whole affair was that there was a second soldier nearby. He apparently then felt some pressure to do something. Had he been alone..."

Zsira

6 **Rimanóczy family Palace** (1739), now used as a retirement home.

Cycle through this long, stretched out place, pass the church and follow the road until the triangular intersection at which point you turn right towards Koszeg. Cross the **Répce** (Rabnitz) and continue until you reach the next stop on our tour.

Répcevis

Kurt-Werner Schulz was shot close to here.

The **Irottkö Natural Park** starts behind here and the route goes gently downhill.

Peresznye

The street names are also available in German.

Continue straight through the village on a quiet road.

Horvátzsidány

This part of the route requires a bit of power before it continues through a forest and then down to **Koszeg** (Güns). There you come across road 87, on the left of which you will find a train station (trains depart directly to Szombathely where you can change into many different directions). Cross the tracks, turn right, pedal a short while on the main road and turn left. Turn left at the next crossing and then continue straight towards the centre. Cross a stream and continue until you get to a main road where you must give way. There is a stone sculpture on the left side. There, turn right, pass the bus station and continue until you hit the main road, into which you turn right. Sty on this road and it will lead you to the main square.

Köszeg

- Distinctive Neo-Gothic **Sacred Heart Church** (19th century) with remarkable stained glass windows
- **Former Esterházy Castle**. Just like the market-place, it has also been referred to as Miklós Jurisics (Nikola Jurišì) since 1932. A bridge leads over the moat to the inner castle, which in 1777 took its present form after the great fire.
- **Large synagogue ruins**, Kiss János utca.
- **Market place Jurisics tér**: Town hall with an attractive façade (1597), at No. 11, the two-story pharmacy museum "Golden Unicorn" and the Heroes' (1932). Intended to remind is of the successful defence of the city during the third wave of the Turkish wars 400 years ago.
- **Portré**, on the main square, ✆ +36/94/363170, ✆ +36/30/2802406

After the collapse of the important textile industry, the "jewel box of Hungary" looked towards tourism for revitalising its fortunes. The potential was good, because the geographical position offers good recreation and winter sports possibilities. In the Koszeg Mountains, the foothills of the Alpine mountain range, there is a diverse range of nature and in the Austria-Hungarian National Park numerous trails, hiking trails and museums can be found. The architecture in the 12,000-inhabitant-strong city comes mainly from Habsburg 18th century. If you start your tour at Fö tér (main square), the

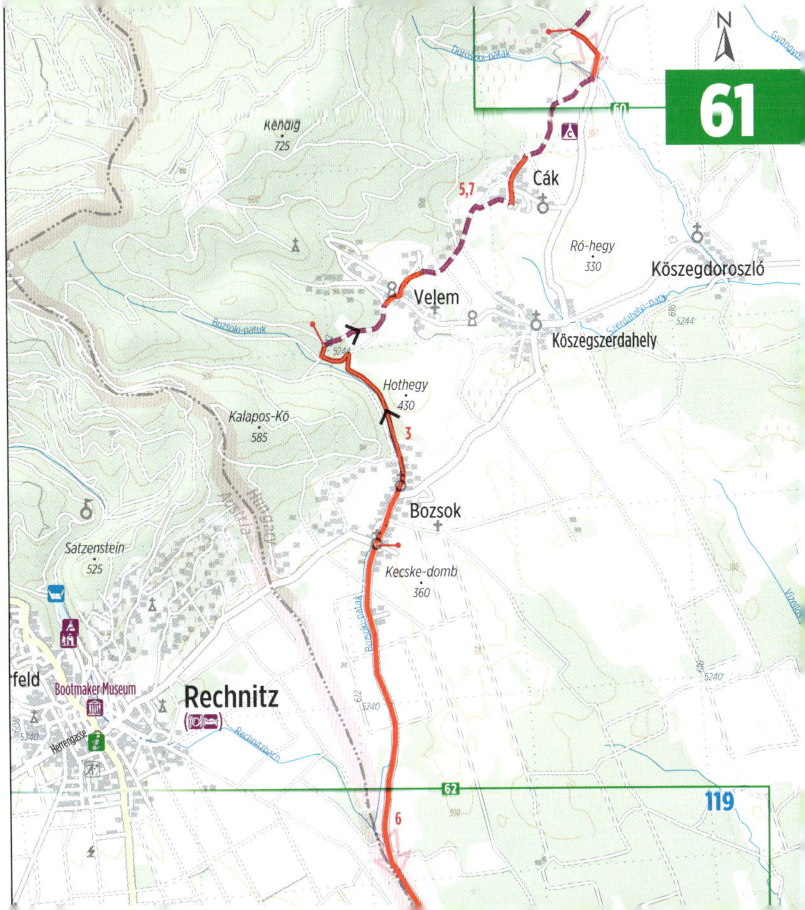

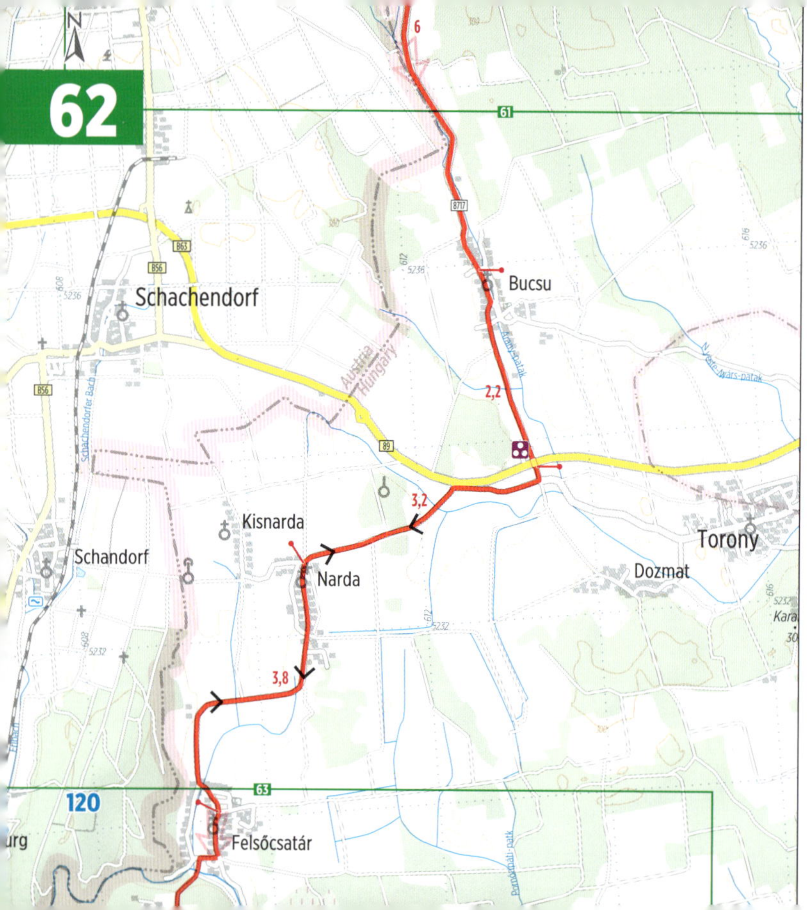

An abandoned building near Buscu, once occupied by former border troops

buildings will probably look much younger because the southern edge of the old town was only built in the late 19th century. This also applies to the Sacred Heart Church and the large-sized Heldentor (Heroes' Gate). Since 1777, the church bells have been rung on a daily basis in honour of the successful defence of the city against the Turks. The Heroes' Gate can be found on the southern side and is the main access point to the city. The actual marketplace is the significantly narrower Jurisics tér, named after the Croatian general, who the city has to thanks for the withdrawal of the Turkish attackers.

On the left hand side is the town hall which is still in use today. The Pharmacy Museum at number 11 is also interesting. The old houses seem very low down, but this is only because the square was increased by a layer of debris after several major fires. There are two very similar-looking churches in the middle, which almost looks as if they are rivals, which is probably because they were in the past. When after 1558 the German Lutherans became stronger, they excluded the Calvinists from using Jacob's Church. This forced them to build a competing church next door which was small but had a higher tower. The church was, however, soon after the Counter-Reformation in Catholic hands. This also affected the Gothic St. Jacob's Church, which has been repeatedly altered in the course of its existence, mostly with Baroque additions. In 1937 a mural from the time the church was built was found in the south part of the church. The former Esterházy castle *is accessible from Rajnis utca. Just beyond the eastern old town square there are some great synagogue ruins. The Jews of Koszeg belonged to the last groups of people who were deported to Auschwitz in 1944. 4,500 people died of typhoid in the local labour camp and the surviving 2,000 were driven on a death march over the Alps to the Ebensee concentration camp before the Soviet army could arrive.*

Köszeg gas chambers

Before the "death march" the sick were eradicated because the guards wanted to make good progress and did not want to fall into the hands of the rapidly advancing enemy. Therefore, in camp "Ziegelofen" the only gas chamber ever to be built on Hungarian territory was constructed and the sick prisoners in the Kőszeg "Ziegelofen" camp and from "Brauhaus" were murdered on 22 March 1945 and on 23 March 1945. As the last forced labourers were removed and put on a train to Steiermark on 25 March 1945 there were still a great number of patients remaining, who were subsequently shot or hanged by the guards so that the camp could be dissolved.

Roman aqueduct near Buscu

From Köszeg to Szentgotthárd 88 km

From the main square, cycle on the right side past the Sacred Heart Church and turn left behind the church into **Ady Endre utka**. Soon you will hit **Temetö utka** where the route is signposted to the right as a cycling path to Cák. From there it is straight uphill past a cemetery. Just past the town exit and the last few houses you

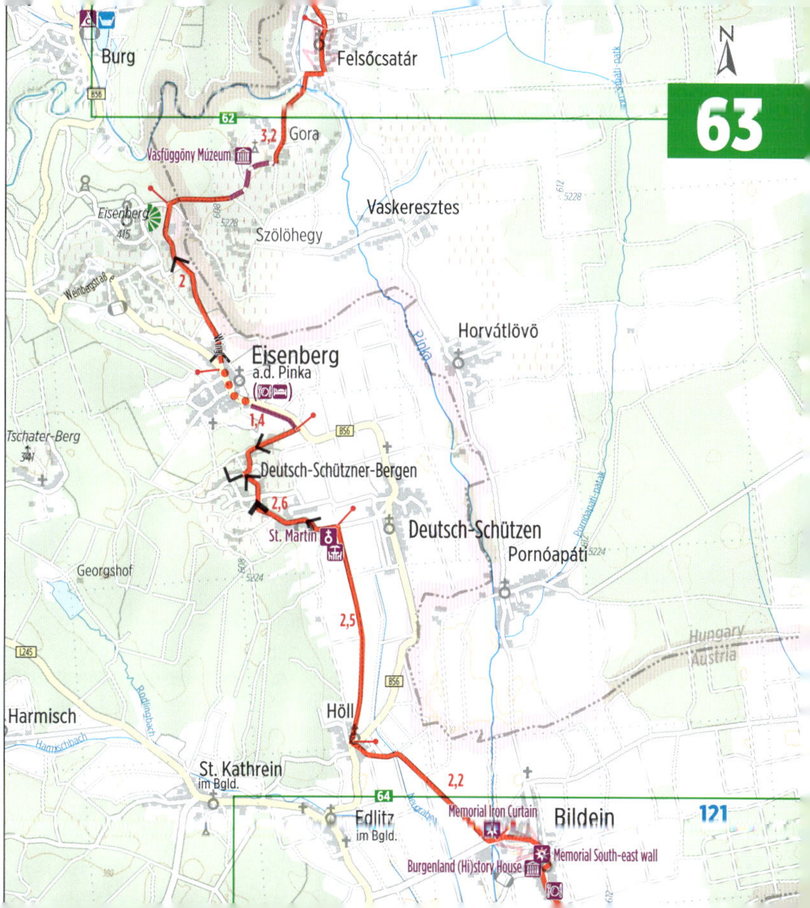

will find the **Gerikba route** signposted. Turn left into **Mohás út** left which is signposted to Cák, Velem and Bozsok. The solid path leads you through the natural park and is easily navigable. You will hit an asphalt road into which you turn left in the direction of Velem.

TIP A footpath will lead you to Cák.

Stay on the signposted **Gerikba route** until you hit a main road, into which you turn towards Szombathely. After a short ascent on the main road, turn right.

TIP The road through Cák and Velem to Bozsok is signposted with the symbol.

Watchtower in the Vasfüggöny Museum

There is also a campsite behind the right bend. Shortly after this the asphalted road disappears, the trail goes downhill and is then asphalted once again in Cák.

Cák

The route takes you right to Velem. Cák is not signposted, but stay on the road, from where you turn left. In the forest, the path is in good condition. At our next stop the road is paved.

Velem

At the next intersection, follow the yellow line straight. The route takes you slightly downhill. Eventually you will intersect with the **natural park route** which is sign-posted to the right. Immediately go left through the gate and follow the signs straight ahead towards Bozsok. You can expect little traffic on this unpaved but decent road. The bicycle sign has a yellow background, an S-curve with a C in front of it. Turn left onto the signposted and paved road, which unfortunately, at the moment of writing, is not in very good condition. A little while later, the road is not paved, but nonetheless easy to navigate. After the exit you will come to a triangular junction on a paved road, into which one turns left and this becomes the Weinstraße route which will lead you to Bozsok.

Bozsok

Bozsok is located just in front of the Austrian border. It once belonged to the Sibrik family who in 1552 had their possessions spread across two areas. Therefore, two castles were built in this area. The older was is located on the northern outskirts and is run as a castle hotel. The southern castle was taken over by the Batthyány family and is sadly now only recognisable as a ruin - similar to the former Trinity Church.

Cycle through Bozsok on an asphalt road.

EXCURSION Turn right to get to Rechnitz in Austria.

Rechnitz massacre

On 24 and 25 March 1945 around 200 Hungarian Jewish forced labourers were killed near Castle Rechnitz when about 600 people (mainly Hungarian Jews) were transported by rail from Kőszeg to the castle which was to be used in the construction of the south-east walls. For around 200 of them, exhaustion and illness meant they were unable to work and were therefore transported back to Rechnitz. Ten days before the Red Army reached Rechnitz, 180 of the sick were shot. The dead were buried by forced labourers, who themselves were also shot the following day. A memorial in Kreuzstadl reminds us of these terrible events.

Follow the signs straight to Bucsu and cycling through some beautiful countryside as you go, heading straight along the border. You will see a white border sign, the border stones, the border river with trees and pass an abandoned border troop building.

Bucsu

Follow the cycle path signs at the roundabout and turn right towards Szombathely. Cycle across the river and then turn immediately left again. On a quiet road look out of a board which gives information about a Roman aqueduct. Pass under the motorway that leads to Szombathely.

CONNECTION Direct trains to Sopron und Budapest leave from the station here.

Szombathely

The city is a shining example of the positive development in the border region following the EU expansion. Until the peaceful revolution, the city was rather discriminated against due to its poor infrastructure links. Now, however, it is a prosperous centre in western Hungary. The roots of the town date back to the Roman period. The reconstructed "Iseum" can still be found in the city centre today.

You can reach the old road from behind the motorway, into which you turn right. Where this street meets a new one, turn left and follow the signs to the Wall Museum.

Narda

Continue following the signs which will take you slightly uphill in the forest. You will have a beautiful view of the foothills of the Alps on the right side. Cycling downhill, pass a cemetery and a church and then continue straight along the main road.

Felsőcsatár

Turn right off the main road onto the road signposted to the museum. Cross a stream on a bridge, follow the signs and reach the museum.

Iron Curtain Museum (Vasfüggöny Múzeum)

Sándor Petofi, a former Hungarian border guard, set up an extensive private outdoor museum about the history of the Iron Curtain from 1949 to 1989. It includes a watchtower, fortifications and information boards. The museum places a particular emphasis on minefields and sentry guns. The friendly operator of the museum even gives tours himself.

Pass the museum and follow a paved road leading slightly uphill that at the end of the village merges into a forest path. Upon leaving the forest, the road is paved again and you immediately turn right into the paved border path which leads to the **Grenzweg** on the Austrian side, in which you turn left. There is a steep descent on the signposted **Weinidylle Cycle Route** (B 57) and **Jubilee Cycle Path** (R 1)..

Eisenberg a. d. Pinka

Leaving the place, continue on a separate bike path, keep right and follow the B57 and the R1 slightly uphill, and then later keep twice to your left and cycle downhill. Look out for an information panel behind

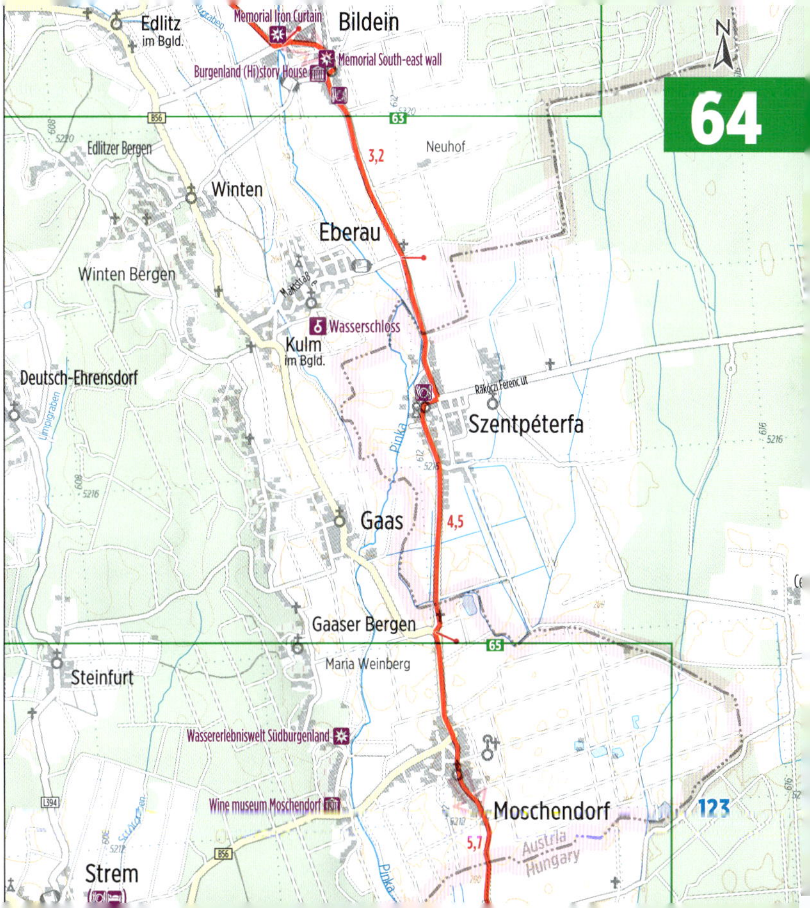

a sports field located to the right of the **St. Martin church** ruins informing us of a massacre on the 27th of March 1945 by German troops.

The Deutsch Schützen massacre

At the same time as Auschwitz was being liberated, Majdanek was being discovered and Budapest was being conquered by the Soviets, about 850 mostly Hungarian-born Jewish forced labourers were selected for the construction of a South-east wall. As the Red Army were making more and more progress, the labourers were forced to march to the Mauthausen concentration camp on 27 March 1945. The next morning 120 of them were brought to St. Martin Church. A little later, 57 of these forced labourers were shot and another while later, those too weak to walk were also shot. After the war, some of the Austrian Hitler Youth recorded what had happened there.

"Iron Curtain" memorial near Bildein

A statement on 31st August 1945 by the Vienna Public Prosecutor read: "Four military policemen and an SS man secured the space around the trenches. The Jews were ordered to put down their tools. They then had to come forward and give up their watches. [...] Once they had done this, the Jews were made to line up together in a ditch. Then the SS junior group leader Adolf Storms fired his pistol at them along with another SS guard and a military policeman armed with a submachine gun. Before the Jews went into a ditch, a woman begged the SS men on her hands and knees to not shoot. But this was in vain, and the SS men kicked several Jews into the ditch who were hesitating."

Martin Church in Deutsch Schützen

The surviving prisoners were marched towards Hartberg. On the 400-kilometre stretch along the South-east wall, another 125 such graves were later found. The mass grave in Deutsch Schützen was located on 23 August 1995 and officially declared a grave. A plaque on the church of St. Martin, where the Jews were rounded up, reminds us of these events.

The SS group lead Adolf Storms, named as being involved and now number 4 on the list of "most wanted Nazi criminals" by the Simon Wiesenthal Centre - lived undisturbed in Germany after the war until he was found by researcher Andreas Förster from Duisburg and convicted for 58 counts of of murder. Before the trial could begin, however, the 90-year-old died in 2010.

In Deutsch Schützen there is nowhere to stay, so turn right at St Martin's Church and then continue straight.

Höll

Pass the church, cross the main road and continue straight ahead on the signposted **eco/green bike path**.

Bildein

- **Burgenland (Hi)story House**, Florianig. 1, ✆ 03323/2597, ✆ 03323/21999, OT: Sat, Sun / holidays 14-17 hrs u n V. insights into the history of the youngest Austrian province from 1921 to today.
- **memorial "Iron Curtain"** opened in 2011
- **memorial for the South-east wall**
- **Rosemaries Bed and Breakfast**, Hauptstr. 113, ✆ +43/3323/21918

Cross the river and turn right into the second street which is the signposted **Grenzerfahrungsweg**. At the next corner you will see a memorial with an excavated trench, a bunker and underground tunnels informing us about the South-east wall and the last few years of the war.

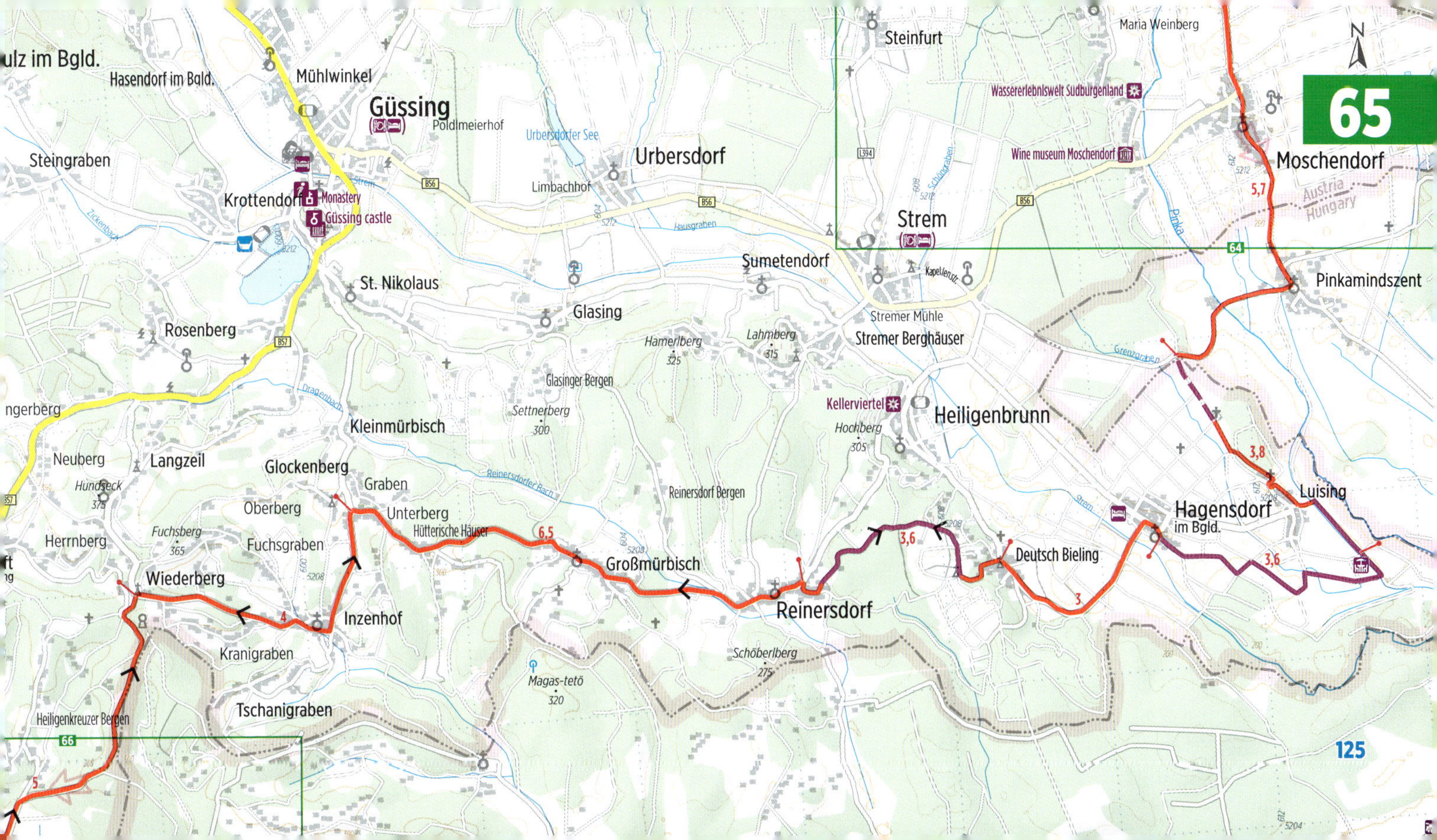
65
Güssing
Mühlwinkel
Hasendorf im Bgld.
Poldlmeierhof
Urbersdorfer See
Urbersdorf
Limbachhof
Steingraben
Krottendorf
Monastery
Güssing castle
St. Nikolaus
Glasing
Rosenberg
Steinfurt
Maria Weinberg
Wassererlebniswelt Südburgenland
Wine museum Moschendorf
Moschendorf
Strem
Sumetendorf
Austria
Hungary
Pinkamindszent
Stremer Mühle
Stremer Berghäuser
Hamerlberg
Lahmberg
Glasinger Bergen
Settnerberg
Kellerviertel
Heiligenbrunn
Hochberg
Kleinmürbisch
Neuberg
Langzeil
Glockenberg
Graben
Hundseck
Oberberg
Unterberg
Hütterische Häuser
Reinersdorf Bergen
Hagensdorf im Bgld.
Luising
Deutsch Bieling
Herrnberg
Fuchsberg
Fuchsgraben
Großmürbisch
Wiederberg
Inzenhof
Reinersdorf
Kranigraben
Schöberlberg
Magas-tető
Tschanigraben
Heiligenkreuzer Bergen
ngerberg
ulz im Bgld.
125

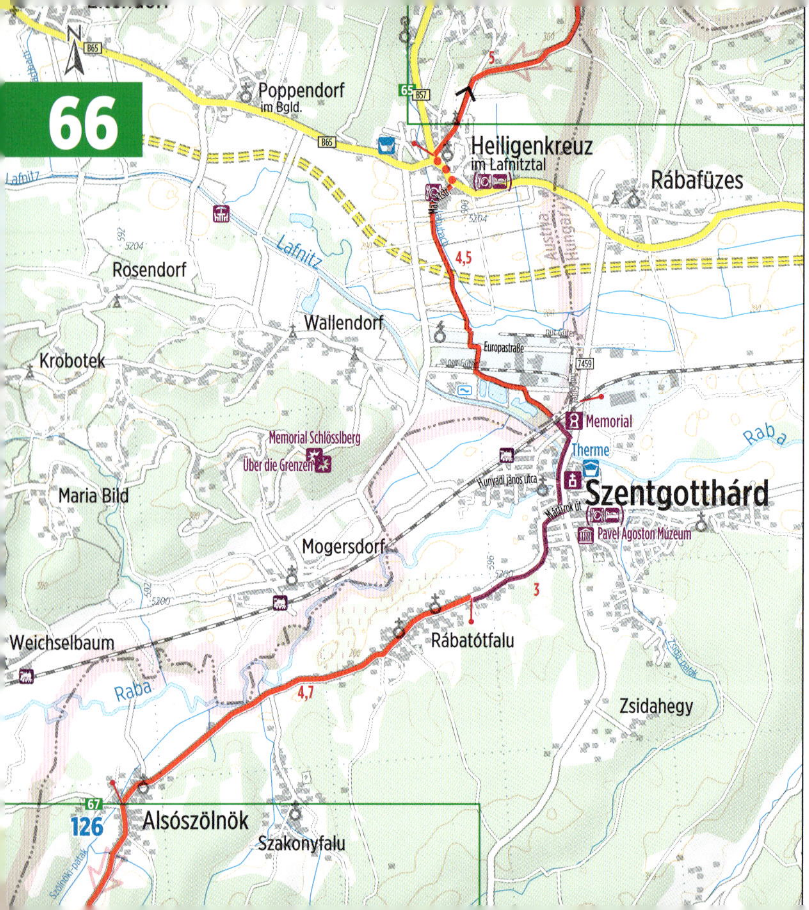

The South-East Wall

The German 6th Army's defeat in Stalingrad at the beginning of 1943 prompted the German leadership to take measures to secure the border of the German Empire. An empire safety system, called the South-east wall by Nazi propaganda, was to extend from Pressburg (Bratislava) over the northern edge of Lake Neusiedl, Odenburg, Schopan and Liebenstein on to Ljubljana and extend all the way to Trieste. The construction started in 1944 and the work was carried out by thousands of conscripted civilians, mostly old people, Hitler Youth, prisoners of war and Hungarian Jewish forced labourers. Only the simplest of tools were available that had to be brought by the local workers themselves. Wine cellars, churches and cemeteries were all to be included in the defence system. The South-east wall was not intended to be a single front. Trenches were created and anti-tank ditches, as here in Bildein, and sometimes shelters could only be made from wood. There were hardly any concrete positions. It was intended that the positions would be occupied by retreating German troops. As a last resort, in 1944 so-called Volkssturm battalions were formed consisting mainly of old men who were poorly trained and armed.

The Empire protection position was built using an immense amount of labour, working without machines and mostly in subhuman conditions and was provisional at best. Not only this, as the Red Army advanced towards the border, it was hardly

War memorial in Szentpéterfa

occupied by any regular troops. There were only a few times where the Red Army was stopped short in their advance.

At the memorial for the South-east wall turn left until you come across the **Grenzerfahrungsweg**, into which you turn right. A little later you can see a bed and breakfast on the left hand side in the main road. At the end of the road, at the transformer hut, turn right and cycle on the Grenzerfahrungsweg past the "Burgenland Story House". The jagged border demarcation causes you to enter and leave different countries multiple times. We pass Eberau in the direction of Szentpéterfa (HU).

Eberau

Large water palace (1400)

Abandoned border crossing Eberau-Szentepéterfa

Szentpéterfa (HU)

Eighty per cent of the people living in this place are Croatian.

Turn right at the guest house and left at the statue reminding us of the two world wars and follow the road to Moschendorf (A).

Moschendorf

The town was devastated three times during the Turkish wars over the course of 100 years. The creation of Burgenland led in 1921 to the fact that the town was surrounded on three sides by the state border. No wonder then, that from 1930 to 1938 so many residents emigrated to the USA because of the economic crisis. The village chronicle reports that today more people from Moschendorf live overseas than here.

Continue on to the border.

Pinkamindszent

At the roundabout in front of the Church, turn right towards Güssing. Cross the Pinka and after a rising S shaped bend, turn immediately left into a non-paved field road. Cycle through a small wood, then through some fields and later onto a paved road past a cemetery towards Luising.

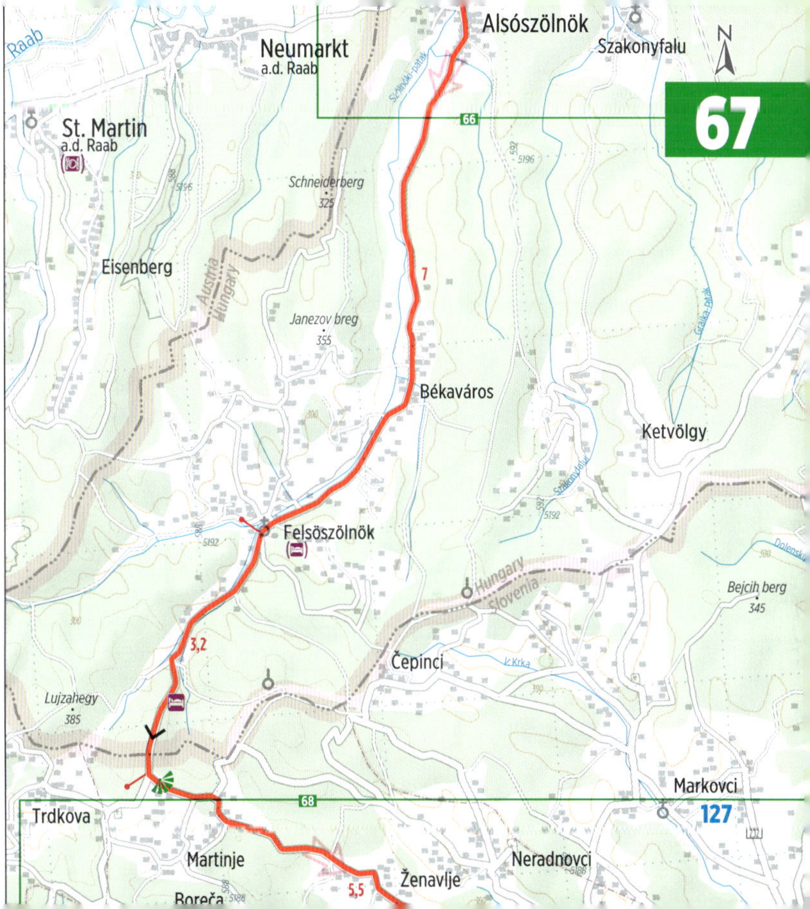

Luising

At the entrance to the village, follow the signposted **cycle path B 61** left, and behind turn right behind a babbling brook.

Continue on an asphalt road along the stream to the next bridge, where you turn right. Stay on the signposted **Schachtblumenrunde** or **ökoEnergieland bike path**, which makes a sharp turn, and goes around to the south side of Luising. Then turn immediately left again, remain on the signposted paved bike path and turn right at the next corner.

Church in Šalovci

Hagensdorf

Cycle past the church, turn left into the B 61 and cross the **Strem**. Ride in the direction of **Deutsch Bieling**, where you turn left at the church and the leave the B 61. Continue slightly uphill and then downhill.

Reinersdorf

Behind here, you have to first deal with a fairly steep incline. It then becomes more undulating as you go through **Großmürbisch** and **Unterberg**. Later on the route takes you left downhill.

Inzenhof

At a sharp right bend in the road you will arrive at the place and at **Wiederberg** turn left. You will then travel downhill on the **bike path R 1**.

Heiligenkreuz

There, turn left into **Untere Hauptstraße**, follow the Jubilee cycle path and turn right at the war memorial into **Marktstraße**, in which the Pummer guest house is located (refreshments and accommodation available). Behind the hotel, turn left onto the **L 252** that is later called the **Heiligenkreuzer Landstraße** and continue across some fields into the **Neuheiligenkreuz industrial area**. Upon reaching a biomass power plant, leave the jubilee cycle path, turn left and cycle past the lakes.

Where the road bends off to the left, cycle on the non-paved road straight across the tracks and then across the border to Hungary. There is a memorial, which was built in the meadow 20 years after the fall of the Iron Curtain. After crossing another set of tracks, join the bike path on the main road, which you follow over the river Raab. You will find Szentgotthárd train station on the right side providing you with direct trains to Sopron, Szombathely and Graz.

Szentgotthárd

These days, the city is the centre of the Slovenian minority in Hungary and owes its origin to the eponymous Cistercian monastery from 1183. The fortress like monastery equipped with a moat was destroyed in 1605 while the Castle Garden is now the city's largest public park. After their return, the Cistercians built a Baroque church in 1750, which as the third largest church in Hungary dominates the cityscape. The new monastery was closed in 1950. The opening of the railway heralded an economic boom, which continued until the First World War. Thereafter, the business side of the city lost the hinterland due to boundary changes in 1921 and the Iron Curtain in 1945 and slipped into obscurity. Since the opening of the border and EU accession, the tide has turned once again. The Industrial Park based in the north is

Border crossing Szentgotthárd

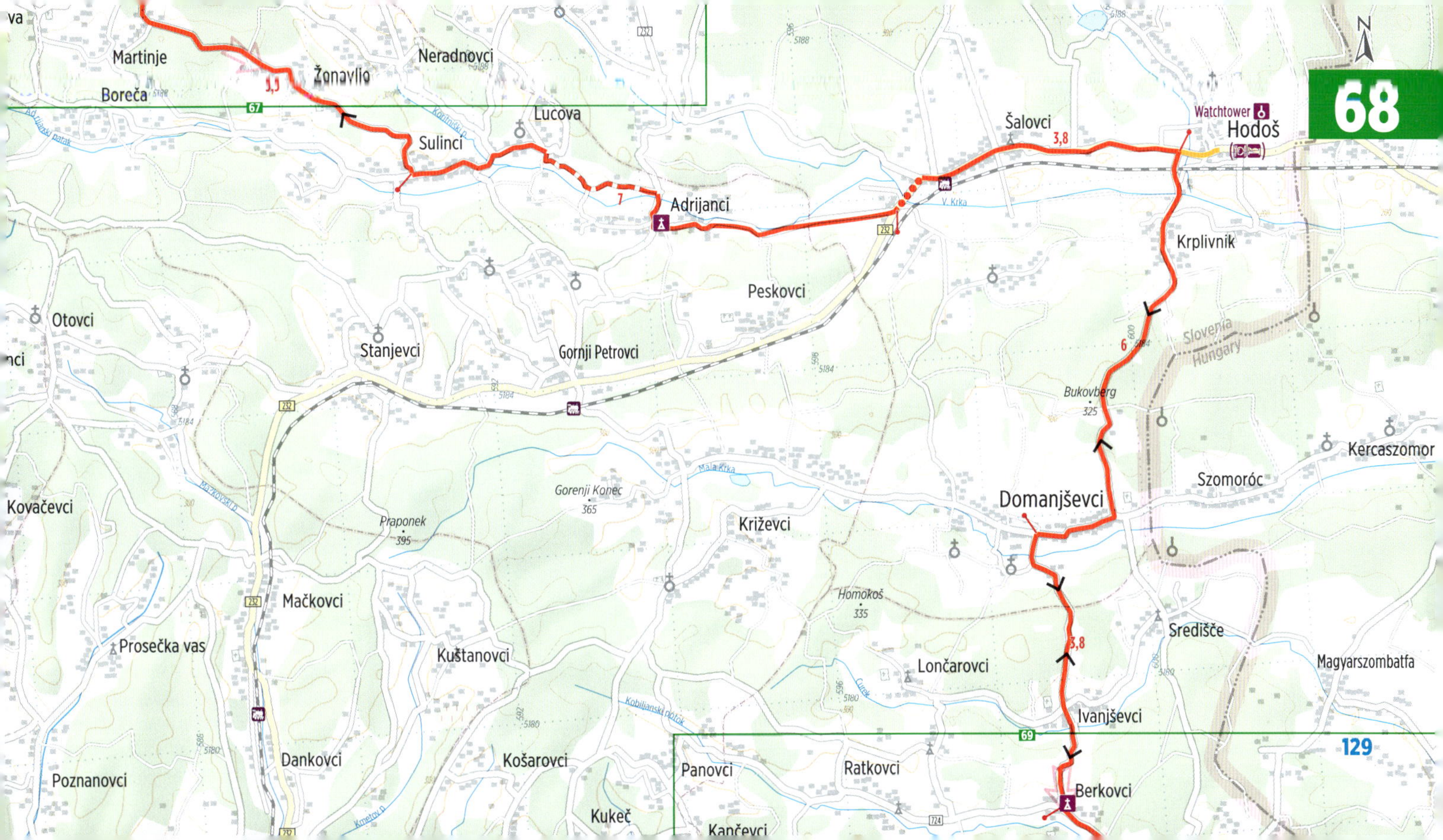
68
129
Martinje
Neradnovci
Žonavlje
Boreča
Lucova
Sulinci
Šalovci
Watchtower
Hodoš
Adrijanci
V. Krka
Krplivnik
Peskovci
Otovci
Stanjevci
Gornji Petrovci
Slovenia
Hungary
Bukovberg
325
Kercaszomor
Szomoróc
Domanjševci
Mala Krka
Gorenji Konec
365
Kovačevci
Praponek
395
Križevci
Mačkovci
Homokoš
335
Središče
Prosečka vas
Kuštanovci
Lončarovci
Magyarszombatfa
Kobiljanski potok
Ivanjševci
Dankovci
Košarovci
Panovci
Ratkovci
Berkovci
Poznanovci
Kukeč
Kančevci
232
67
69
724
3,8
7
6

a cross-border joint venture with Holy Cross and a thermal park attracts visitors from far and wide.

From Szentgotthárd (HU) to Hodoš (SL) 33 km

Stay on the bike path on the main road, cycle past the large church and at the next roundabout follow the signs right towards Felsöszölnök. On a fairly flat road, continue towards **Rábatótfalu**.

Alsószölnök

Stay on a nice and flat road in the valley.

Felsöszölnök

Julianna Panzio, ✆ +36/94/434428, ✆ +36/20/3132539, after leaving the village

The route takes you initially uphill. Turn left directly behind the border in the direction of Hodoš.

At the top of the hill you can enjoy a beautiful view and then continue downhill through **Ženavlje**.

Sulinci

Turn left onto the main road. When leaving follow the sign left to Lucova and behind Bach **Koritniški potok** turn right. Once in **Lucova**, do not follow the paved road across the river, but instead turn left into the unpaved but well-maintained road. Continue straight and at the end of the road turn right. Cycle over the river.

Adrijanci

Beautiful **little church** (1928)

Turn left into the paved road and continue to Šalovci. Soon you will hit road **232**, into which one turns left. Cross the river **Velika Krka**, then turn right and pass the train station.

Šalovci

Stay on the main road, cycle past the church and follow the next roundabout signs to Hodoš.

Hodoš

The municipality consists of the two villages Hodoš and Krplivnik and with around 400 residents is the smallest independent municipality in Slovenia. Due to the fact that most of the population come from Hungary, the place name signs and other public inscriptions in the town are bilingual. It is possible to visit Hodoš and spend the night there. There is a café opposite the train station which is also open on Sundays. Direct trains to Ljubljana and Budapest are available from the station.

There is an old Yugoslavian watchtower east of Hodoš. The accompanying land was purchased by the city with the aim to restore the guard tower. A former military camp was converted into a hostel. Groups as well as individuals can stay there.

Yugoslavian watchtower near Hodoš

The History of Slovenia

The Slovenes as a western South Slavic nation came into being at the end of the 8th century and beginning of the 9th century under Frankish, later Habsburg, rule. Until the end of World War I, the Slovene settlements in Krain, Styria, Carinthia, Gorizia-Gradisca and Istria belonged to the Austrian half of the Habsburg Monarchy, where there was not a Slovenian administrative unit. The beginnings of an ethnic-cultural awareness among Slovenians go back to the Reformation and Counter-Reformation. Under the reign of Empress Maria Theresa (1740-1780) compulsory education concerning Slovene teaching was introduced in the first grade. Her son, Emperor Joseph II. succeeded in 1782 abolished serfdom and granted everyone the right to freedom of religion. The first Slovenian newspaper appeared in 1797. As a result of all these measures, the ethnic and cultural awareness was strengthened among Slovenians. However, the formation of a nation proved to be extremely difficult, because the majority of the nobility and the bourgeoisie was German or loyal to German culture. The second half of the 19th century saw an increase in confrontation with the German hegemony in politics, economy and culture and gradually a Slovenian Emancipation nationalism emerged from the Slovene heartland Krain and its

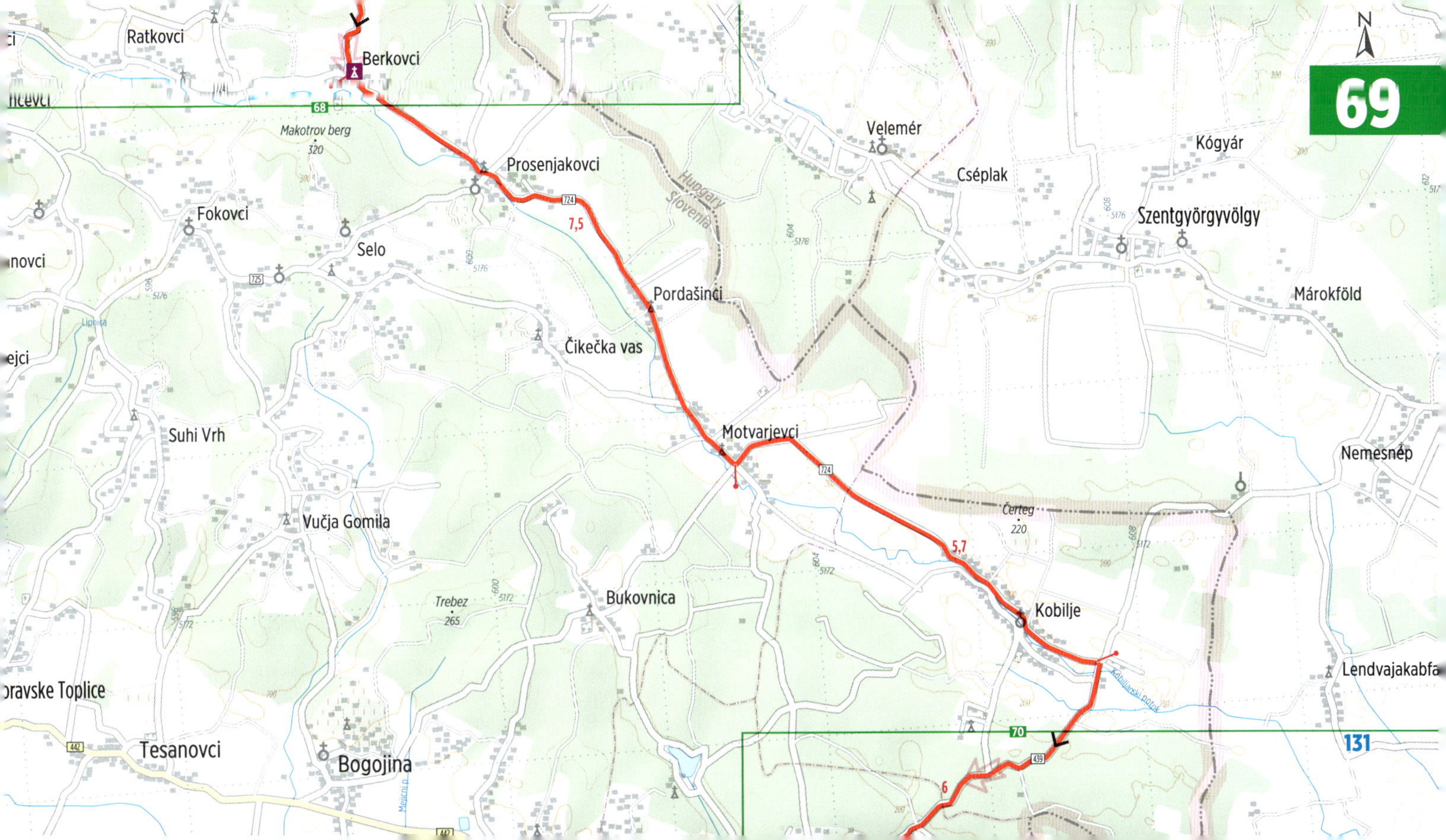

69
Ratkovci
Berkovci
Makotrov berg
320
Prosenjakovci
Fokovci
Selo
7,5
Pordašinci
Čikečka vas
Suhi Vrh
Motvarjevci
Vučja Gomila
Bukovnica
Trebez
265
Kobilje
5,7
Čerteg
220
Velemér
Cséplak
Kógyár
Szentgyörgyvölgy
Márokföld
Nemesnép
Lendvajakabfa
Hungary
Slovenia
Tesanovci
Bogojina
6
68
70
131
724
725
439
442

capital Ljubljana. This led to the South Slav unification movement and contributed to the First World War. The Slovenes fought on Austria-Hungary's side and the collapse of the Habsburg Empire on 1.12.1918 led to the creation of the first Yugoslav state, that with the 1922 border treaty Rapallo had to cede territory to Italy. In the "Kingdom of Serbs, Croats and Slovenes", that was called the "Kingdom of Yugoslavia" in 1929, in the face of increased Italian territorial demands and the struggle for the unification of all Slovenians – including those in Austria – politicians favoured a strong Yugoslavia and with this were able to achieve a de facto autonomy. Due in a small part to Habsburgian heritage, Slovenia was the most economically and culturally developed region within Yugoslavia. The resulting wealth gap between North and South was one of the great unsolved problems of the two Yugoslav states and continued to cause regional conflicts that were additionally exacerbated by cultural differences and religion including Catholicism versus Orthodoxy and the language. During World War II, after the Yugoslav capitulation in April 1941, Slovenia was divided up between Germany and Italy, with a small part also going to Hungary. Rigorous attempts to reduce the nationalism of the population and the reign of terror by the occupying powers only strengthened the resistance of the population and the communist-dominated National Liberation Movement "Osvobodilna Fronta (OF)" quickly gained the upper hand under Josip Broz Tito. He managed to drive out the German and Italian occupiers from occupied Yugoslavia without relying on Soviet support.

After the war, Slovenia became a republic in the socialist Yugoslavia, which under Tito, was composed of six republics with two autonomous provinces (Kosovo and Vojvodina). Tito's Unity Party ruled the state which included five nationalities, four languages, three religions and two alphabets. He was not only adamant in his opposition to Stalin's hegemony, but also wary of Western influence.

According to the terms of the Paris Peace Conference, a part of the coastal region was returned to Slovenia in 1947 and then after the London Agreement of 1954 the southern part of the Free State of Trieste, except the city of Trieste itself. Slovenia strengthened its national cultural and educational insti-

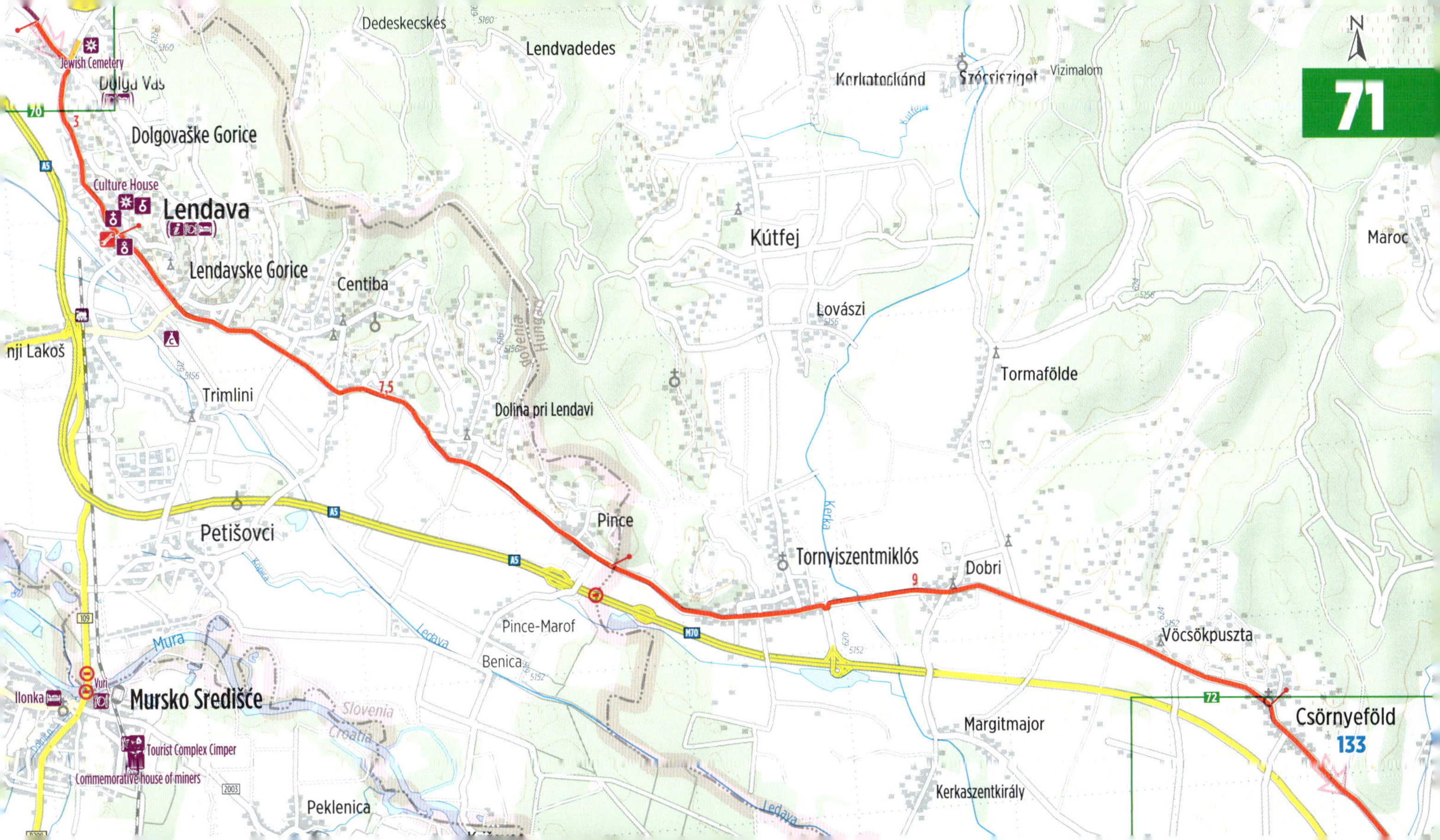

71
Dedeskecskés
Lendvadedes
Szécsisziget
Vizimalom
Jewish Cemetery
Dolga Vas
Dolgovaške Gorice
Culture House
Lendava
Lendavske Gorice
Centiba
Kútfej
Maroc
Lovászi
Tormaföld
nji Lakoš
Trimlini
Dolina pri Lendavi
Slovenia
Hungary
Petišovci
Pince
Tornyiszentmiklós
Dobri
Pince-Marof
Benica
Mura
Ledava
Kopica
Kerka
Völcsökpuszta
Vuri
Ilonka
Mursko Središće
Slovenia
Croatia
Tourist Complex Cimper
Commemorative house of miners
Margitmajor
Csörnyeföld
Kerkaszentkirály
Peklenica
A5
M70
70
72
3
7,5
9

tutions in socialist Yugoslavia. Many of its politicians were part of the reform wing of the Communist League and sought independence from the other republics. With the constitutional amendments in the late 1960s / early 1970s and the Yugoslav constitution of 1974 the powers of the republics were significantly strengthened at the expense of the federal government.

The solidarity of the Slovenes began to unravel along with the rest of Yugoslavia during the 1980s as the mismanagement and the regional conflicts continued in Yugoslavia alongside the struggle for the equality of the Slovene language. This was made worse by the fact that an external threat was no longer recognisable to bind them. On April 8th, 1990 Slovenia's first free elections on Yugoslav soil were held and on the 23rd of December 88.5 percent of Slovenes voted for independence with a turnout of 85 per cent. Independence was declared on the 25th of June.

However, this prompted an invasion by the Yugoslavian national army. This was successfully rebuffed by the Slovenian Territorial Defence in the "ten-day war" who ensured that Slovenia became a sovereign and democratic state. Since 2004, the country's two million inhabitants have been members of NATO and the EU. Since 2007 it has also been a member of the European Monetary Union and the Schengen agreement. The small country held the first Presidency of the European Council in 2008.

From Hodoš to Lendava — 43 km

In Hodoš cycle along the bridge over the railway tracks and then over an undulating path towards **Krplivnik**.

Domanjševci

Turn left towards Prosenjakovci and cycle through **Ivanjševci**.

Berkovci

Little old **wooden church**

Keep left as you cycle through here.

Prosenjakovci

At the crossroads, cycle straight ahead and after **Pordašinci** you will reach **Motvarjevci**, where you turn left towards Kobilje. The route is flat, has no traffic and you can see the edge of the forest, the Hungarian landmarks.

TIP: The numerous raised blinds were built for hunters, not for the military.

Kobilje

Cross through the town, turn right at the exit, cross Kobiljanski potok and continue in the direction of Dobrovnik.

Dobrovnik

The name was first mentioned in 1270, later as a market and then even as a city. In the second half of the 19th century and beginning of the 20th century, it enjoyed a relatively large growth in population, and crafts (pottery) and trade flourished. The first inn was opened in 1878 and in 1911 a brick factory was completed, which remained in operation until 1979. Three quarters of the 1,400 inhabitants belong to the Hungarian minority. In the economically difficult time during the First World War a sawmill brought progress to the village. 1930 saw a post office in Dobrovnik, the first telephone exchange, and after the Second World War electricity came to the city.

TIP: If you want to visit Dobrovnik, turn right at the roundabout towards Moska Sobota. After about 1km you will see two restaurants where you can drink some coffee and have a bite to eat, but cannot stay the night. If you wish to stay, go straight at the roundabout until you reach a guesthouse.

In Dobrovnik, turn left at the roundabout towards Lendova and cycle on a street with little traffic towards **Žitkovci**. Once you arrive, turn right at the small church on the right.

Kamovci

Use the bicycle path on the left side of the road until you reach **Genterovci**. The bicycle path is missing within the village itself, but behind the village it starts up again. The shared pedestrian and cycle path goes through **Mostje** (Hungarian Hívdég) and is then set further apart from the road.

TIP: Unfortunately, the bike path is repeatedly interrupted because the bridges over the streams and rivers were built too narrow. When or even if these gaps in the bike path will be filled, is currently unknown.

Cross the motorway on the bike path and behind the roundabout you can find the bike path again on the left side. Once you arrive in **Dolga Vas**, the

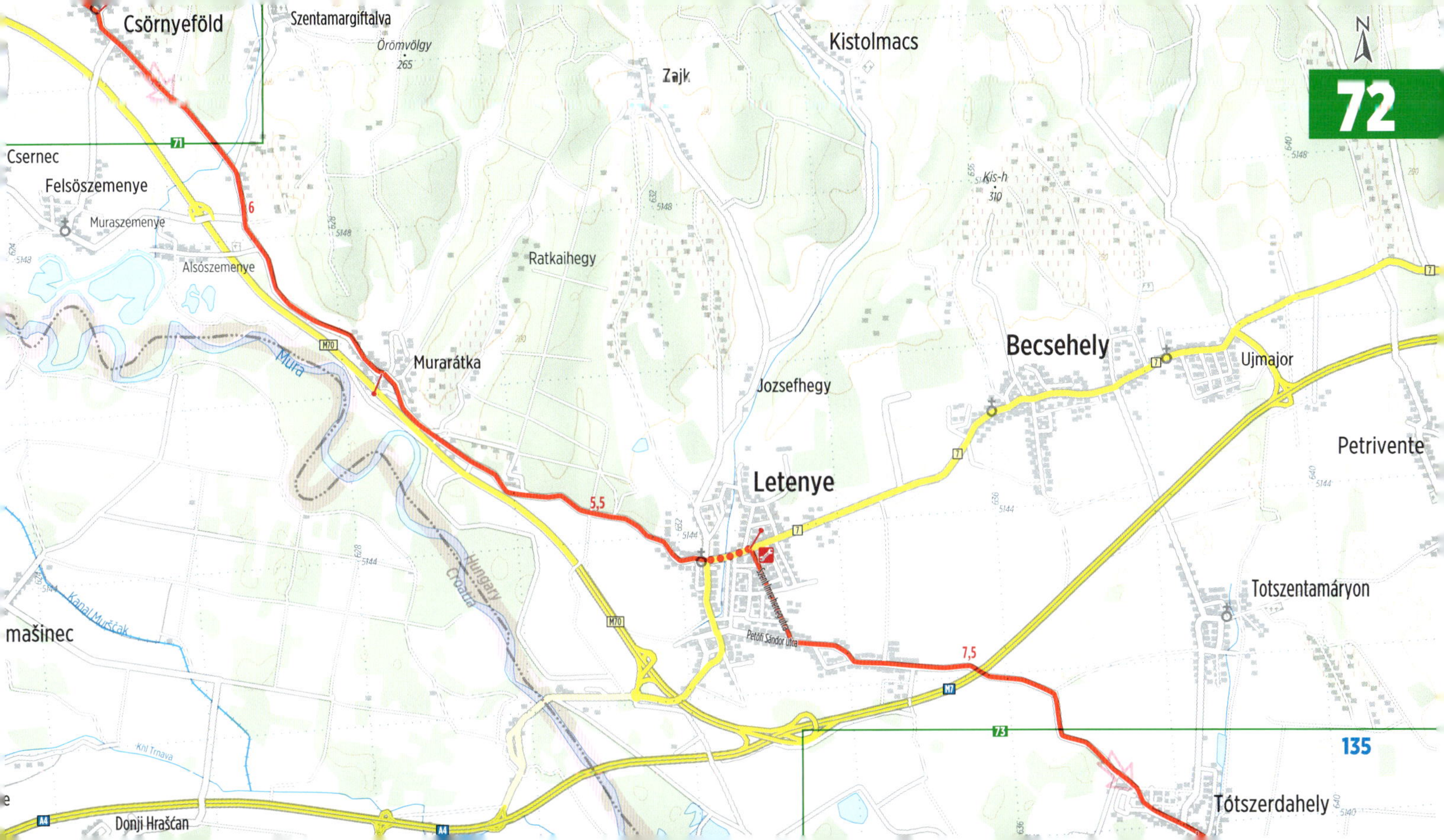

72
Csörnyeföld
Szentamargiftalva
Örömvölgy
265
Kistolmacs
Zajk
Csernec
Felsöszemenye
Muraszemenye
Alsószemenye
Ratkaihegy
Kis-h
310
Murarátka
Mura
Jozsefhegy
Becsehely
Ujmajor
Letenye
Petrivente
Hungary
Croatia
Kanal Muršćak
Totszentamáryon
mašinec
Petőfi Sándor utca
Knl Trnava
Tótszerdahely
Donji Hrašćan
135
6
5,5
7,5
71
73
M70
M7
A4
7

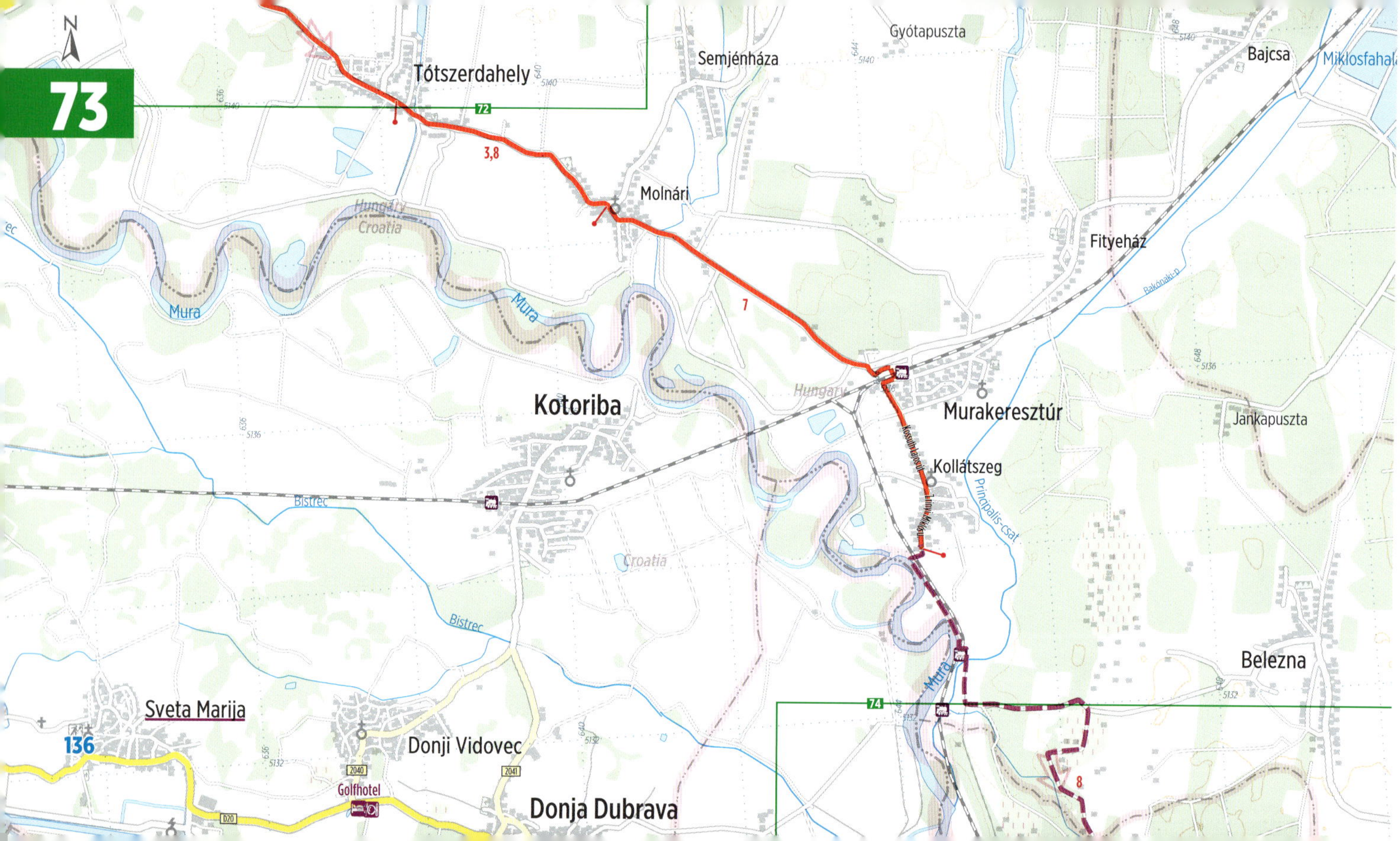
73
72
Tótszerdahely
Semjénháza
Gyótapuszta
Bajcsa
3,8
Molnári
Hungary
Croatia
Mura
Mura
Fityeház
Bakonaki-p.
7
Hungary
Kotoriba
Murakeresztúr
Jankapuszta
Kollátszeg
Principális-csat.
Bistrec
Croatia
Bistrec
Belezna
Mura
74
8
Sveta Marija
136
Donji Vidovec
2040
2041
Golfhotel
D20
Donja Dubrava

74
Surd
Somogybükkösd
Legrad
Murmündung
Pansion Legradanka
Hungary
Croatia
Mura
Drava
Visszafolyó-p
Porrog
Porrogszentpál
Porrogszentkirály
Örtilos
Zákányfalu
Zákány
Đelekovec
War memorial
Gyékényes
Dózsa utca
8
3,6
3,6
7
73
75
137
20
41

Wayward Culture House in Lendava

cycle path will end. If you like, you can stop here and spend the night. At the crossroads, turn right to Lendava.

EXCURSION Approximately 300m to the left there is the well-maintained Jewish cemetery of Lendava, the only one in the region that has remained intact. The missing gravestones are testament to the fact that the cemetery does not have many visitors these days.

Continue straight, passing through the long town and past the large church and tourist office.

Lendava

Turizem Lendava d.o.o., Glavna ulica 38, 9220 Lendava, ✆ +386/2/5788390

St. Catherine's church, marketplace. The church has a double onion-shaped roof and has a beautiful Baroque pulpit.

The **castle** is particularly impressive because of its size and elevated position. It houses a museum with various exhibitions, including one on the late Bronze Age, because a lot of things have been found on the Western Pannonian plain from this period.

Wayward Culture House (1991), opposite the castle. The Hungarian architect Imre Makovecz (*1935) mainly used natural materials, referring to design elements influenced by history and mythology surrounding the place. He therefore obtained a highly impressive portfolio that occasionally recalls the great Antoni Gaudí. The building is used for theatre, music and dance events, but also for conferences and - among other places - also for the summer doll festival.

42 percent of the people in the easternmost municipality in Slovenia at the beginning of the peninsular speak Hungarian. Many major companies in the chemical and petrochemical industries have developed in the transit station surrounding the gas and oil pipelines.

TIP Near the market square there is a fully restored synagogue – one of only two in the whole of Slovenia. It is used for exhibitions and events.

Von Lendava (SL) nach Murakeresztúr (HU) 43 km

Continue on the road for 7km past some vineyards.

Pince

Cross the border here and cycle parallel to the motorway in the direction of Letenye.

TIP After the motorway was completed the street was closed to truck and heavy vehicle traffic and now very few cars are in evidence as well. Nevertheless, it is prohibited for cyclists to use this road and they are sometimes diverted to narrow bike paths.

Tornyiszentmiklós

Behind this cross the **Cserta (Kerka)** river and cycle past some fields and vineyards.

Csörnyeföld

The area to the right belongs in part to the Mura flood plains.

After **Murarátka**, where the motorway and country roads are squeezed between the hills and the Muraschleifen pass, the valley widens a little again and we continue to Letenye. Soon you will come across an intersection and main road 7. Cycle straight along the main road towards Budapest (**Bajcsy-Zsilinsky utca**).

Letenye

Gyula Kovacs, Bajcsy-Zsilinsky utca 41, ✆ +36/30/2387753

Here you can find the most fragrant, fresh white wines that you can taste in many an old cellar. After repeated plundering by Turkish troops and the heavy losses to the population due amongst other things to the plague, the city lost its status as a market town. An important border crossing to Croatia has existed since 1923, and since the 1930s, Letenye has been on the up. In 1989 Letenye's status was raised to that of city.

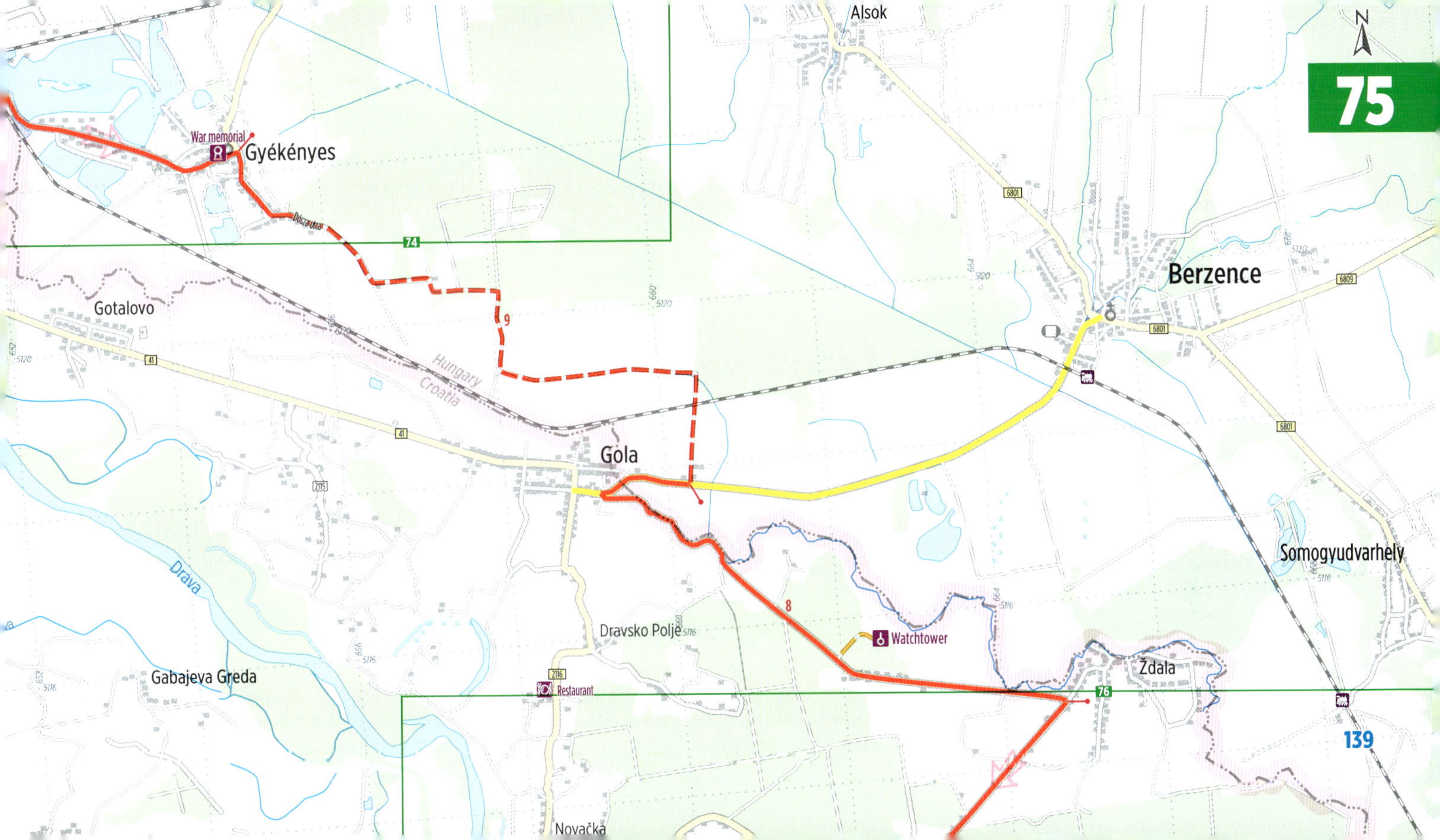
75
N
Alsok
War memorial
Gyékényes
Dózsa utca
74
9
Gotalovo
Hungary
Croatia
Berzence
6801
6809
Gola
41
2115
8
Watchtower
Drava
Dravsko Polje
Somogyudvarhely
Ždala
76
Gabajeva Greda
2116
Restaurant
Novačka

Turn right into **Szent Imre herceg utca** and at the end of this street turn left into **Petőfi Sándor utca** towards Murakeresztúr. Cross the motorway.

Tótszerdahely

Cycle through Tótszerdahely until you get to Molnári.

Molnári

Here you turn right at the beautifully situated little church. Cross a small river and you will see ahead of you overhead train power lines.

After the left bend turn right onto the paved road. You will see a tower. Continue cycling parallel to the tracks. At the next possibility turn right into a non-paved road, keep to the right and cross the tracks to reach the road. The train station can be found on the left side, where you can catch direct trains to Budapest and Zagreb.

Murakeresztúr

Vom Murakeresztúr (HU) to Gola (HR) — *34 km*

The main route takes you right and after a left bend, cycle on **Kossuth Lajos út** in a southerly direction. Cycle right past the church, into **Zrinyi Miklós utka**, at the end of which turn right into the unpaved but decent path. Cross the railway line and behind the tracks, turn immediately left, where you will be between the border river and the railway. Just before the station in **Belezna** you cross the tracks again and the little stream via a wooden bridge. Continue over St. Michael's mount on the forest path which is signposted with a red cross and easy to travel on, with the stream following alongside the path. Follow this red cross, taking a left turn through the forest and a little while later you will pass a vineyard. Continue straight once you arrive at two houses belonging to the vineyards. Shortly thereafter, the path will take you right into a path running through a meadow, then after a short time turns into a well-maintained field road. Where trail with the red cross goes right, take the parallel and wider path.

TIP: This is easier to cycle.

Church in Gyékényes

After 6 km through the forest you will come to a wide, unpaved road, into which you turn left and which after a little while turns into a paved road. Pass **Ettero Vilag Turistas Falloz** and a white church. Take the seldomly-traveled road, marked with the red cross, to reach Őrtilos.

Őrtilos

Within Őrtilos, turn right at the first possibility. At the next possibility to turn right, do so again and then immediately left again. Before the train tracks, the path takes you left. Ride parallel to the tracks.

Zákány

CENTRE: Keep going until you hit a road behind the station that leads straight to the centre, where you can shop and take a break.

Leaving the place, turn right, cross the railroad tracks and reach Gyékényes. At the end of the road turn right, passing a war memorial commemorating the First World War and a church.

Gyékényes

On **Dosza utca** cycle past cornfields and after a right bend you will come across an unpaved but decent road. After a long stretch through some cornfields you will come across a paved road, into which one turns right. After a left and a right turn cross the railroad tracks and look out for a paved road on the other side, into which one turns right. Pass the Croatian-Hungarian border, turn right and reach Gola.

CENTRE: Continue straight to reach the town centre.

Gola

The history of Croatia

In 879, Prince Branimir was approached by Pope John VIII with the "dux Croatorum", which at the time amounted to a recognition

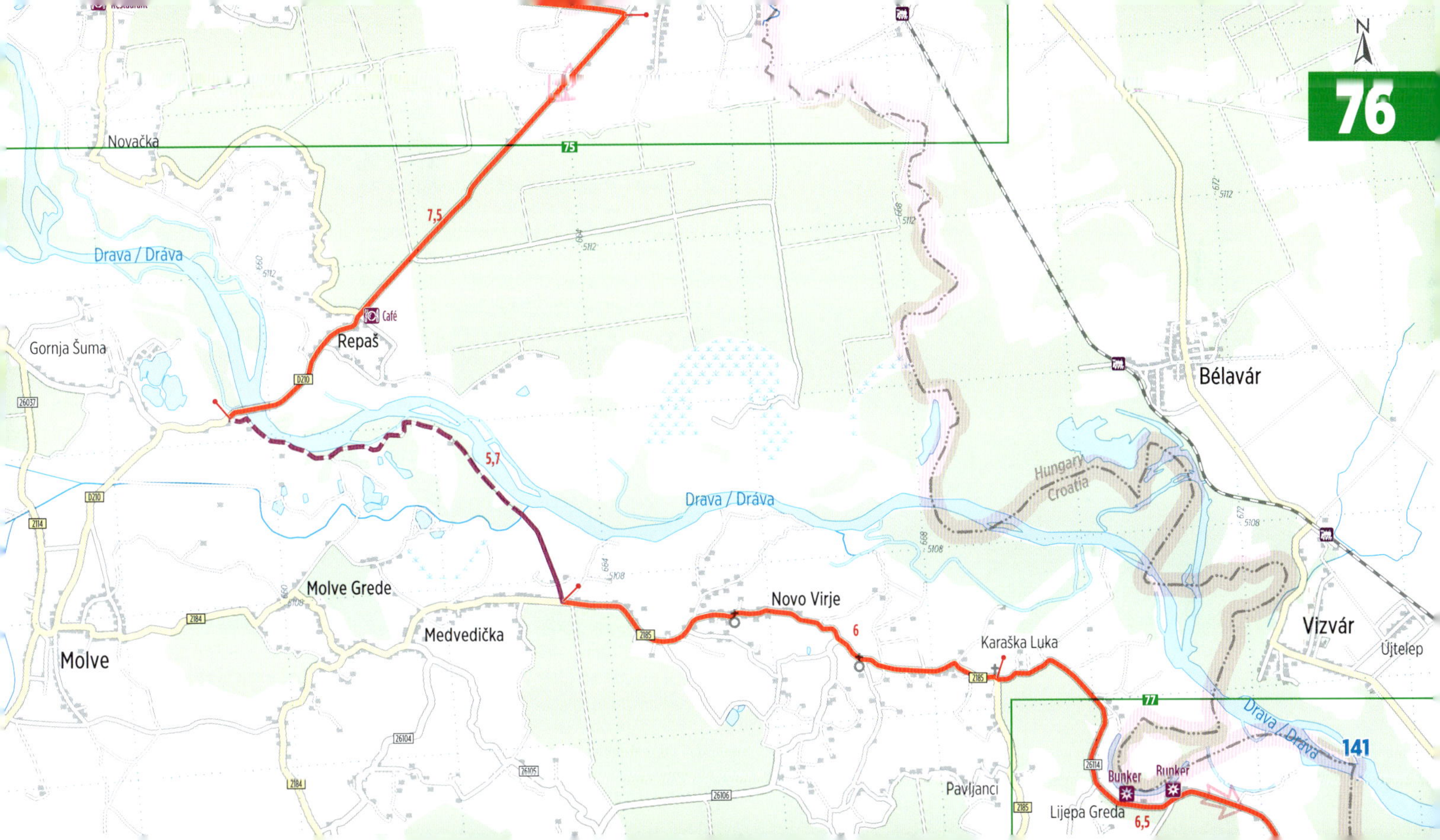

76
75
77
141
Novačka
Drava / Dráva
Café
Repaš
Gornja Šuma
D210
26037
7,5
5,7
Bélavár
Hungary
Croatia
Molve Grede
Novo Virje
6
Medvedička
Molve
2184
2185
Karaška Luka
Vízvár
Újtelep
26104
26105
26106
26114
Pavljanci
Bunker
Lijepa Greda
6,5
2114

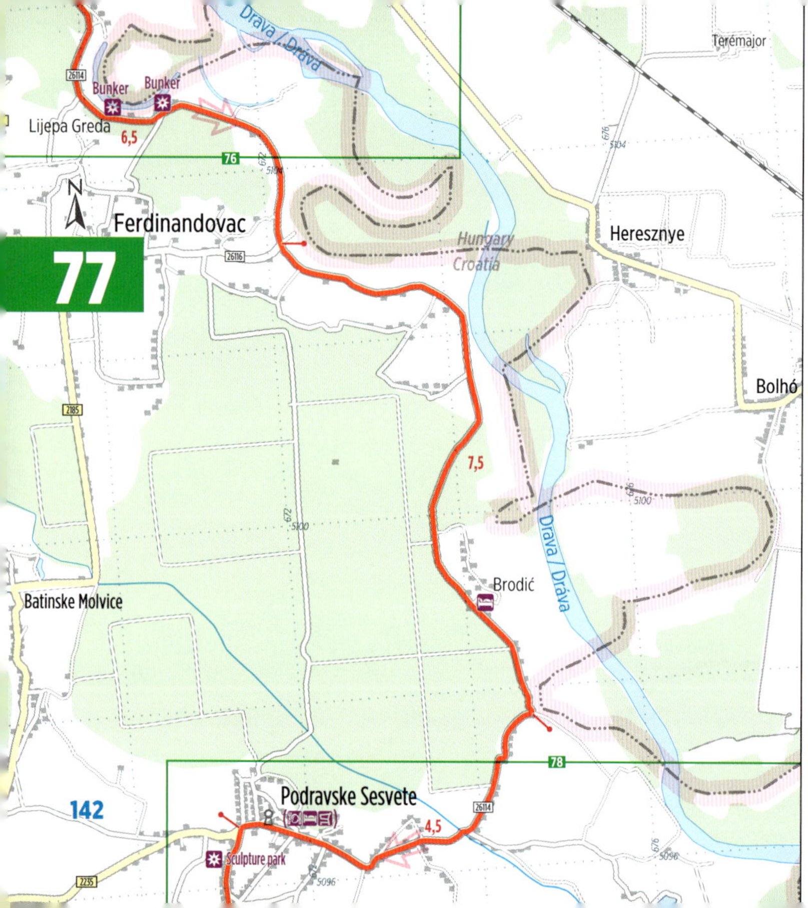

of the medieval Croatia. King Tomislav (910-928) was the first king of Croatia and was crowned in 925. As a result of the coronation of the Hungarian king Koloman as Croatian king in Biograd near Zadar in 1102, Croatia entered into an agreement (pacta conventa) and union with Hungary. This Union remained for the most part in various different forms with just a few interruptions until 1918. Large areas of Hungary and Croatia came under the rule of the Ottoman Empire (1451-1699) in the mid-15th century. After the Napoleonic Wars in 1815, some parts of Croatia came under Austrian rule, others, such as the Kingdom of Croatia-Slavonia, belonged to the Hungarian part. In the second half of the 19th century the desire for more self-determination rights grew among the Croatian population.

After the First World War, Croatia began to detach itself from the Austro-Hungarian Empire. Croatian territories along the Adriatic coast were occupied by Italy, as promised by the terms in the Treaty of London 1915. At the end of 1918, the Kingdom of Serbs, Croats and Slovenes was formed. Many Croats rejected the monarchy felt discriminated and demanded the establishment of a Republic for Croatia. The Constitution stipulated a centralised state organisation that secured for the Serbs, the numerically largest nation, a de facto supremacy. In 1929 King Aleksandar I dissolved Parliament and renamed the state to the Kingdom of Yugoslavia. He ruled as a dictator mainly supported by Serbian officers. In response, Ante Pavelić founded the Ustasha movement supported by Mussolini. Soon after Germany attacked the Kingdom of Yugoslavia it capitulated on April 17, 1941. Croatia became a German vassal state. With the support of the Axis powers, Ante Pavelić announced the birth of the Independent State of Croatia (NDH) and declared himself head of state on April 10. He established a fascist dictatorship and Jews, Serbs, Roma, and Croatian antifascists were systematically persecuted and murdered. The Jasenovac concentration camp attained notoriety and became known as the Croatian Auschwitz due to the killing of between 80,000-100,000 people. An armed uprising of Croatian Communists against the Ustasha regime began in the summer of 1941 and – without relying on Soviet support – by 1942 and 1943 controlled a large part of the country. In addition to Josip Broz Tito, Andrija Hebrang was one of the leaders. After the war, Croatia became a republic in socialist Yugoslavia, which was composed of six republics with two autonomous provinces (Kosovo and Vojvodina) under Tito. Tito's Unity Party ruled the country

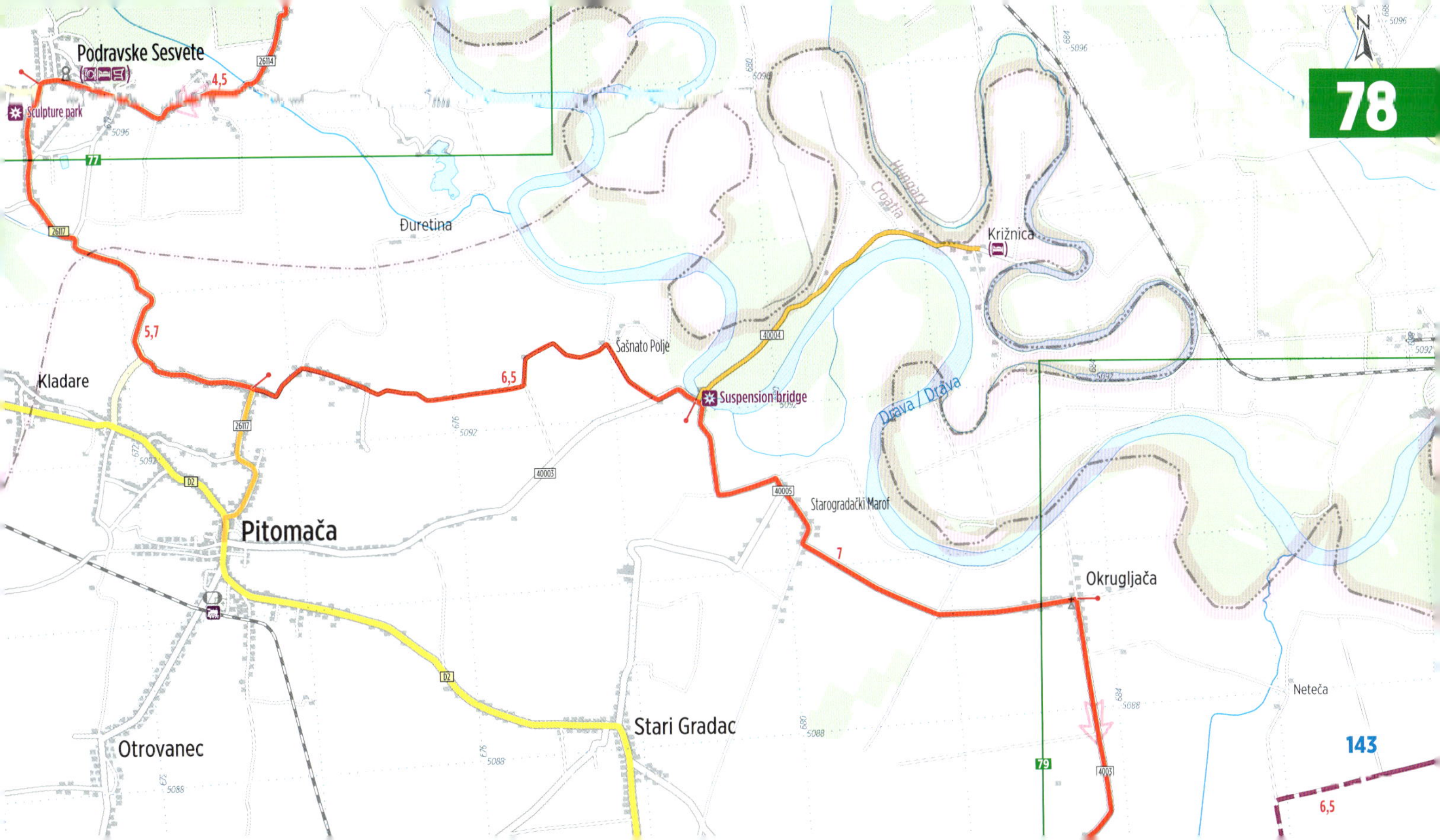
78
Podravske Sesvete
Sculpture park
4,5
26114
5096
77
26117
Đuretina
Hungary
Croatia
Križnica
40004
Šašnato Polje
5,7
6,5
Kladare
26117
Suspension bridge
Drava / Drava
5092
D2
40003
40005
Starogradački Marof
Pitomača
7
Okrugljača
Neteča
79
4003
Stari Gradac
Otrovanec
5088
6,5

comprising five nationalities, four languages, three religions and two alphabets and not only rallied against Stalin's hegemony, but also against Western influence.

After Tito's death in 1980, tensions between Croatia and the Serb-dominated Yugoslav government increased. In the late eighties, this grew into a demand for independence and a desire for greater autonomy. The Croatian Franjo Tuđman who had fought on Tito's side against the Ustasha regime, gained popularity among the Croatian population. After the weakened Yugoslav government allowed a multiparty system Tuđman founded the Croatian Democratic Union (HDZ) in 1990. It soon took on the characteristics of a People's Party, and won the elections in 1990 with a majority of parliamentary seats and chose Franjo Tuđman to be president. On May 19th, 1991 95 percent of the electorate voted in a referendum in favour of Croatia's independence. Turnout was "only" 83 percent because of a boycott by the Krajina Serbs. On the 25th of June 1991, the parliament in Zagreb declared Croatia's independence, which was then internationally recognised. Soon after, the Serbian Slobodan Milošević conquered almost a third of Croatian territory and supported by the Yugoslav People's Army, had driven about 80,000 Croats from Serb-controlled areas by the end of the year. That was the beginning of the "ethnic cleansing". Although Tuđman's Croatia still supported in 1992 the "war within a war" against the radical Bosnian government in Sarajevo, the nearly four-year war between Serbia and Croatia only ended with "Operation Storm" on 5 August 1995, when Croatian forces managed to retake parts of Krajina in 72 hours and expel the formerly superior Serb forces from Croatia. The war in Yugoslavia ended in late 1995 with the Treaty of Dayton.

Croatia, with its 4.5 million inhabitants, has been a member of NATO and the EU since 2013.

From Gola to Ferdinandovac 34 km

Turn left just over the border and cycle along a rarely-used road along the signposted border towards Ždala. Where you see the first houses of Ždala, just before a left bend in the road, turn left into a gravel road. Continue down this road until you reach a well-preserved watchtower, which you can also climb. Since you cannot ride along the Drava dam, go back to the road and continue towards Ždala.

Ždala

Zdala is a city with a significant Hungarian minority, whose special accent can hardly be understood by many Hungarians. A memorial stone commemorates the victims of the war with Serbia, and there is a bust of Franjo Tuđman (1922-1999) in the restored church, who was the first president of Croatia (1990-1999).

Turn right and in Ždala cycle in the direction of Repaš on a street with little traffic through one of the largest and oldest oak forests in Europe, where there are two three-hundred-year-old oaks.

Repaš

Behind the place, cross the **Drava** and directly after the bridge turn left into an unpaved field road.

The Drava (Dráva)

The Drava (Dráva) is a 749 km long tributary of the Danube. It starts in Italy and passes through Austria, Slovenia and Hungary before emptying in Croatia into the Danube. In some sections, it acts as a border river for a length of almost 200 kilometres between Austria and Slovenia, as well as between Croatia and Hungary. The border between Hungary and Croatia was established in 1919 along the Drava. While most rivers have been channelled in Europe, the Drava is still wild and untamed. It therefore meanders back and forth between borders. During the time of the Iron Curtain islets emerged between states - a no man's land with important sanctuaries for nature. It was allowed to develop and the river remained untouched and a large biodiversity took shape. The natural bed of the Drava river is constantly changing, sandbanks can arise and the river is not always a border. Due to its relevance as a settlement area many archaeological sites can also be visited. But their existence is under threat however, because parts of the river banks have been fortified and dredgers as well as huge pipes took sand and gravel from the river, which changed the natural flow of the river. Fortunately, a project for the construction of a hydroelectric power plant was prevented which would have destroyed even more. Environmentalists fought against such projects and were successful. In 2008, the Croatian government put the Green Belt and the Drava under protection, making the future of sand martins- about

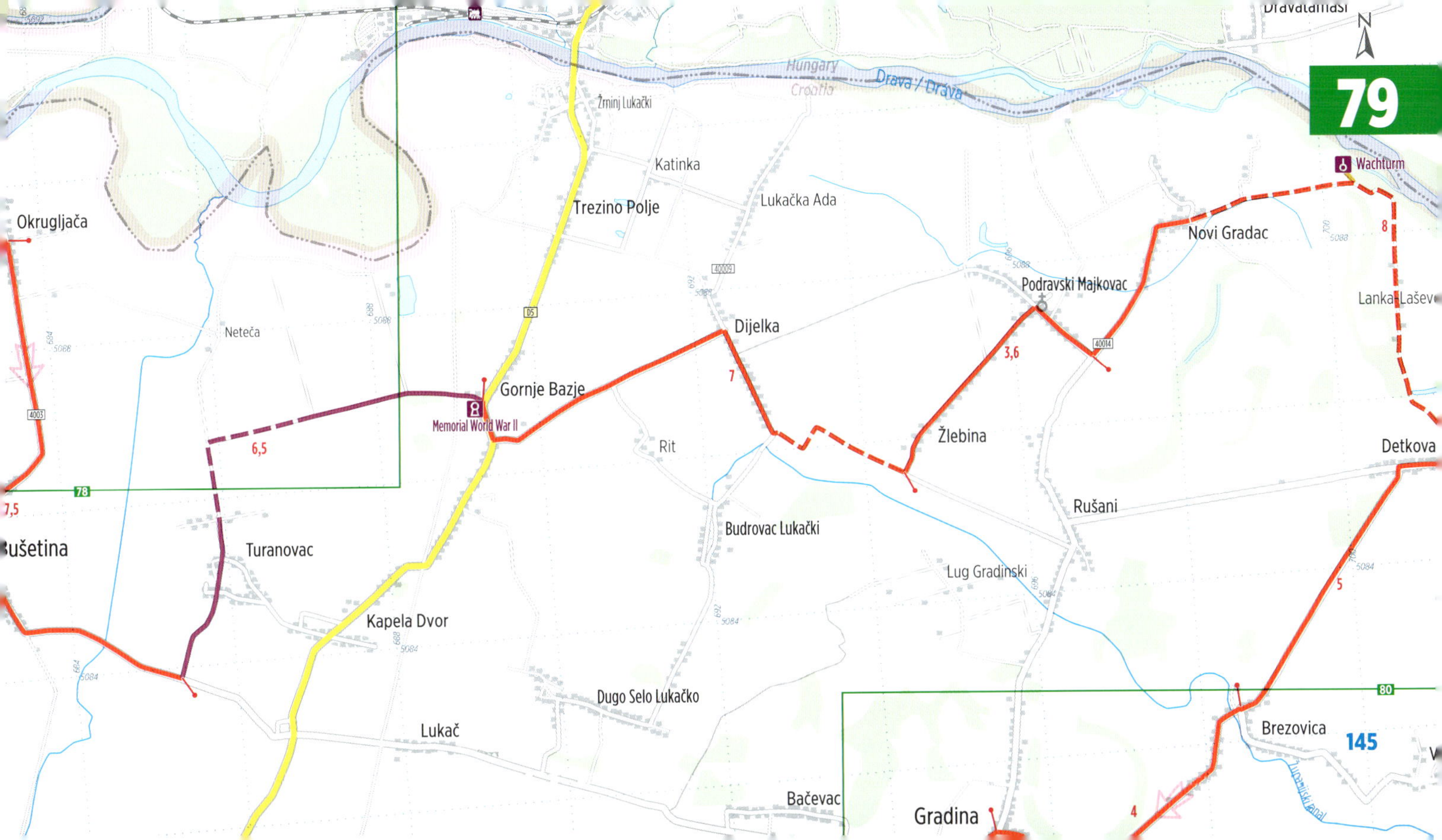

79
Drávafamási
Hungary
Croatia
Drava / Dráva
Wachturm
Žrninj Lukački
Katinka
Trezino Polje
Lukačka Ada
Okrugljača
Novi Gradac
Lanka-Laševo
Podravski Majkovac
Dijelka
Neteča
Gornje Bazje
Memorial World War II
3,6
7
8
6,5
Žlebina
Rit
Detkova
78
7,5
Rušani
Bušetina
Turanovac
Budrovac Lukački
Lug Gradinski
Kapela Dvor
5
Dugo Selo Lukačko
80
Brezovica
145
Lukač
Bačevac
Gradina
4
D5
4003
40009
40014
5088
5084

Suspension bridge over the Drava near Križnica

10,000 of which breed in the mud and sand walls of the river – far more secure. In Austria, Slovenia and Croatia, the Drava, with a maximum capacity of 1,200 MW, plays an important part in power generation.

The Drava bike path

The Drava bike path from Italy to Slovenia via Austria won an award by the German Cycling Federation (ADFC) in 2012 and its description (all the way from the spring of the Drava to Maribor) was published in the bikeline guide series. In Croatia, an extension from the dam to the Danube is being planned, and it is hoped that the route will be developed in a cyclist-friendly way and signposted. Once you are there, you can inquire about the progress of the construction work.

Stay on the wide lakeside path and turn right at a bridge over a Drava tributary into an asphalt road. Turn left on road **2185**.

Novo Virje

At the church follow the signposted Drava route around a left bend on the little-travelled road towards Ferdinandovac.

Karaška Luka

You will find a bunker with a statue of Our Lady at the intersection, which was built before World War 2 and is a useful landmark that indicates that the border is 104 metres away. After the crushing of the Hungarian uprising (1956) Hungarian soldiers tried to stop refugees from running away. Yugoslav soldiers shot into the air above the soldiers to protect the refugees. Thanks to their actions, 400 civilians were able to escape across the Hungarian border.

Do not go right at this junction, but straight. Similarly, at the next branch in the road, do not turn right towards Ferdinandovac, but instead remain on the road.

TIP You will find a border stone and another bunker about 100 metres away from Drava. In the river, the actual borderline is marked with sticks. Three quarters of the Drava is Croatian territory and a quarter belongs to Hungary. A little further there is a second bunker, which is overgrown with ivy.

Ferdinandovac

From Ferdinandovac to Novaki — 90 km

Where the road bends sharply, cycle straight into a paved road, which is closed to lorries.

Brodić

Etno kuće obitelji Karlovčan, ✆ 091/55/66524, ✆ 091/442/0548

Cycle through Brodić and cross the Drava canal.

Podravske Sesvete

Cycle through Podravske Sesvete and on the right hand side you will see a memorial commemorating the war in Yugoslavia. Follow the signposted Drava route and turn left before Pitomača.

Šašnato Polje

Turn right here. On the road that leads to the river Drava, turn left and you will see the suspension bridge.

EXCURSION If you want to stay the night, cross the Drava and cycle 5km to Križnica.

Suspension bridge

The bridge was built in 1968 by the military, so that the soldiers could quickly cross the Drava. Today it is not officially a public road. The use is not prohibited but one uses it at one's own risk. There is also a ferry parallel to the bridge, which can take you across the river Drava.

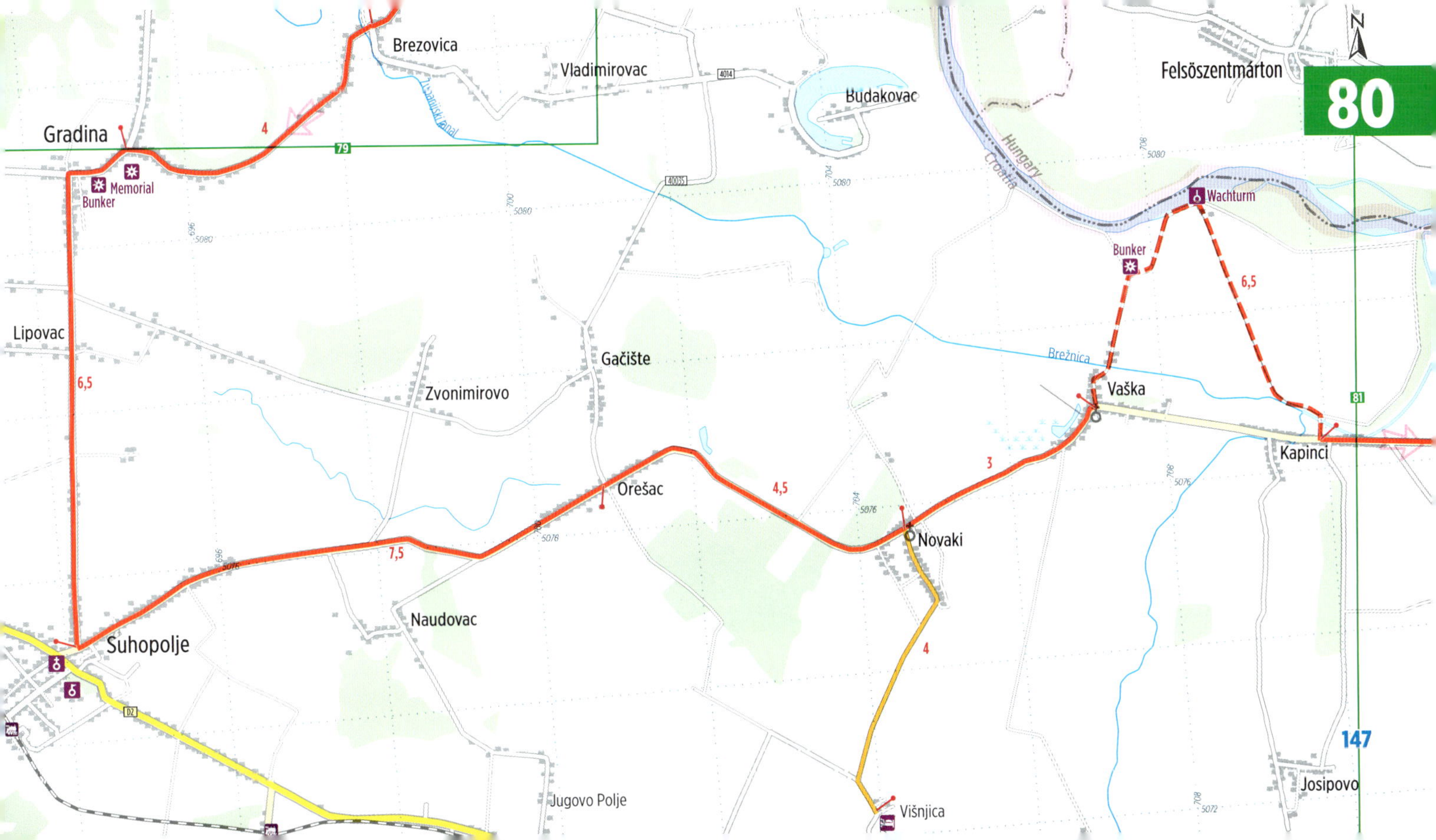
80
Brezovica
Vladimirovac
Budakovac
Felsőszentmárton
Gradina
Memorial
Bunker
Hungary
Croatia
Wachturm
Bunker
Lipovac
Gačište
Zvonimirovo
Brežnica
Vaška
Kapinci
Orešac
Novaki
Naudovac
Suhopolje
Jugovo Polje
Višnjica
Josipovo
147
79
81
4014
40035
D2
4
6,5
6,5
3
4,5
7,5
4

Křižnica

After the bridge, follow the road to the right until you come across a street, into which you turn left. Turn right again towards **Starogradački Marof.** Continue through Křižnica and turn left.

Okrugljača

A memorial stone can be found at the end of the village, commemorating the locally born politician Đuro Basariček (1884-1928).

Behind the church, turn right and stay on the road. Follow the windy road and reach the next location.

Bušetina

Cycle through the village whilst keeping the left. Behind Bušetina you can see some large tobacco plantations and after crossing the canal and upon seeing the first few houses, leave the main road and turn left.

Turanovac

At Turanovacride cycle straight along a narrow road that later ceases to become paved. Turn right at the next possibility - the gravel road is a little bit better and is even paved a little while later - reach Gornje Bazje where you turn right at the stop sign onto the main road.

Gornje Bazje

There is a monument here for the victims of WW2.

At the next opportunity, turn left, signposted to Veliko Polje. In Dijelka turn right into a tarmacked road. At the next intersection, turn left onto the signposted, 2km-long Žlebina, where corn cobs are abundant in the gardens. The gravel road becomes paved a little later.

Podravski Majkovac

Turn right at the church. Behind the exit sign, turn left onto the road signposted to Novi Gradac. Continue straight, follow the winding paved main street past the church. At this point a gravel road begins which is in good condition. A little later, you will reach a dam.

EXCURSION Turning left, you will reach a watchtower, which is still well preserved.

Follow the gravel road, turn right and just before the next place, the road becomes paved again.

Detkovac

Turn right into the main street and at the next branch in the road, turn left onto the road signposted to Gradina.

Tobacco plantations near Bušetina

Brezovica

Cross the **Županijski canal** and you will get to Gradina, which is nestled between three side arms of the Drava.

Gradina

Due to its dispersed settlements, it is hard to believe the village has 4,500 inhabitants. There is a post office, a store and no less than three bakers at an intersection.

EXCURSION On the right where a sign indicates the presence of a church, the pilgrim route takes you left towards a memorial with many wooden crosses.

Memorial in honour of an apparition of the Virgin Mary

On Friday, 13th June 1997 on the feast of St. Anthony, on the last day of school, students gave their textbooks back. After this they had some free time. Some decided to play in the school yard, and some went to a playground, where there were swings and seesaws. One group of students during a walk, claimed to see an apparition of the Virgin Mary in the distance. The children ran excitedly and frightened back to school to report it. Three teachers followed them to the spot and confirmed that they could also see the silhouette of the Virgin Mary in the distance. This memorial commemorates this event.

A little while later you can see an old bunker standing in front of a school. It is painted with the famous cartoon Snoopy. There is another bunker which is not painted. At

Kemse
Drávasztára
Zaláta
81
Drava / Dráva
80
3,5
4024
Sopje
Sv. Marija Magdalena
St. Florian
Sopjanska Greda
Watchtower
2,6
Gornje Predrijevo
7,5
4024
Noskovci
Bunker
Noskovačka Dubrava
4026
Hungary
Croatia
82
Martinci Miholjački
Bunker
8
Ilmin Dvor
Gezinci
D34
Čadavički Lug
Voćin-Drava-Kanal
8
D34
Čadavica
Nova Šarovka
Vranešfevci
Sladin
Šaševo
D34

the end of the village, turn left onto the road signposted to Suhopolje. On this somewhat busy street cycle through **Lipovac**.

Suhopolje

- **St. Teresa of Avila**. The immense, temple-like classical church does not seem to belong to a village with its balanced proportions and its brilliant white colours.
- The **Castle** (late 18th century) belonged to the Janković family and is the foundation of the village. It is located at the back of the village and since 1964 has been in a protected park on the southwest side of the road. The municipality acquired it and wants to renovate it.

The town founded by Croats and Germans with about 8,000 inhabitants is spread over 23 villages. A memorial from 1999 at the church commemorates the victims of the war in former Yugoslavia (1991-1995). The train station has direct trains to Zagreb and Koprivnica.

At the church turn left into a road sign-posted as Drava Route in the direction of Vaska and Sopje and this quiet road will take you to Orešac.

Orešac

Although the streets seem to be quiet, the people here are quite lively and busy. It is a common occurrence for the "exotic" cyclist to be greeted in the remote villages with a friendly wave. In the surrounding area you can see the equipment used to dry tobacco plants. Had John Lennon grown up here, the Beatles song would have been: "Tobacco Fields Forever".

Pass a small lake at the end of Orešac where you can also see cornfields on the left and right of you.

A few moist woodland areas have been allowed to remain in Orešac, but the rest of the landscape is conspicuous for its use of intensive farming.

Novaki

A monument from 1986 commemorates the unnamed civilian and military victims of fascist terror.

EXCURSION: If you wish to stay here, turn right at the church and cycle almost five kilometres to Višnjica.

Višnjica

Hotel „Višnjica", +385/33/401650

On a former Pustara (an extensive patch of grasslands) in the 19th century a holiday resort has been constructed which was rated excellent in 2011 by the European Commission (EDEN). During the Austro-Hungarian Empire, when Croatia still belonged to it, there were some huge estates with buildings where farm workers lived with families. Many of these estates that were confiscated during the communist period, stood empty since 1991. Ksenija Plantak, the former mayor of Slatina, bought this Pustara, and turned it into an excellent resort. Horses are also bred here and GMO-free crops are also produced on the estate and consumed by the guests. The hotel specialises in local specialties such as sweet potatoes, which also withstand periods of long droughts very well.

From Novaki to Donji Miholjac — *61 km*

Cycle straight on the main road.

Vaška

Pass a fish pond and a church and then cycle straight on a gravel road past a bunker towards a dam on the river Drava. On the dam, keep right and soon you will sees a green painted watchtower. Since the Drava cycle path on the dam is not yet finished, take the next right and after crossing the **Brežnica** arrive in **Kapinci** where you turn left in the road towards Sopje.

Sopje

- Church of Sv. Marija Magdalena

Here is the centre of administration for the surrounding villages.

Cycle past the church. The road bends to the left at the Memorial of St. Florian, the patron saint of firefighters - "Save my house, set fire to another" (St. Florian principle). Shortly before the exit you will see some installations for the drying of tobacco leaves.

Gornje Predrijevo

Pass a standalone steeple and join the signposted Drava route to get via **Noskovci** to the next location.

Noskovačka Dubrava

Since it is not possible to travel further at the dam, stay on the rarely travelled road until you reach Čađavica.

Čađavica

- Rebuilt Baroque **church** with Campanile

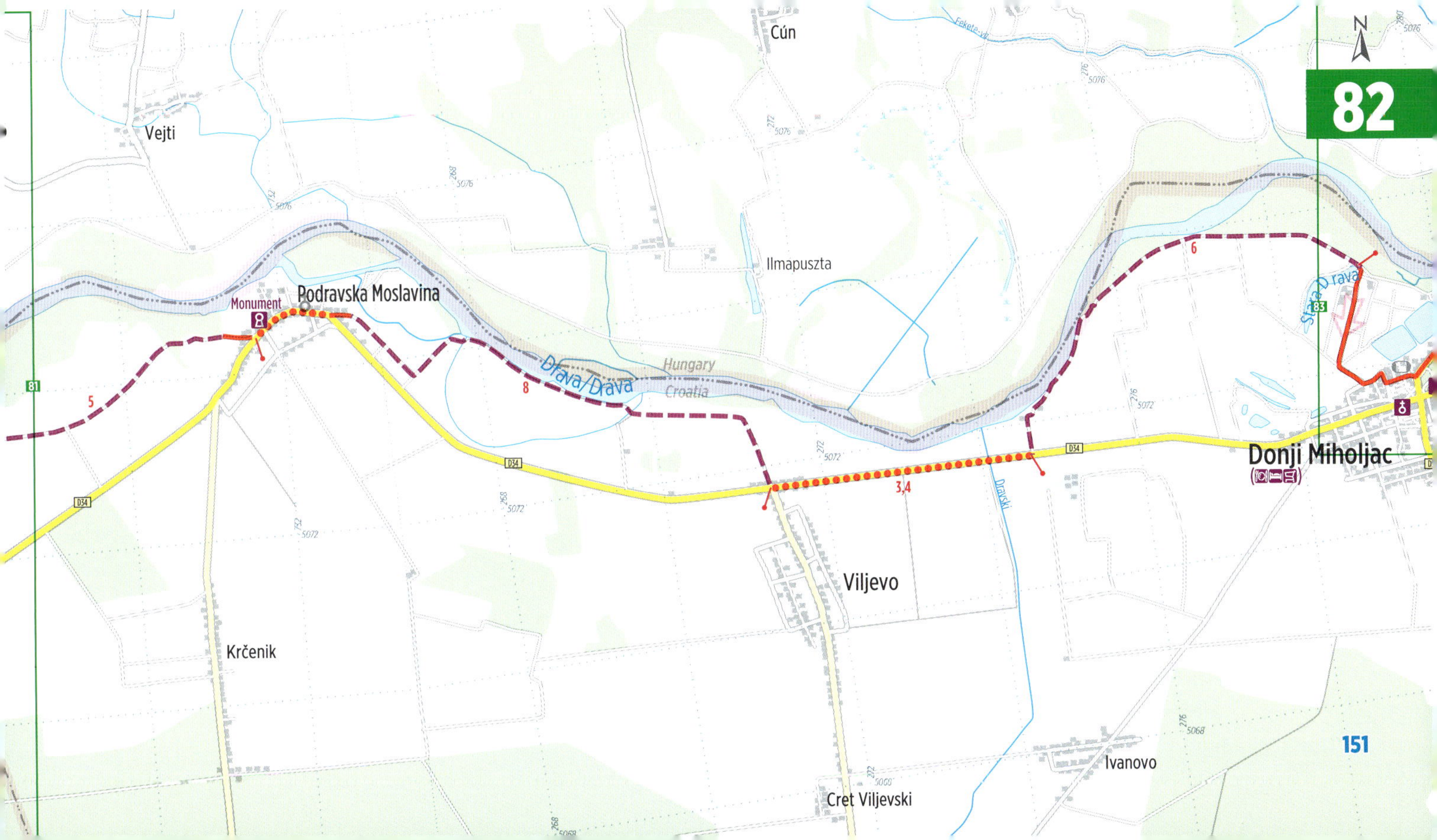
82
Cún
Vejti
Ilmapuszta
Monument
Podravska Moslavina
Drava/Drava
Hungary
Croatia
Stara Drava
Donji Miholjac
Viljevo
Krčenik
Ivanovo
Cret Viljevski
Dravski
D34
81
83
5
6
8
3,4
Fekete-víz

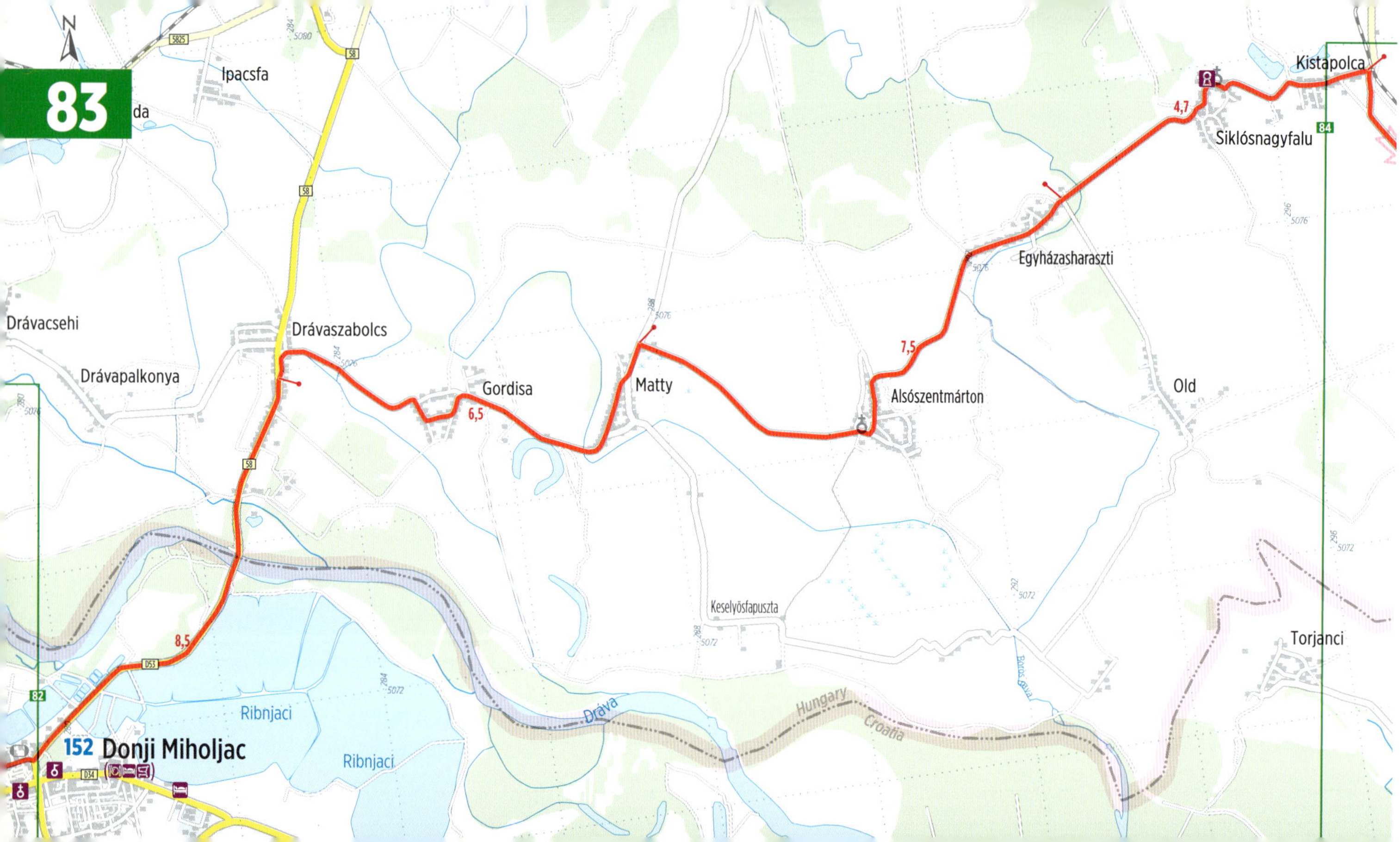
83
Ipacsfa
da
Drávacsehi
Drávaszabolcs
Drávapalkonya
Gordisa
Matty
Alsószentmárton
Egyházasharaszti
Siklósnagyfalu
Kistapolca
Old
Keselyősfapuszta
Torjanci
152 Donji Miholjac
Ribnjaci
Ribnjaci
Dráva
Hungary
Croatia
Boros-gyava
58
58
58
5825
D53
D34
82
84
4,7
7,5
6,5
8,5
5080
5076
5076
5076
5076
5076
5072
5072
5072
5072
N

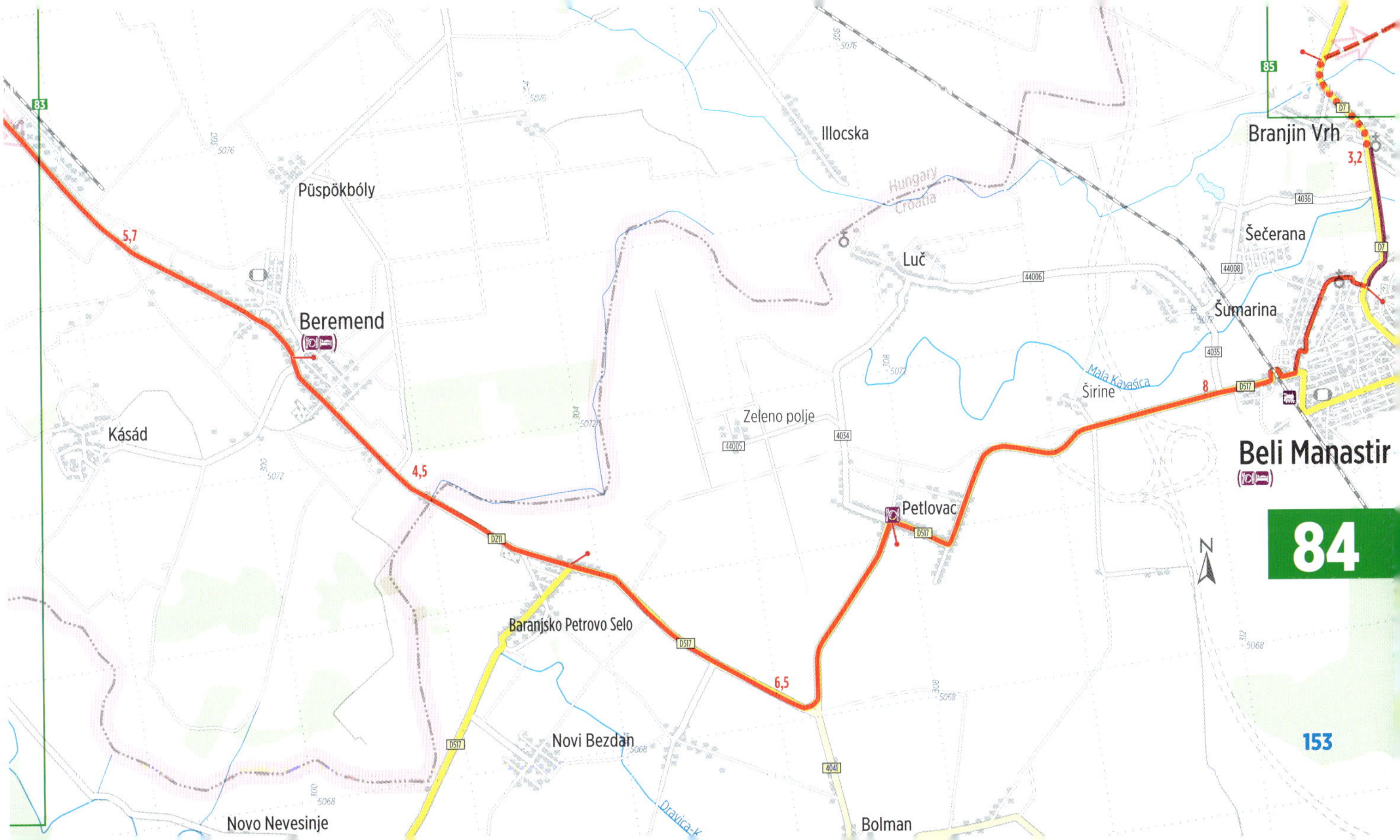

83
85
Püspökbóly
Illocska
Branjin Vrh
3,2
5,7
Hungary
Croatia
Luč
Šećerana
Beremend
Šumarina
Kásád
Zeleno polje
Širine
Mala Kavašica
8
Beli Manastir
4,5
Petlovac
84
Baranjsko Petrovo Selo
6,5
Novi Bezdan
Novo Nevesinje
Bolman
D7
D211
D517
4036
44008
44006
4035
4034
44005
4041

South of the city, the oldest Slavic traces of Croatia (6th-7th century.) have been found.

TIP The unpaved road along the Drava is not in good condition, but the alternative would be the almost 50km long state road 34. The bicycle-friendly Drava route on the dam is in the process of being planned. So long as it is not finished, the described onerous, but car-free road is recommended. It is a lot easier to navigate in dry weather, but the road is also still useable in wet weather.

In Čađavica turn left at the crucifix behind house number 197 into a non-paved road. When you reach the Drava, the road bends right. The Drava does not need a dam here because the river banks are high, and the river bed is so deep. At the first opportunity after the cornfield turn right into a field road that leads you to a very old wooden bridge used to cross the **Voćin-Drava channel**. After a few metres through some tall grass, ride on a wide road along some fields. When the first trees appear, continue straight ahead and the field road will eventually turn into a gravel road. Follow this beautiful road around a bend to the right.

Martinci Miholjački

You hit an asphalt road close to a house. There is an old bunker in the garden. Continue cycling down the road for a little while and then turn left before the church into a field road which is signposted to the cemetery. The initially bumpy road turns into a paved country road later on. Soon you will come across a wider gravel road on which you continue straight ahead. At the next branch in the road, go straight, leave the gravel road and continue cycling through a meadow. You can sense the river Drava nearby, because there are the familiar trees, but you cannot see the river because the fields are in between. The meadow path leads straight to the forest, where it bends to the right. Here you will already be able to see the road and the first houses of Podravska Moslavina. You have to conquer a small slope before reaching an asphalt road that leads you to the main road.

Podravska Moslavina

On the left side is a monument that was built in 2009 to commemorate the Yugoslav war. Three young people are mentioned and we are told that they should "rest in peace, in the awareness that they have brought peace to the Croatian people".

After the church, on the outskirts of Podravska Moslavina, switch to the left side of the street and continuing straight, leave the main road. After a short time, the road is not paved anymore. On a gravel road, turn left into the direction of the Drava. Turn right at the forest, and then continue close to the River Drava. Various roads go off to the right to get to the street. After a sharp right bend at the river banks you will reach an asphalted busy main road in **Viljevo** into which you turn left. Behind the river **Drava**, turn left into the field road, which later turns into a path leading you through a meadow towards a dike. There, keep to the right and cycle along the dike until you reach Altarm **Stara Drava**, where you turn right into the asphalt road. Follow this road until you can reach the centre of Donji Miholjac.

Donji Miholjac

- Baroque **church of St. Michael**, located on the bypass, first mentioned in the 11th century.
- **Castles.** After the expulsion of the Turks, a noble family deemed to be deserving of reward received some land and built in 1818, the 80 m long single-storey building in late Baroque style, which runs along the road. After Emperor Franz Joseph I's visit a much larger castle in the very popular Neo-Tudor style was built behind it with a covered walkway connecting them. It was completed in 1906. The city administration has its headquarters there today, which is also surrounded by a landscaped park.
- **Hotel Borik**, ✆ +385/31/631228, ✆ +385/31/631268, at the exit, after the petrol station on the left side.

The town with its 10,000 inhabitants has many different types of accommodation and lots of areas to explore. Illyrian tribes, Romans and Avars as well as Croats have all settled here throughout the centuries. The name is associated with the Church of St. Michael. Limex, well-known throughout Europe for its metal products has a thriving production facility. Donji Miholjac's location at the intersection of two motorways with a bridge over the river Drava coupled with the possibilities for sustainable tourism hold a lot of potential for the town. The Miholjačko sijelo (Miholjac meeting), the most important event of the year, is well worth seeing with costumes, music and dance in the second week of July.

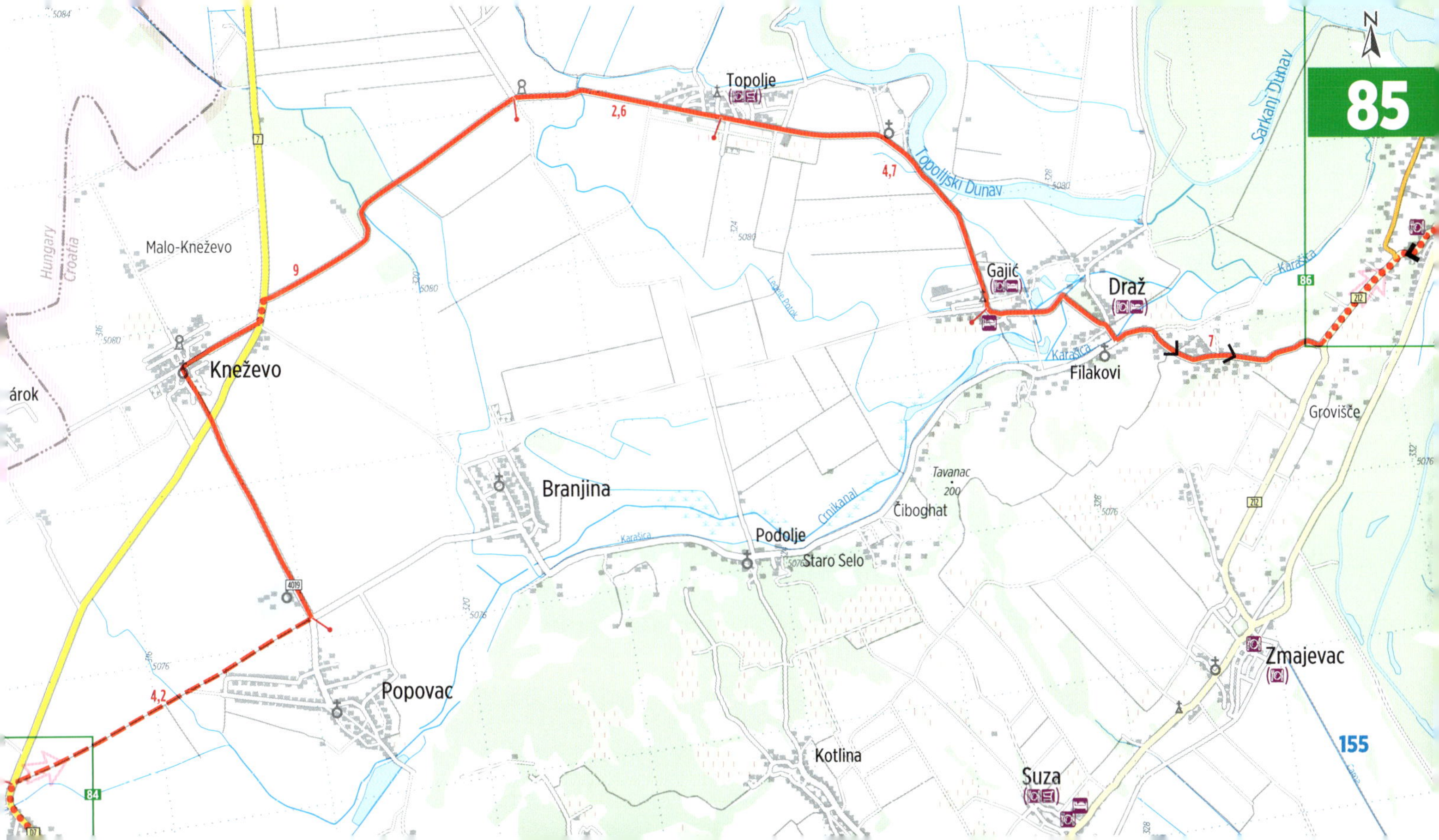

85
Topolje
Topoljski Dunav
Sarkanj Dunav
Malo-Kneževo
Hungary
Croatia
Kneževo
árok
Branjina
Gajić
Draž
Filakovi
Karašica
Grovišče
Tavanac
200
Čiboghat
Crnikanal
Podolje
Staro Selo
Popovac
Kotlina
Suza
Zmajevac
155
84
86
2,6
4,7
9
7
4,2
4019
212
7
D7

From Donji Miholjac (HR) to Bezdan (RS) 87 km

At the palace, turn left into the **D 53**, cycling over the Drava towards Hungary and continue on the **D 58** with little traffic.

Drávaszabolcs

Turn right into a paved road towards Gordisa, which is closed to heavy vehicles. On the left side you can see a pyramid mountain.

Matty

Cycle on the road without any town signs and turn right at the exit.

Alsószentmárton

At the church a memorial stone commemorates the 1st World War.

Pyramid mountain near Drávapalkonya

Turn left and upon leaving the place, turn right. Passing through **Egyházasharaszti** reach the next stop.

Siklósnagyfalu

A memorial put up in 2004 commemorates the 2 August 1944, when more than 3,000 Sinti and Roma were murdered in the Auschwitz-Birkenau concentration camp in the course of just a few hours.

Reach **Kis Tapolca**, where you turn right and pass a cement factory.

Beremend

It is possible to stay a few nights in the 2500 people strong village.

Go past two churches. After the border, in Croatia, after reaching Baranjsko you will then reach Petrovo Selo.

Baranjsko Petrovo Selo

The community has a regionally important border crossing. But it is also more well known for the Petaračke Buše which is a three-day carnival. Those who opt for the beautiful "Busa" (mask), must clothe themselves in the traditional costume of the opposite sex. Men can also wear an ugly, horned and very heavy wooden mask. On the last day, the evil spirit of the past year is burned, and there can even be an artificial "Chicken with a cold" as a symbol for the bird flu.

Continue straight, remain on the **517** and after some time bend left behind the village.

Petlovac

Turn right at a sign with a red star, which was erected in 1955 and honours the brigades. There is also a coffee bar

Church of Branjin Vrh

here. The centre of Beli Manastir is reached via the 517 and after passing under the railway tracks.

Beli Manastir

You can stay the night and explore the 8,700-population-strong city. There is a pedestrianised area and the train station has direct trains to Pécs and Osijek. The city belonged to Hungary until 1920. Over time the name for the monastery in the village of Pel, originally named Pel Monostor, changed to the similar sounding Beli Manastir, the white monastery. The population has always been multi-ethnic – in 1910 is was 61 percent German - and it is multi-ethnic today due to the return of non-Serb residents who were displaced during the Croatian Serb war in the 1990s. Croats, Serbs and Hungarians are well represented today but there are very few Germans.

Cycle straight through the pedestrian zone until the road makes a right bend at the end, passing a small church and emerges after a couple of S bends onto a road with heavy traffic **D 7** (E 73). Turn left onto the separate cycle lane and cycle along it to the church of Branjin Vrh.

Branjin Vrh

At the church a memorial stone with a five-pointed red star commemorates 11 deaths from 1941-45.

At the exit, turn right after the bridge over the **Karašica** into a decent but unpaved road. Continue straight the whole way.

Bridge over the Danube near Batina

VIEW You will see a sugar factory (Šećerana) on the right side of the Popovac church and on the left side of the tower.

After 2 km you will reach a junction. Continue straight to Branjina. Here, turn left and after 2.5 km cross the main road.

Kneževo

At the impressive church, turn right, cross main road 7, keeping left as you do, and after a few kilometres reach Topolje.

Topolje

Continue through Gajic to the next place.

Draž

Here you can stop off and stay the night if you want. Draž is also the administrative headquarters for Batina which is only six kilometres away, and only half as big.

Turn left and cycle along road **212**, which is signposted as the **Danube Bike Trail**, towards Batina. You can see the Euro Velo. 13 symbol next to the symbol for the Euro Velo 6.

EXCURSION Before it goes downhill to the Danube Bridge, a sign points left to the tourist information centre and to a

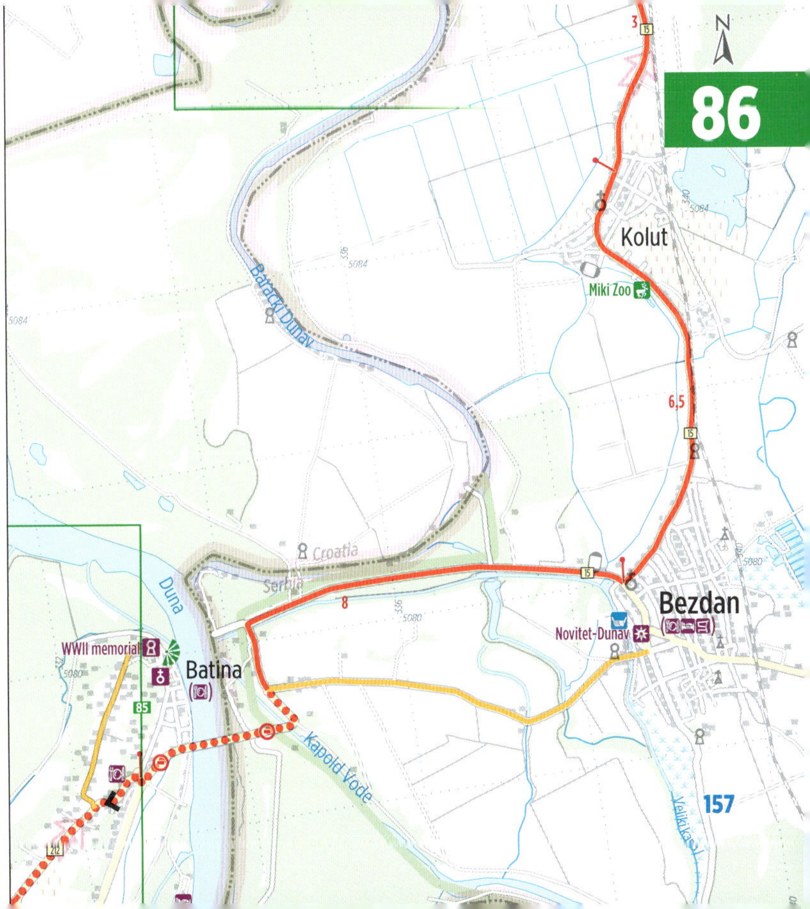

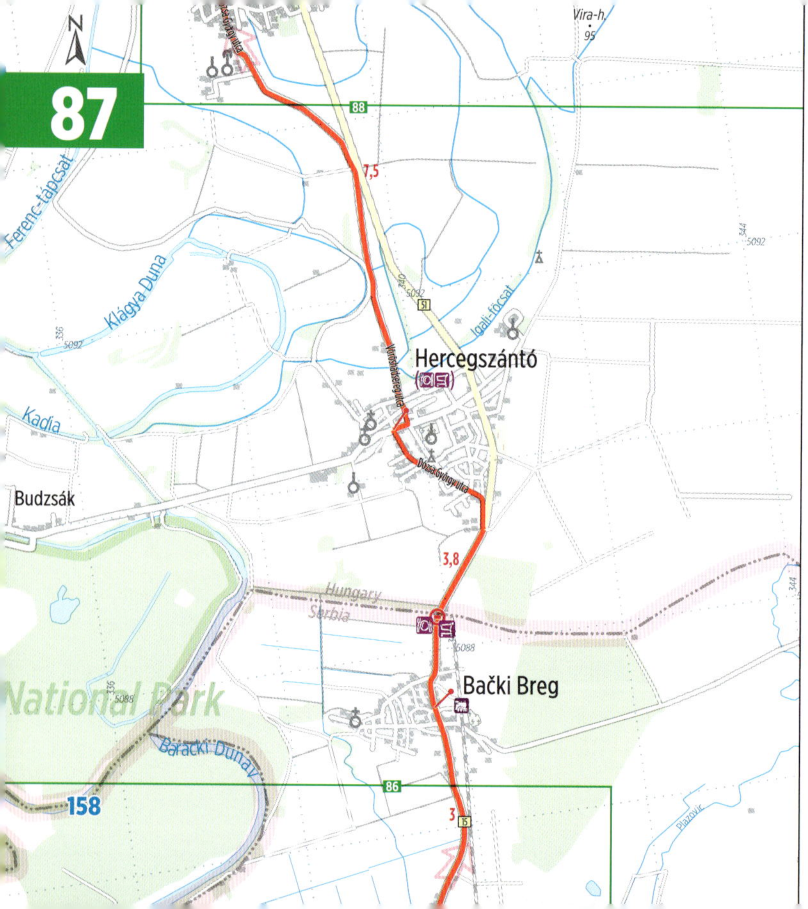

Monument to the battle of Batina

memorial 2km away which commemorates the Battle of Batina. On a steep cliff, one can see the nearly 30m tall monument by the Croatian sculptor Antun Augustinčić and a permanent exhibition on the Battle of Batina (1944), when the Soviet and Yugoslav federations liberated the territory from German troops. In addition, you will be rewarded with a magnificent view over the Danube and its numerous oxbow lakes. (For more information on the Danube, see p.s. S. 97)

Continue downhill on cobblestone before reaching a bridge. The Croatian border control is before the bridge and Serbian one behind it.

EXCURSION Already at the entrance to the place, the concrete bridge leading to Serbia encourages you to have a quick visit to this hardly spectacular but still nicely situated small place.

Batina

Baroque church **Parish Valentine**

Already on the approach you can see the wine cellars on your left. They are built into the rocks and look like old huts from the road. The rather regular looking church would hardly be worth a visit in any other place but looks great here through its elevated location. The border town with 1,500 inhabitants narrows to the north, where it is dominated by a steep cliff with a monument to the Battle of Batina. The small port is still dominated by agriculture, but offers tourists a few things and provides a nice residence for artists.

The road crosses a tributary of the Danube on the Serbian side and then bends to the north, where the signs for the Danube cycle

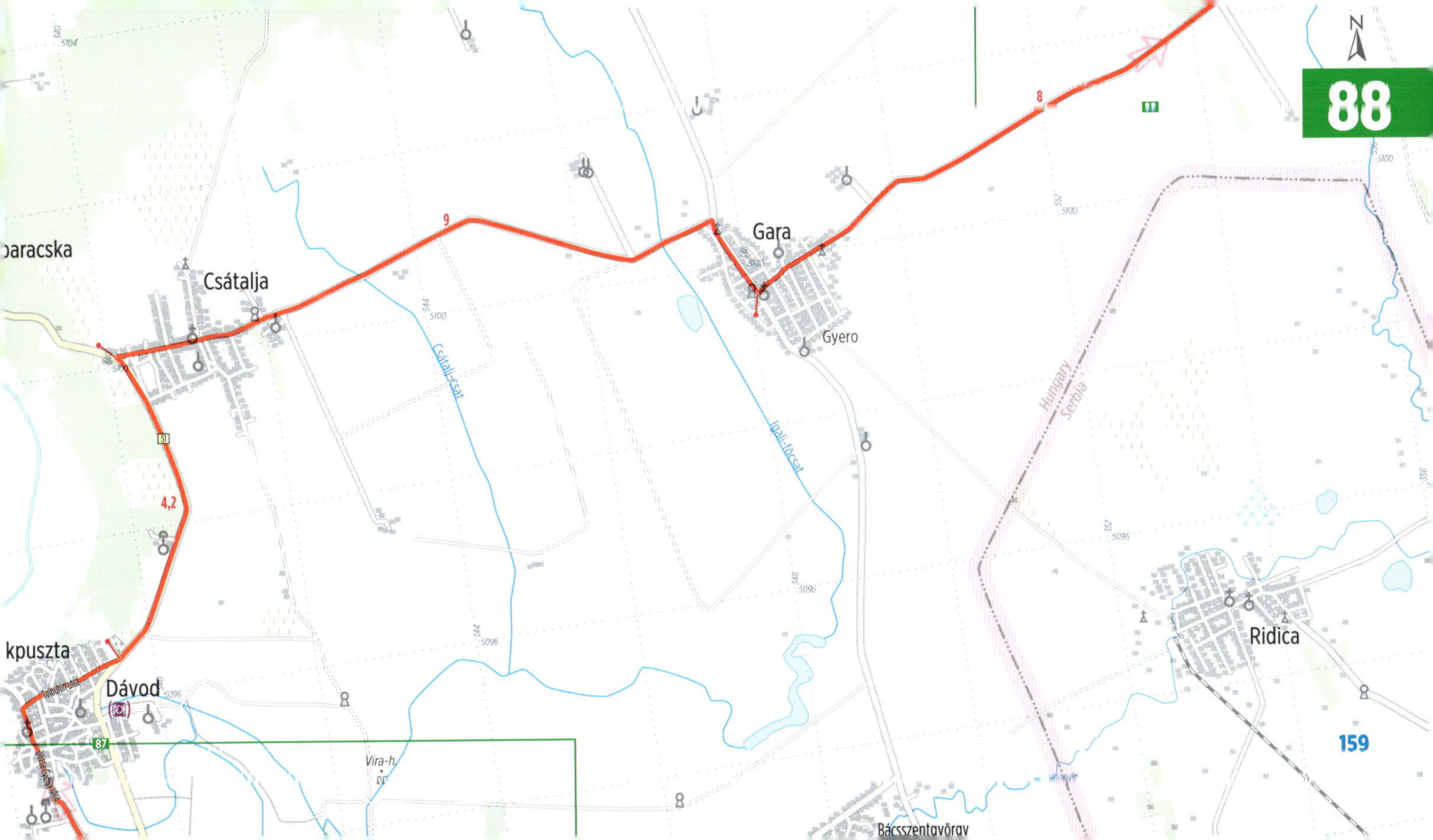
88
Gara
Csátalja
baracska
Gyero
Csátalji-csat
Igali-főcsat
Hungary
Serbia
Ridica
kpuszta
Dávod
Vira-h.
Bácsszentgyörgy
9
8
4,2
51
87
5100
5096
5104
159

path as well as the symbol for the Euro Velo. 13 are displayed in both directions,

ALTERNATIVE Turn right after nearly 500 metres and continue through the fields towards Bezdan. Cross two more tributaries and a channel. However, the route changes part way into a dusty gravel road, so that they are generally not used, even by local cyclists.

For this reason, stay on the road, turn right, pass through the lock on the tributary of the Danube and reach the trilingual two signpost of Bezdan.

Bezdan

The settlement with 5,200 inhabitants has little in the way of urban character, but offers shopping, refreshments and a variety of accommodation options. It is characterised by crafts and agriculture and has a textile factory and a shipyard and a little bit of industry. The natural wealth lies in the forests, streams and lakes. In addition, there are thermal springs, which have been used to create a modern spa and rehabilitation centre. After the expulsion of the Turks and the establishment of the Habsburg rule, Poles, Czechs and German settled here. Bezdan is still quite mixed, but the composition of nationalities has changed. The latest change in the population was due to the influx of Serbian refugees in the 1990s and simultaneous exodus of Hungarians. Despite this, the latter still comprise the majority at nearly 60 percent.

From Bezdan (RS) to Bácsalmás (HU) 63 km

At the gas station at the entrance, turn left into road **18** to the border.

The road is not very busy, but the parallel disused railway line would be ideal for the two Euro Velo routes 6 and 13.

Kolut

Pass a dilapidated church and reach the border town.

Bački Breg

Germans and Hungarians settled in both places in the 18th century, but today in Kolut, the Serbs dominate and in Bački Breg, the Šokci a population group commonly referred to as Croats in censuses. They maintain their own dialect, costumes and customs, for example the mask carnival, as already mentioned in Baranjsko Petrovo Selo shortly before Beli Manastir.

TIP Before crossing the border, you can grab some refreshments from a small Balkan hotel or swing by a shop for some drinks, because the border crossing can take a long time.

Hercegszántó

After the border the Danube Bike Trail shifts to the side street. Turn left twice, cycling from **Dózsa György utca** right into **Vöröshadsereg** utca straight through the town. On the east side of the church is a great square where you can shop and stop for a break. The Vöröshadsereg utca leads you out of town onto the **Dózsa György utca**, on which you reach the centre of Dávod. Cycle towards the church.

Dávod

Go past the church and turn right into **Tolbuhin utca**, which leads to road **51**, into which you turn left. Later turn right.

Csátalja

Pass the church and follow the signs to Gara. Pass through the surrounding area, and reach Gara after travelling through some field roads. Turn right to enter Gara.

Gara

Gara is said to have been originally located on a distant hill four kilometres away and therefore bear this name, because it is named after a Slavic word for hill. Word has it that the original settlement was destroyed by the Turks and later rebuilt, which Germany also played a role in. A stone in front of the church commemorates the Hungarian Germans who were deported in 1945 to Russia. The larger monument is dedicated to the victims of World War II.

Monument for the Hungarian German victims in Gara

89
Bácsbokod
Takarmány
Bácsborsód
Madaras
9,5
9,5
Bokodi-Kígyós-csat.
Vájaspusztai-csat.
88
90
N
356
5108
360
5108
364
5108
5104
368
5104
5100

Monument dedicated to the victims of World War II in Gara

Turn left again in front of the church. The next 11km is rather lonely. The corn and sunflower fields stretch as far as the eye can see.

Bácsborsód

Keep to the left and cross the tracks.

Bácsbokod

Behind the church square, which is decorated with two hero monuments, turn right, crossing what is, in the summertime, a dry river and you will find yourself between two fields. 1km behind this, turn right at the fork and after two track crossings and 11 km reach Bácsalmás.

Bácsalmás

Csauscher-House, behind the church. It is worth seeing this domed building with classical decorations.

Sárga Csikó Panzió, ✆ +36/79/342569

The perpendicular scale town with 7,000 inhabitants gives the impression that it was a very planned town. The conquest of the area by the Turks caused the local population to disappear, so that the Bunjevci (bunjevci) could take their place. This Croat minority that speaks their own dialect, settled in the region of Bácska that until 1918 belonged to Hungary, but then for the most part fell to Serbia. The cultural centre of the Catholic Bunjevci is Subotica, a town 25 kilometres away, behind the Serbian border. In the 1780s, with the country under Habsburg control, almost three times as many German were settled here. The so-called Danube Swabians called their new home Heimerskirchen. Even in 1941, when the city reached 13,000 - its biggest ever population- two-thirds of them were German. Today, after the German expulsion and the settlement of Hungarians from Slovakia, only 230 residents Germans remain. There is a monument commemorating the forced resettlement in the park. The Croats have largely been assimilated, so that only 125 people actually call themselves Croatian. The population declined and it took until 1986 to get back over 8,000. After the closure of some firms and some debt-laden cooperatives many people began to leave the rural town again. A large number of unemployed people are there today with little in the way of perspective. Nonetheless, you can stop there for a while, shop and stay the night. The train station offers direct trains to Kiskunhalas.

From Bácsalmás to Kelebia 29 km

At the major junction, turn right and then left towards Csikéria and cross the abandoned railway line that once led to Subotica and Bácsalmás. Cycle through vineyards and you will probably also see large flocks of sheep. After a left turn you will reach the elongated municipality of Csikéria.

Csikéria

Neo-Gothic **Church**

The tradition of Bunjevci is still alive here.

Cycle past the church and leave the place to the north with a right turn in the direction of Kelebia. Again, it is rather lonely between the fields.

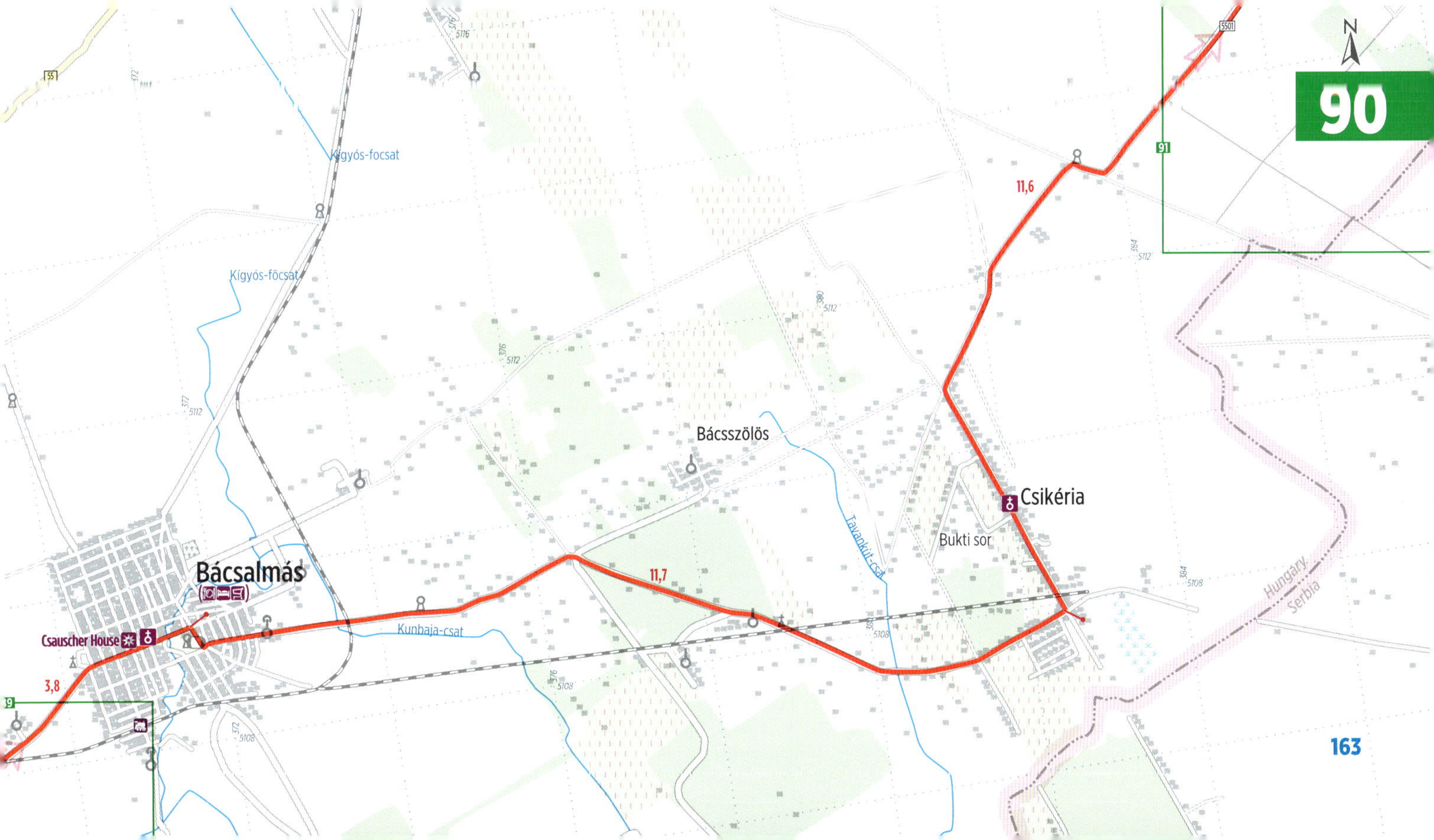
90
Bácsalmás
Csauscher House
Csikéria
Bácsszölös
Bukti sor
Kígyós-focsat
Kígyós-föcsat
Kunbaja-csat
Tavankút-csat
Hungary
Serbia
3,8
11,7
11,6
55
5501
91
9
5116
5112
5108

Your loneliness turns to joy, however, when you encounter a nice and shady grove and then suddenly a little pink church pops up.

Church of St. Anna

In terms of style and ornamentation, the Neo-Gothic church is like a great cathedral. It is decorated with beautiful stained glass windows and belongs to Baron Meierhof (Bárómajor) Redl whose castle building is partially hidden behind. This is also a neo-Gothic building, but rather reflects an elegant English style. It currently serves as a nursing home.

EXCURSION If you are interested in seeing a few of the sights in Tompa and/or stay the night, turn left onto the busy major road (53) which is the fastest route. Or better yet, you can approach it from the eastern edge of Kelebias.

Tompa

The 5,000-strong community, which since 2004 has the right to be called a city, had to build the number 53 road around the settlement area because of the Yugoslav war and specifically the high volume of trucks. For tourists to the Adriatic regions, the place is mostly a transit station and for Serbian workers it is a place to go shopping - now somewhat hampered by the situation at the EU's external border. Although 70 limited liability companies have settled there, agriculture remains a significant part of the area with the production of peppers, tomatoes and rearing of livestock.

EXCURSION Those who want to visit Subotica, turn right onto road 53 and look out for a Yugoslav watchtower on the Serbian side.

Refuge for Jörg Berger

In March 1979, in Subotica, near the Hungarian border, a junior team from the DDR played against Yugoslavia. The night before the football game, the National Coach of the GDR, Jörg Berger, left the hotel unnoticed, and took a train to Belgrade at 5am. Once there, he received fake papers (in the name of Gerd Prenzel) from the West German Embassy and travelled on the "Orient Express" from Belgrade to Frankfurt. His disappearance was reported immediately in the Yugoslav media. When his ticket and papers were checked between Yugoslavia and Austria, he told the border guards that his passport had been stolen which is why the West German Embassy had provided him with a replacement passport. Jörg Berger describes the most important moment on that journey in his book: "Meine zwei Halbzeiten – Ein Leben in Ost und West" (My two halves - A life in East and West) as follows: The inspector "gave me my (fake Gerd Prenzel) papers back, looked me straight in the eye, smiled and said: "And now, Mr. Berger, good luck in the West!" He was able to continue his career as a football coach for many Bundesliga teams. He made his name primarily as a "rescuer" of teams and twice kept Eintracht Frankfurt from being relegated. In the West, he continued to be watched by the Stasi, as in the GDR, he was

Church in Kelebia

considered a "traitor". He turned down a position for West Berlin football club Hertha BSC because the risk there for him was even greater than in West Germany. Jörg Berger said in an interview in 2009: "I had the same nightmares for two years: I was back in the GDR, had been kidnapped or went

91
Tompa
Kelebia
Kelebija
Watchtower
Watchtower
St. Anna
Hungary
Serbia
9,5
4,7
3,8
6
7,5
53
5501
92

Watchtower near Ásotthalom

there for my job and could not go back. I always woke up drenched in sweat, with a feeling that was so intense, that at first I did not know if it had really happened."

In Kelebia that is just 4 km away, cross road 53 straight and continue cycling through a beautiful forest.

EXCURSION

The best way to reach Tompa is from the eastern outskirts.

Kelebia

The town is a curiosity due to its connection and history with the Iron Curtain: The settlement was divided by the border, and even today, exists twice. However, in this case, the division was done after the First World War, when Vojvodina mostly fell to Serbia. The Serbian village Kelebija, which developed as a north-westerly settlement in the foothills of Subotica in the 1930s is now a larger built-up community and finishes at the border crossing to Tompa. Hungarian Kelebia is located in the north and is now larger than its twin sister, has large water reserves and decent forests and is close to Subotica. The train station has direct trains to Budapest and Belgrade.

From Kelebia to Szeged 60 km

Turn left at the church (turning right will bring you to the station), cross the railway line, pass a couple of ponds and turn right at an angle behind it. Continue through a forest and over fields, passing a wood factory, on whose premises an old, concrete watchtower can still be seen.

Ásotthalom

Turn right behind Csongrad Megye into a paved road in the direction of Fatima-Haz (Curfillo). After a zig-zagging route you will reach the asphalt road, where you arrive from a southerly direction in Mórahalom.

Mórahalom

In Mórahalom, turn right before road no.55 towards Röszke. After a left bend, cross a river (dry in the summer), pass a few scattered farms and after crossing the M5 / E75

Saint Michael in Szentmihály

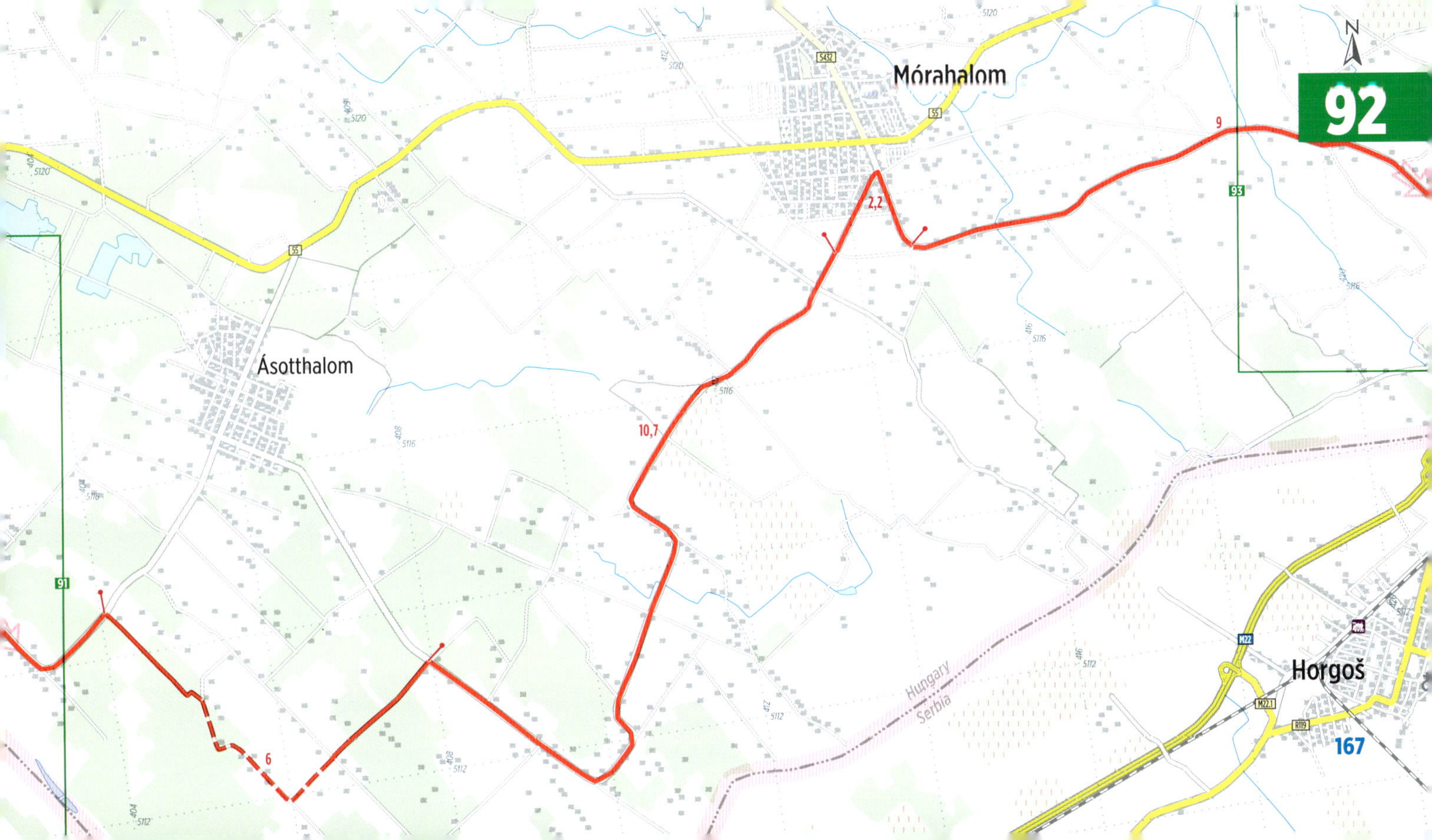
Mórahalom
Ásotthalom
Horgoš
Hungary
Serbia
92
93
91
2,2
10,7
9
6
55
5432
M22
M22.1
R119

Saint Stephan

motorway and the railway line to Horgos and Subotica, reach the border village of Röszke near a tributary of the Tisza.

Röszke

Here you can find relief of Imre Nagy.

Imre Nagy

Today's national hero Imre Nagy (1896-1958) fell into Russian captivity in 1915 and took part in the October Revolution in 1917. After the First World War, he returned to Hungary and in 1919 was a member of the communist government of Bela Kun for a short time. Under the Horthy government, he emigrated to the Soviet Union in 1929 and returned to Hungary in 1944 with the Red Army. As Minister of Agriculture for the MDP Communist Party he led from 1945 the Hungarian land reform and was in the context of de-Stalinization Prime Minister in 1953. Because he advocated the idea of "national and human socialism", he was deposed as prime minister in April 1955 and expelled from the party. When the "secret speech" of the Soviet party leader Nikita Khrushchev against Stalinism became known in February 1956, the Poznan began an uprising in Poland. In Hungary, student protests began in October, which officially were in support for the workers of Poland, but were the start of the Hungarian Revolution. Soon after this, Imre Nagy became the Prime Minister once again. On October 28, he officially recognised the revolution in Hungary, formed a multi-party government and called for parliamentary democracy and Hungarian neutrality. Even the army and police were on his side. After he proclaimed neutrality on November 1st, 1956 and terminated the membership of his country in the Warsaw Pact, Soviet tanks advanced in Hungary and bloodily put down the revolution. 2,500 Hungarians were killed. Nagy himself fled to the Yugoslav embassy. With the new prime minister János Kádár (1912-1989) assuring him of impunity to any charges, he left the embassy on the 22nd November 1956 but was arrested with his companions by the KGB and quietly deported to Romania. In a secret trial in which he rejected any charges of treason and attempting to overthrow the "people's democratic state order" and refused to plead guilty, he was sentenced to death on June 16th 1958 to death and executed the same day.

After the verdict, he said: "My only consolation is that the Hungarian people will absolve me from those serious allegations. I do not ask for mercy. "

The small road leads to the left.

Szentmihály

A statue of St. Michael can be found here on a bridge over a stream.

Pass the Church of St. Michael on the opposite side of the bike path and reach the entrance to Szeged. There, the cycle path changes to the other side and after crossing the railway line you reach the centre.

Szeged

Votive Church, in Neo-Romanesque style. Work started on the church before the First World War and in 1930 the fourth largest church in Hungary was completed.

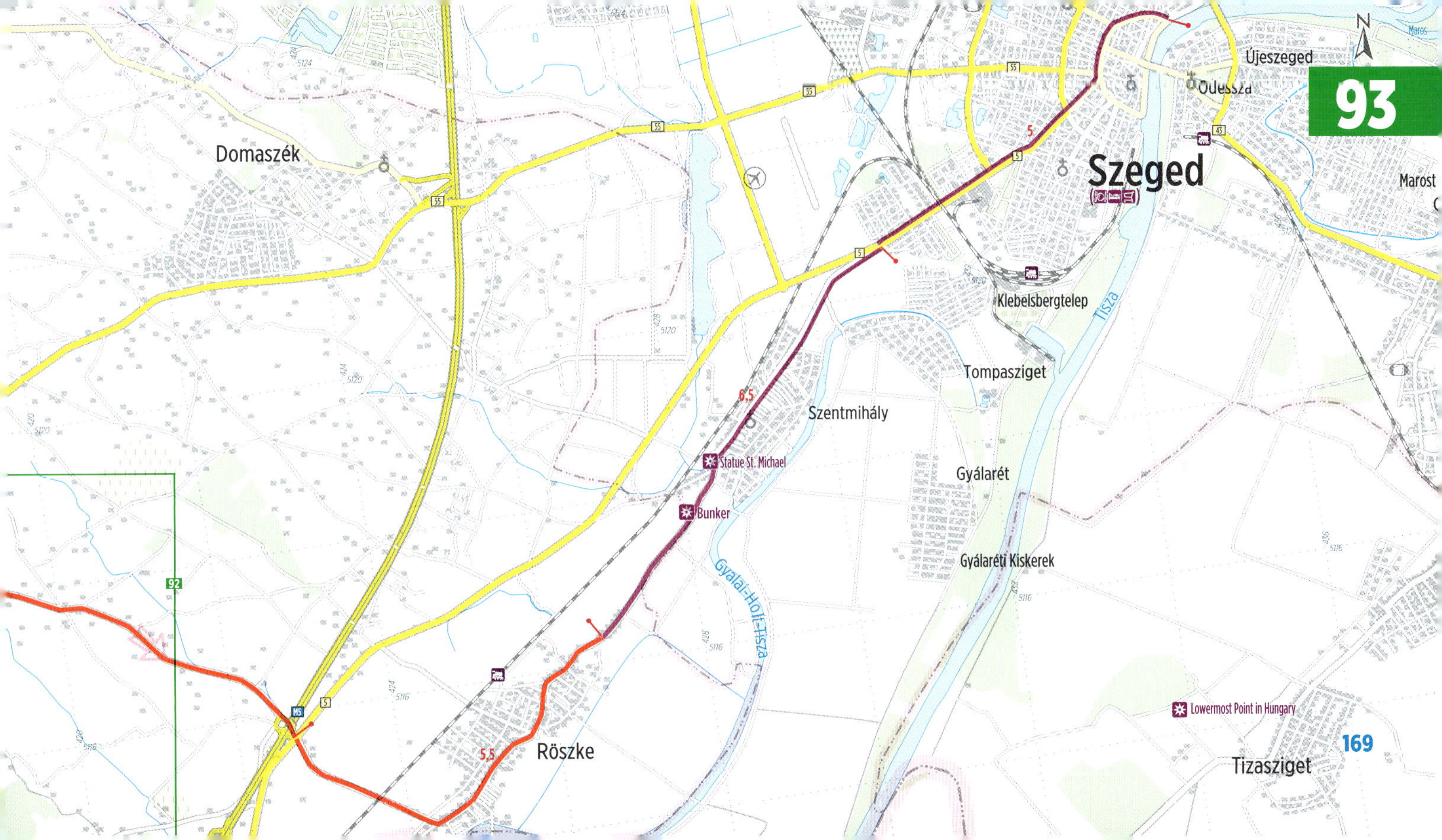

Domaszék
Szeged
Újeszeged
Odessza
Marost
Klebelsbergtelep
Tisza
Tompasziget
Szentmihály
Statue St. Michael
Bunker
Gyálarét
Gyálaréti Kiskerek
Gyálai-Holt-Tisza
Röszke
Lowermost Point in Hungary
Tizasziget
Maros
5
6,5
5,5
92

Serbian Orthodox Church with a Baroque tower. Inside, a carved wooden iconostasis in rococo style with 80 icons.

Reök Palais with an Art Nouveau façade and simple roof.

Demetrius Tower. The octagonal tower was discovered during construction and dates back to the 13th century. It is the oldest building in town.

Dóm tèr (Domplatz) with the **National Memorial Hall**. In the arcades, famous people are honoured with busts. The musical clock on the facade plays at 12:15 and 16:15 for 9 minutes and involves a little dancing figure.

Dugonics tér. Administrative building for the university and beyond, and is located on the corner of Kárász utca. The Unger-Mayer-house, which in 1911 received a specially-crafted Art Nouveau roof scape.

New Synagogue, Gutenberg utca. It was built in the 1907 with the usual mixture of styles. The outside is not particularly attractive but the interior radiates with its interesting shapes and colours and is an impressive treat.

Many connect the name of this city to "Szeged goulash", which is a dish served with sauerkraut and sour cream. The town lies on a sharp bend of the River Tisza (szeg = corner) and was established under the name Partiscum by the Romans. Later, it seems to have served as a base for Attila the Hun. After the arrival of the Hungarians in the 10th century the city became the centre of the salt trade. The Turks plundered the city in 1526 and occupied it for 143 years. With the re-conquest, a period of growth began, although this was hampered by a number of witch trials. In 1879, 95 per cent of the town was destroyed by a

Szeged Town Hall

catastrophic flood, but from that incident an opportunity emerged. With international assistance it was possible to plan a completely new city, which led not only to the radial structure with the ring roads, but also to the uniform cityscape with a mixture of historicism and art nouveau. The renewed upturn slowed in 1918 due to the loss of the southern regions of Romania and Serbia. After the Second World War, a period of prosperity took place. Food production was expanded into an industry, major oil discoveries were made, services jobs created and numerous educational institutions were established. There is an abundance of things to do here and for that reason a longer stay here seems advisable. Highly visible, despite the mass of buildings around it, is the impressive Votive Church. In front of the tower, on the left, is the octagonal Demetrius Tower. Operas, dramas and folklore take place in the summer on the Dóm tér, which roughly corresponds in size to the Piazza San Marco in Venice. It is particularly well suited for these activities because it is U-shaped and is surrounded by the National Memorial Hall. Right behind the cathedral you can see the Baroque tower of the Serbian Orthodox Church. You can leave the square through a large archway which is located right from the building with the musical clock. Keep right and on the second occasion go right again through Jókai utca. You will come to the almost triangular Dugonics tér where on the right the administration building of the University stands and behind it, on the corner of Kárász utca, you can find the Unger-Mayer-House. Visits can be difficult, as it is on the end of a long shopping street and often extremely well attended. Around the next corner, hidden on the right in a much smaller triangular space, is the Reök Palais. Enter Ringstraße Tisza Lajos körút and follow it up to the second street on the left, which is the Gutenberg utca. This will lead you to a new, large synagogue. Through Hajnóczy utca, which runs on the other side of the building, you can now go straight through to Klauzál tér and visit the most famous cafe in town, the Virág-kávéház. The place is popular because the revolutionary Lajos Kossuth held his last speech in 1849 on the balcony of the large white building of the Kárász House, before being forced to flee into exile. Direct trains to Budapest and Subotica are available from Szeged.

Index of Places

Index of Places